LEARNINGEXPRESS®'s

ACT™
EXAM SUCCESS
In Only 6 Steps!

LEARNINGEXPRESS®

NEW YORK

Library of Congress Cataloging-in-Publication Data:
ACT success / Elizabeth Chesla . . . [et al.]—1st ed.
     p. cm.
Includes bibliographical references.
ISBN 1-57685-436-1 (pbk. : alk. paper)
  1. ACT Assessment—Study guides. I. Chesla, Elizabeth L.
LB2353.48 .A293 2003
378.1'6621—dc21   2002015278

Printed in the United States of America
9 8 7 6 5 4 3 2 1
First Edition

ISBN 1-57685-436-1

For more information or to place an order, contact LearningExpress at:
  900 Broadway
  Suite 604
  New York, NY 10003

Or visit us at:
  www.learnatest.com

About the Authors

Elizabeth Chesla is the author of *TOEFL Exam Success* and many other writing and reading guides and test preparation books. She lives in South Orange, New Jersey.

Nancy Hirsch is a writer and education editor in New York, New York.

Melinda Grove is a high school math teacher from New Britain, Connecticut.

Jelena Matic is a doctoral candidate for chemical engineering at Polytechnic University, in Brooklyn, New York. She works as an adjunct instructor of chemistry and has written for McGraw-Hill's *Chemical Engineering*.

Kurt Haste, **Julie Barker**, and **Carol Ivers** are high school science teachers in the Cheshire Public School District in Cheshire, Connecticut.

Contents

Contents

Introduction

The ACT Assessment® is an important exam; so the more you know about it, the better off you will be in the end. This chapter will introduce you to the essentials of the ACT and all of its separate parts.

▶ Part 1: Introduction to the ACT Assessment

Taking the ACT Assessment or SAT exam as a part of the college admissions process is a rite of passage for millions of teenagers across the country and in many parts of the world. It is probably not something you look forward to, but it cannot and should not be avoided for long.

Why the ACT, Why Me?

Because of the simple fact that high school standards and quality vary widely, colleges look to standardized tests to level the playing field for all students. Unlike the SAT, the aim of the ACT is to test what you have learned in high school. It is not an "aptitude" test, as the SAT claims to be, nor is it an intelligence test. So if you have taken challenging courses in high school, you have already set the foundation to do well on the ACT. Your score on the ACT is used in conjunction with other factors including grades, application essays and extracurricular activities to help colleges decide on whom to admit. Different schools give different weight to the importance of ACT scores, but a high score can only help you get into the college of your choice.

ACT vs. SAT

The SAT has gotten a lot of bad press in recent years, and talk has turned to altogether eliminating standardized testing from college admissions. ACT has long avoided much of this controversy, partly because it does not claim to test aptitude or forecast your ability to do well in college—both very subjective factors. For the same reason, many educators and students alike prefer the ACT to the SAT, as they judge it to be a fairer test of students' knowledge.

Subjective opinions aside, there are some concrete differences between the SAT and the ACT:

- The ACT tests limited vocabulary.
- The ACT tests trigonometry, English grammar, and science reasoning.
- All ACT questions are multiple-choice.
- Points are not deducted for incorrect answers on the ACT.
- Colleges can view all SAT scores, while students can send their best ACT scores.

Who Takes the ACT?

If you are planning on attending college, chances are you are going to have to take either the SAT or ACT in order to even apply to almost any school. Historically, the ACT has been more popular with schools in the Midwest and West, while the SAT has been the test of choice for students on the East and West Coasts. The popularity of the ACT all over the country has been growing, in part because it is seen as fairer than the SAT in testing students' knowledge. Today, nearly every college accepts ACT scores and many educators and students alike prefer the ACT because its content more closely matches what is actually taught in school.

When to Take the ACT

The first step in preparing for the ACT is to decide on the date you want to take the test. Your application must be postmarked by the registration deadline, and the cost for normal registration is $24 ($27 in Florida and $40 outside the United States), which includes the reporting of your scores to four colleges. If you miss the deadline, you can still take the test, but you must pay an additional fee of $15. If you manage to miss both the original deadline and the late deadline, there is still hope. You can go standby and hope to get a spot by just showing up early (with an extra $40, in addition to the late fees).

2003/2004 Dates

For a complete update of future dates beyond those listed below, log onto www.act.org.

April 12, 2003
> Registration deadline: March 7, 2003; late fee applies: March 21, 2003

June 14, 2003
> Registration deadline: May 9, 2003; late fee applies: May 23, 2003

It is never too early to start preparing for the ACT. In fact, choosing which courses to take in school should be your very first test-prep step. Taking a demanding course load is the best way to begin to prepare. And remember that colleges take into account the courses you choose, too, regardless of your ACT score.

September 27, 2003

> (available *only* in Arizona, California, Florida, Georgia, Illinois, Indiana, Maryland, Nevada, North Carolina, Pennsylvania, South Carolina, Texas, and Washington)
> Registration deadline: August 22, 2003; late fee applies: September 5, 2003

October 25, 2003

> Registration deadline: September 19, 2003; late fee applies: October 3, 2003

December 13, 2003

> Registration deadline: November 7, 2003; late fee applies: November 20, 2003

February 7, 2004

> (test not available in New York)
> Registration deadline: January 2, 2004; late fee applies: January 16, 2004

April 3, 2004

> Registration deadline: February 27, 2004; late fee applies: March 12, 2004

June 12, 2004

> Registration deadline: May 7, 2004; late fee applies: May 21, 2004

How to Sign Up

If you have never registered to take the ACT before, there are two ways to do it. You can either register online or fill out the forms found in the student packet, which is available at your guidance office or by contacting ACT directly (see contact information). If you have taken the test within the last two years, you can re-register by phone.

1. Student Registration Form

Even if you plan on registering online for the ACT, you should still pick up a copy of the student registration form. In it you will find important information such as test center codes, testing information, and a practice test. You *must* register through the paper student packet if:

- You plan on taking the test outside the United States or
- You are requesting special accommodations because of a disability or

Making Changes to Your Registration

If you must change your test date or location, you should call ACT at 319-337-1270 (between 8:00 A.M. and 8:00 P.M. Central time, Monday through Friday) before the late deadline for the test you are taking. You will need to provide your Social Security Number, test date, and code number for the test center you are choosing.

ACT will charge you $15 to change your test location or date (plus an additional $15 if you make a change after the registration deadline of the new date you are choosing), so be sure to have a VISA® or MasterCard® handy when you make the call.

If you are registered to take the test and miss all the deadlines to change your test date or location, you can try your luck by just showing up. If there is still space once all the registered students have been seated, you will be given a spot before the standby students. ACT will charge you $15 to change location and $30 to take the test on a different date. Remember to bring your admission ticket with you.

- You would like to request a fee waiver or are using a state-funded voucher to cover the basic fee or
- You are currently enrolled in grades 6, 7, 8, or 9

If you are taking the ACT outside the United States, you should contact ACT directly for the appropriate registration materials. In general, the testing dates remain the same, but fees are higher. You must register with the supervisor of the test center where you choose to take the ACT on or before the Friday two weeks before the test date you choose.

2. Online Registration

You can register online to take the test by going to the ACT website (www.act.org). The whole process should take about an hour or an hour and a half, but you do not have to do it all in one sitting. Once you log on to the site, you get a password and you will be able to work on your registration as often as you need to for the next 72 hours. Registering online for the ACT costs the same, and the process is shortened by the time your registration would spend going through the mail.

To register online you must pay with a VISA® or MasterCard®, and your online registration still has to be completed by midnight of the registration deadline. It is a good idea to print out a copy of your online registration for your own records since the only thing you will receive from ACT is your admission ticket (which should arrive in one or two weeks).

► Part 2: About the ACT Assessment®

What's On the Test

The simple answer to the question of what is tested on the ACT is: reading comprehension, English, math, and science reasoning (see the overview of the four sections on page 10 for a detailed description of the subjects covered). This does not mean that you will ace the test if you have somehow managed to memorize every grammar rule, math equation, and scientific formula you were ever taught in school.

The ACT also tests how well you are able to infer the answer to a given question from the information presented on the test. This requires you to think about a question in a specific way, rather than simply regurgitate facts. You will learn how to do this through practice questions and specific pointers presented later in the book. On the bright side, if you did manage to get through your classes without memorizing every fact you were taught, that will not keep you from doing well on the ACT.

Length

Be prepared for about three hours of total testing time, not including short breaks between sections. The entire test is made up of 215 questions broken down as follows:

- English test: 75 questions in 45 minutes
- Math test: 60 questions in 60 minutes
- Reading test: 40 questions in 35 minutes
- Science Reasoning test: 40 questions in 35 minutes

Format

The ACT is broken into four different tests that, while taken on the same day, are totally separate. You are given a specified amount of time to complete each test, and you cannot return to other tests once the time for that specific test is up. The format of the reading, math, and science reasoning tests is very straightforward: a problem or a piece of information is presented and followed by a multiple-choice question. The English test may look a little more complicated, with its underlined passages and boxed numbers, but once you are used to the types of questions you will encounter (through practice questions in this book), you will realize they are just as straightforward. The format of the ACT never varies. Once you familiarize yourself with the question types, you will know exactly what to expect.

Multiple-choice

The ACT Assessment Test is made up entirely of multiple-choice questions. Each question on the English, reading, and science reasoning tests has four possible answers; the questions on the math test have five possible answers.

English

Five prose passages of varying lengths make up the ACT English Test. The format of the questions that follow each passage are a bit more complicated than the Reading Test questions, although they are still multiple-choice. Each question is numbered and refers to the corresponding numbered section in the text. Most questions correspond to an underlined or numbered portion of the text, and you are asked to choose the best answer from the group, including the option "no change." Some questions, however, refer to the text as a whole and are clearly noted as such.

MATH

The ACT Math Test is made up of 60 multiple-choice questions, each of which refers to a graph, chart, word problem, or straight equation. In some instances, more than one question may be asked about the same problem.

READING

The ACT Reading Test consists of four prose passages that are about 800 words long, and each passage is followed by ten multiple-choice test questions. The passages are identified by a heading that will tell you what type of text you are about to read (fiction, for example), who the author is, and might also give you more information to help you understand the passage. The lines of the passage are numbered to identify sections of the text in the questions that follow.

SCIENCE REASONING

The 40 multiple-choice questions on the ACT Science Reasoning Test refer to seven sets of scientific information. This information appears in three different formats: data representation (graphs, tables, and other diagrams), research summaries (descriptions of scientific experiments), and conflicting viewpoints (differing scientific hypotheses or opinions).

Strategy Overview

The best way to attack the different sections of the ACT depends on both your own test-taking style and the subject section of the ACT itself. Detailed strategies for each part of the ACT will be covered later in this book, but some basic points can be applied to the test as a whole (see more specific strategies in Chapter 2 of this book).

- *Take notes on the test.*
  Mark up the test booklet as much as you need to as you take the ACT. If you find something that looks important, underline it, make notes in the margins, circle facts, cross out answers you know are wrong, and draw diagrams. Even if you use a calculator on the math test, you should still work out the problem on the test itself. This will help you spot careless errors.
- *Answer questions on the test booklet.*
  Circle the answers for all the questions in one section of the test before you transfer them to the answer sheet (for the English and reading tests, transfer your answers after each passage, and for the math transfer them at the end of each page). This serves two purposes: first, it allows you to concentrate on choosing the right answer and not filling in ovals. Second, it will keep you from skipping an oval and misnumbering your entire test if you decide to come back to a difficult question later.
- *Never leave an answer blank.*
  ACT does not deduct points for wrong answers. This means there is no penalty for guessing. With this in mind, you should absolutely answer every question, even if it is a total guess. If you do come across a question that completely stumps you, look through the answers and try to find at least one that you know is

wrong. The more answers you can eliminate, the better the odds that your guess will end up being the correct answer. (See specific strategies for answering multiple-choice questions on page 23.)

■ *Know what to do before the test.*

The directions for each section of the ACT never change, so you should familiarize yourself with them before the exam. The directions for all four tests are provided in the relevant sections of this book. If you study them carefully before you take the test, it will save you time when it counts—on the test date.

■ *Read each question carefully.*

It is all too easy when you are pressed for time to misread a question and get the answer wrong. Missing a word like "except" can lead you to answer the question incorrectly. All parts of the ACT except for the math section ask you to choose the "best" answer. Be sure you read and understand each question before you try to answer it.

■ *Read all the answers.*

If one answer jumps out at you and you are sure it is right, read all the other answers anyway. Something may seem right just because the ACT has put it there to make you think it is the right answer. Spend the time to at least quickly go through all the answers.

■ *Answer the easiest questions first.*

Questions are not in order of difficulty on the ACT, but you should still answer the easiest questions first. If you come across a question that seems too hard, skip it and come back later (be sure to circle it on the test book).

■ *Pace yourself.*

With the practice questions, you will get a good idea of how long you have to answer each question. Answer the easy questions first. If you find one question is taking too long, circle it in the test book and come back to it later. (Remember to leave space on the answer sheet so your answers are in the right order.)

■ *Ignore all distractions.*

You may have tried to recreate the exact test-taking atmosphere during your practice exams. But when you go for the real thing you will be in a room with many other people—maybe even someone with a cold who is sneezing or coughing, or an ex-boyfriend or ex-girlfriend you don't want to talk to. Ignore it all and concentrate on your test.

■ *Do not talk about the test during the break.*

The temptation is huge to talk about particularly hard questions you are sure you blew. Resist! You have no idea if the person you are talking to got the same questions right or wrong. This will only rattle your nerves. Instead find someplace quiet and eat the snack you brought with you until the test starts up again.

■ *Spot-check your answers.*

Because you have been marking the correct answers on the test pages before transferring them to the answer sheet, you can pick a few questions at random to make sure that you have filled in the right ovals on the answer sheet.

■ *Relax.*

Take a deep breath. Put everything in perspective; this is just one factor that goes into how colleges decide their admissions. If you totally blow it, you can always take the test again. In fact, you probably should take the test a second time. Give yourself a pep talk, you are prepared, you know exactly what to expect.

Scoring the ACT

The way that ACT arrives at your test scores is more complicated than their just adding up your correct answers. The first thing they do is take the number of correct answers on each test and then convert them to scale scores, which allow each test, regardless of the number of questions, to have the same range: 1 being the lowest and 36 being the highest. The composite score is the average of all four scores, rounded off to the nearest whole number. The average ACT score in 2001 was 21, and only one student in 12,000 scored a perfect 36 that year.

Subscores

The seven subscores break down the English, math, and reading scores into more specific subject-area scores. These scores are made up of the questions on each test that apply to that specific area. Two subscores are reported for the Reading Test: a social studies/sciences reading skills score and an arts/literature reading skills score. Two subscores are also reported for the English Test: usage/mechanics and rhetorical skills. The Math Test includes three subscores: pre-algebra and elementary algebra, intermediate algebra and coordinate geometry, and plane geometry and trigonometry. There are no subscores for the Science Reasoning Test; only the main score is reported. These subscores are computed the same way as the main scores, but on a different scale: 1 being the lowest and 18 the highest.

Score Reporting

The ACT puts together three different score reports: the High School Report, the Student Report, and the College Report. If you include your high school code when you register for the test, ACT mails a copy of your High School Report to your high school counselor for your school records. They also automatically mail a copy of your Student Report to your school. ACT will send your scores to your home if your high school requests they do so or if your scores are reported from May through August.

When you register for the test, you may choose up to six colleges or scholarships to receive a copy of the College Report. The College Report also includes grades you reported in up to 30 high school courses and possibly predictions about your performance in college programs and courses.

If you plan on taking the ACT more than once (which you should), do not have the ACT automatically send your tests to any schools. This way, the schools you choose will see only your best score. It will cost you a little extra to send the scores separately, but it is worth it. You can expect to receive your scores four to seven weeks after you take the test.

▶ Part 3: How to Use This Book

Like it or not, an important factor in whether you are going to get into the college of your choice is decided by how well you perform on the ACT. You have made an important first step in ensuring you will get the highest score possible by buying this book, but now what? *ACT Exam Success* will guide you through the entire process of taking the ACT, from how to register to what to bring with you to the test center. More specifically, *ACT Exam Success* will:

- explain the format of each section of the ACT.
- offer specific test-taking strategies that you can use on the exam.
- help you identify the areas on which you need to concentrate your study time.
- provide exercises that help you build the basic skills and practice the test-taking strategies you learn in each section.

Remember that many factors go into getting into the school of your choice, but your score on the ACT is the easiest to improve.

Preparing for the ACT

Your approach to preparing for the ACT will be different from the way you have studied for any other test in the past. Because of this, it is important to adjust your study habits to get the most out of the time you have to prepare. In later chapters of this book, you will find detailed explanations of how to best manage your study time. Cramming for the ACT is likely to do you very little good, which is why this book will help you to identify what you need to study, create a study plan, and help you stick with it.

One of the simplest ways to prepare for the ACT is to go into the exam knowing exactly what to expect. To this end, *ACT Exam Success* provides the complete instructions to all sections of the ACT broken down and explained clearly, as well as numerous practice questions that follow the same format as those on the ACT. Once you have worked through the sample questions, nothing on the ACT will surprise you.

Standardized exams like the ACT end up testing more than just what you have learned in school; they also test how good of a test taker you are. In the following chapters, you will learn how to increase your chances of getting test questions right, even if you do not necessarily know the answer. You will also get pointers on how to spot misleading answers, how to identify what the questions are *really* asking, and how to pace yourself so you do not run out of time.

Using Test-prep Books

A trip to the local library or bookstore proves that there are plenty of test-prep books out there. Most of these books focus on sample tests as a means of preparing you for the ACT. It is important to take as many practice tests as you realistically can (a free sample test is included in the ACT registration booklet available from your guidance office), and this book can help you learn from the results of these tests.

For Remediation

Each chapter of this book includes a skill assessment, which will allow you to pinpoint areas you need to focus on to improve your score. Armed with this information, you can create a study plan (see Creating a Study Plan, page 17), that will devote more time to areas that need extra work.

To Boost Your Score a Second Time

Most students take the ACT more than once, and more than half improve their scores. Unless you are absolutely thrilled with your score, you suffer from uncontrollable test anxiety, or time will not permit it, you should take the ACT a second time. And because you have the option to send only your best score to the colleges you choose, you really have nothing to lose.

If you have already taken the ACT and are not happy with the score you received, you probably have some idea why you did not do as well as you had hoped. Perhaps you did not pace yourself properly or the Reading Test threw you for a loop. You should also look to your subscores to get an idea of which subjects need more attention. But even if you have no idea why you did not do well, this book will help you do better the second time.

▶ Part 4: Overview of the Four Tests

Four distinct tests make up the ACT Assessment: English, math, reading, and science reasoning. Familiarizing yourself with exactly what to expect when you are handed the ACT test booklet is one of the most important ways to prepare for the exam. Because we fear the unknown, having confidence in the fact that nothing will take you by surprise will remove a lot of pre-test anxiety. The only way to perform well on the ACT is to relax and concentrate. Below you will find exactly what makes up each section of the ACT Assessment. Using this information in combination with sample questions found in each section of the book will guarantee that you will be prepared for what you will see on test day.

English

The ACT English Test assesses your ability to write clearly, organize your thoughts, and follow the rules of grammar and punctuation. The 45-minute test is made up of five prose passages, each followed by 15 multiple-choice questions for a total of 75 questions. The questions can be broken down into two categories:

Rhetorical skills
- writing strategy (12 questions)
- organization (11 questions)
- style (12 questions)

Usage and mechanics
- punctuation (10 questions)
- grammar and usage (12 questions)
- sentence structure (18 questions)

Common questions in the English test involve reordering passages to make the text more clear, substituting alternate passages, fixing basic punctuation like commas, apostrophes and semicolons, eliminating redundancy, and improving the clarity or word choice in a passage.

Math

The 60-minute, 60-question ACT Math Test covers subjects taught in most high schools up to the start of 12th grade:

- Pre-algebra (14 questions)
- Elementary algebra (10 questions)
- Intermediate algebra (9 questions)
- Coordinate geometry (9 questions)
- Plane geometry (14 questions)
- Trigonometry (4 questions)

Like the other sections of the ACT, the math test requires you to use reasoning skills. This is good news since it generally means that you do not need to remember every formula you were ever taught in algebra class. You will, however, need a strong foundation of all the subjects above in order to do well on the math test.

Reading

The 35-minute ACT Reading Test assesses your ability to read and understand what ACT considers college freshman-level material. The test presents four passages, each of which is followed by ten multiple-choice questions. The four passages (each around 800 words) come directly from original sources in four subjects or genres:

- Prose fiction: either a short story or a novel
- Social studies: anthropology, archaeology, business, economics, education, geography, history, political science, psychology, and sociology
- Humanities: anthropology, archaeology, business, economics, education, geography, history, political science, psychology, and sociology
- Natural science: anatomy, astronomy, biology, botany, chemistry, ecology, geology, medicine, meteorology, microbiology, natural history, physiology, physics, technology, and zoology

The ACT includes different types of passages to test your ability to read and understand many styles of writing. Thankfully, this does not mean that you have to brush up on your meteorology or archaeology, or even your vocabulary, for that matter, since all the information you need to answer the questions can be gleaned from the passages themselves. In fact, 14 of the 40 questions ask for information that is taken word for word from the passages (ACT calls these "referring" questions). Where do you get the answers to the other 26 questions? Some of the answers must be "inferred" from the information you read in the passages (ACT calls these "reasoning" questions). In order to answer these questions, you need to fully understand the passages as well as be able to infer meaning from them and draw some reasonable conclusions from the passages themselves.

Science Reasoning

The 35-minute ACT Science Reasoning Test aims to test your ability to think scientifically. You are given seven passages, which are followed by 40 multiple-choice questions that test your ability to interpret, analyze, and evaluate data.

The seven passages fall into three categories:

- Data representation (15 questions on scientific data in the form of charts or graphs)
- Research summaries (18 questions on the outcome of scientific experiments)
- Conflicting viewpoints (seven questions based on scientists' differing hypotheses on the same subject)

Like the math test, you will not need to memorize a lot of facts, but you will be asked to draw upon your knowledge of biology, earth and space sciences, chemistry, and physics to answer the questions.

▶ Contacting ACT

If you have any questions about taking the ACT that are not answered here or you need any additional forms, you should contact ACT directly:

ACT Universal Testing
P.O. Box 4028
Iowa City, IA 52243-4028
Tel: 319-337-1448
Fax: 319-337-1285
Website: www.act.org

CHAPTER

2 ▶

ACT Assessment Study Skills and Test-Taking Strategies

The advice in this chapter will help you set up an effective learning environment and create a successful study plan. You will also learn important study strategies and test-taking tips.

▶ Part 1: Study Skills

You probably feel as though you have spent practically your entire life studying, so why do you need to learn how do study for the ACT? The ACT Assessment is different from any other test you have ever taken. Not only is it longer and more important than any test you have had to study for, but multi-subject, standardized tests require their own unique form of preparation.

You certainly do not have to scrap all the good study habits you have already learned, but you will most likely have to adapt them to the specifics of the ACT Assessment. You may already be using some of the techniques found in this chapter, but now is a good time to reevaluate your study habits and tailor them specifically for the ACT.

In studying for the ACT, you will also learn which study habits do not work and be able to eliminate wasted study time for good. Remember that the more effective your studying, the less time you will spend studying and the more free time you will have to do what you really enjoy.

Study Environment and Attitude

THE RIGHT MOOD

It will probably be pretty tough to carve out extra time to study for the ACT on top of your regular school-work, your extracurricular activities, and your social life. These are all reasons that may lead you to procrastinate. But procrastinating can cause lots of trouble at test time. If you procrastinate too much or for too long, you will not be prepared for the exam.

One of the best ways to beat procrastination is to use a reward system. We all like to be rewarded for a job well done. And if we know there is going to be a reward at the end of our work, it is easier to get started. So promise yourself a small reward for each study session. For example, you might promise yourself an hour of watching TV or playing video games as a reward for an hour of study. You might promise to treat yourself to a movie or a new CD after you finish a chapter in a test-prep book. Get your parents involved with your reward plan, and maybe they will provide some rewards of their own.

Remember, your attitude is very important. It can dramatically affect how much you learn and how well you learn it. Make sure that you have a positive attitude. You will study, you will learn, and you will do well. Your study time will be time well spent.

THE RIGHT CONDITIONS

You can have the best attitude in the world, but if you are tired or distracted, you are going to have difficulty studying. To be at your best, you need to be focused, alert, and calm. That means you need to study under the right conditions.

Everyone is different, so you need to know what conditions work best for you. Here are some questions to consider:

1. What time of day do you work best—morning, afternoon, or evening? How early in the day or late in the night can you think clearly?
2. Do you work best in total silence? Or do you prefer music or other noise in the background?
3. If you prefer music, what kind? Classical music often helps people relax because the music is soft and there are no words. But you may prefer music that energizes you. Others work best with music that has special meaning to them and puts them in a positive state of mind.
4. Where do you like to work? Do you feel most comfortable sitting at the kitchen counter? At the dining room table? At a desk in your bedroom? (Try to avoid studying in bed. You will probably be relaxed, but you may be *too* comfortable and fall asleep.) Or do you prefer to study out of the house, in the library or a local coffee shop?
5. What do you like to have around you when you work? Do you feel most comfortable in your favorite chair? Do you like to have pictures of family and friends around?
6. What kind of lighting do you prefer? Does soft light make you sleepy? Do you need bright light? If it's too bright, you may feel uncomfortable. If it is too dark, you may feel sleepy. Remember that poor lighting can also strain your eyes and give you a headache.

7. How does eating affect you? Do you feel most energized right after a meal? Or does eating tend to make you feel sleepy? Which foods give you a lot of energy? Which slow you down?

8. Can you put problems or other pressing concerns out of your mind to focus on a different task? How can you minimize distractions so you can fully focus on your work?

Think carefully about each of these questions and be honest with yourself. You may like listening to music, but do you really study better in silence? Do you usually study in your room, but are tempted by talking on the phone or using the computer? The more honestly you evaluate your study environment, the more effectively you will use your time, and the less time you will have to spend studying. Write down your answers so you can develop a good study plan.

STUDY GROUPS

The majority of your study time should be spent alone in the environment that is best for your study style. However, a good way to get motivated and add some variety to your studying is by forming or joining a study group. Not only will studying with a group be more fun than studying alone, but if you are stuck on a problem, there will probably be someone in your group who can explain it to you. And do not underestimate the value of helping other people in your group. Explaining a difficult concept to someone else is a great way to reinforce what you know or help you figure out what you do not really understand. There are a few things to keep in mind when you form your study group:

- find an appropriate place to study, somewhere where there are few distractions
- keep your group small; three or four people is best
- include only other students who are as serious about studying for the ACT as you are
- set an agenda for your meeting, keep it specific, and decide on one concrete goal for your meeting

THE RIGHT TOOLS

Help make your study session successful by having the right learning tools. As you study for the ACT, have:

- a good dictionary, such as Webster's 10th Edition
- a calculator
- paper or legal pads
- pencils (and a pencil sharpener) or pens
- a highlighter, or several in different colors
- index or other note cards
- folders or notebooks
- a calendar

Keep your personal preferences in mind. Perhaps you like to write with a certain kind of pen or on a certain kind of paper. If so, make sure you have that pen or paper with you when you study. It will help you feel more comfortable and relaxed as you work.

Learning How You Learn

Imagine that you need directions to a restaurant you have never been to before. Which of the following would you do?

- Ask someone to tell you how to get there.
- Look on a map.
- List step-by-step directions.
- Draw a map or copy someone's written directions.

Most people learn in a variety of ways. They learn by seeing, hearing, doing, and organizing information from the world around them. But most of us tend to use one of these ways more than the others. That's our *dominant* (strongest) learning style. How you would handle getting directions, for example, suggests which learning style you use most often:

- **Visual.** Visual learners learn best *by seeing*. If you would look at a map for directions, you are probably a visual learner. You understand ideas best when they are in pictures or graphs. You may learn better by using different colors as you take notes. Use a highlighter (or several, in different colors) as you read, to mark important ideas. Mapping and diagramming ideas are good learning strategies for visual learners.
- **Auditory.** Auditory learners learn best *by listening*. If you would ask someone to tell you directions, you are probably an auditory learner. You would probably rather listen to a lecture than read a textbook, and you may learn better by reading aloud. Try recording your notes on a tape player and listening to your tapes.
- **Kinesthetic.** Kinesthetic learners learn best *by doing*. (*Kinesthetic* means *feeling the movements of the body*). They like to keep their hands and bodies moving. If you would draw a map or copy down directions, you are probably a kinesthetic learner. You will benefit from interacting with the material you are studying. Underline, take notes, and create note cards. Recopying material will help you remember it.
- **Sequential.** Sequential learners learn best *by putting things in order*. If you would create a step-by-step list of driving directions, you are probably a sequential learner. You may learn better by creating outlines and grouping ideas together into categories.

Think carefully about how you learn. Which is your dominant learning style? Keep it in mind as you read about Learning Strategies in Part 2 of this chapter.

Learning Styles and Finding the Methods Right For You

The best way to tackle the preparations involved in studying for the ACT is to first think about the way you study now. Do you set aside a specific time to do your homework? Is there a place that you always go to study? Do you take on all your subjects at once or start with the easiest? Once you have given some thought to your current study habits, it is time to honestly evaluate how well they actually work.

Creating a Study Plan

You will probably spend more time studying for the ACT than you have spent studying for any other test. So even with the best intentions, if you sit down with this book and say "I'm going to master the ACT," you will most likely get discouraged and give up before you sharpen your number 2 pencil. But, if instead you create a study plan by breaking down your tasks into manageable parts and scheduling time to tackle them, you will almost certainly succeed.

The first step you should take is to make a list of everything you need to study in order to do well on the ACT. Make this list as detailed as possible. Instead of "study English" or "practice math," for example, appropriate tasks should be "take a practice English test" or "go over missed questions on the last math practice test." Make your list long. The smaller the tasks, the faster you will be able to cross them off your list. The effort you put in at the start will more than pay off in the end by eliminating wasted time.

What You Know and What You Need to Know

In order to make your list, you need to find out what you already know and what you need to learn. To create an effective study plan, you need to have a good sense of exactly what you need to study. Chances are you already know some of the test material well. Some of it you may only need to review. And some of it you may need to study in detail.

Each chapter of this book includes a skills assessment, which you can use to create your list. You should also take a practice ACT Assessment to find out how you would do on the exam. How did you score? What do you seem to know well? What do you need to review? What do you need to study in detail?

Scheduling Study Time

You next need to set a time frame. Once you have a good sense of how much studying is ahead, create a detailed study schedule. Use a calendar to set specific deadlines. If deadlines make you nervous, give yourself plenty of time for each task. Otherwise, you might have trouble keeping calm and staying on track.

To create a good schedule, break your studying into small tasks that will get you to your learning goals. A study plan that says "Learn everything by May 1" isn't going to be helpful. However, a study plan that sets dates for learning specific material in March and April *will* enable you to learn everything by May 1. For example, if you need to focus on building your reading comprehension skills, you might create a schedule like the following:

Week 1	Review basic reading comprehension strategies.
Week 2	Practice finding the main idea.
Week 3	Practice vocabulary in context questions.
Week 4	Practice specific detail questions.
Week 5	Practice inference questions.
Week 6	Practice finding the references.
Week 7	Take reading practice test.
Week 8	Begin reviewing grammar/usage rules.
Week 9	Continue reviewing grammar/usage rules.
Week 10	Start overall review.
Week 11	Continue overall review.

Every day: Read the editorials in the local newspaper.

As you set your deadlines, think carefully about your day-to-day schedule. How much time can you spend on studying each week? Exactly when can you fit in the time to study? Be sure to be realistic about how much time you have and how much you can accomplish. Give yourself the study time you need to succeed.

STICK TO YOUR PLAN

Make sure you have your plan written on paper and post your plan where you can see it. (Do not just keep it in your head!) Look at it regularly so you can remember what and when to study. Checking your plan regularly can also help you see how much progress you have made along the way.

It is very important that you do not give up or get discouraged if you fall behind. Unexpected events may interrupt your plans. You may have a big test coming up at school or you may even come down with the flu. Or it might just take you longer to get through a task than you planned. That's okay. Stick to your schedule as much as possible, but remember that sometimes, "life gets in the way." So if you miss one of your deadlines, do not despair. Instead, just pick up where you left off. Try to squeeze in a little extra time in the next few weeks to catch up. If that does not seem possible, simply adjust your schedule. Change your deadlines so that they are more realistic. Just be sure you still have enough time to finish everything before the exam.

You will need to revisit your list often, allotting more time to areas you feel less comfortable with and reducing the time needed on areas you have mastered.

How Do You Know What You Know?

One of the keys to successful studying is knowing what you know, and knowing what you don't know. Practice tests are one good way to measure this. But there are other ways.

One of the best ways to measure how well you know something is how well you can explain it to someone else. If you *really* know the material, you should be able to help someone else understand it. Use your learning style to explain a difficult question to someone in your study group. For example, if you are an auditory learner, talk it out. If you are a visual learner, create diagrams and tables to demonstrate your knowledge.

Rewrite your notes or make up your own quizzes with questions and answers like those on the exam. Provide an explanation along with the correct answer.

How do you know what you *do not* know? If you feel uncertain or uncomfortable during a practice test or when you try to explain it to someone else, you probably need to study more. Write down all of your questions and uncertainties. If you write down what you do not know, you can focus on searching for answers. When you get the answers, you can write them out next to the question and review them periodically. And notice how many questions you answer along the way—you will be able to see yourself making steady progress.

If you are avoiding certain topics, it is a good sign that you don't know those topics well enough for the exam. Make up your mind to tackle these areas at your next study session. Do not procrastinate!

▶ Part 2: Learning Strategies

How successful you are at studying usually has less to do with how much you know and how much you study than with *how* you study. That is because some study techniques are much more effective than others. You can spend hours and hours doing practice tests, but if you do not carefully review your answers, much of your time will be wasted. You need to learn from your mistakes and study what you do not know. The best method is to use several of the following proven study techniques. You may already be taking advantage of many of these study skills in your normal schoolwork, but they can help you make the most of your learning style and store information in your long-term memory.

Asking Questions

Asking questions is a powerful study strategy because it forces you to get actively involved in the material you want to learn. That, in turn, will help you better understand and remember the material. And there is another important benefit—asking and answering your own questions will help you be comfortable with the format of the exam.

For example, when you are reading something you can ask yourself questions like those you would see on the ACT, such as:

1. What is this passage about?
2. What is the main idea?
3. What is the author's purpose and point of view?
4. What is the mood or tone?
5. What is the meaning of this word as it is used in the sentence?
6. Is this sentence a main idea or a detail?

Highlighting and Underlining

Here is a good habit to get into: Whenever you read or study, have a pen, pencil, or highlighter in your hand. That way, as you read books, notes, or handouts that belong to you (not the school or library), you can mark the words and ideas that are most important to learn or remember. Highlighting and underlining help make key ideas stand out. Important information is then easy to find when you need to take notes or review.

The key to effective highlighting or underlining is *to be selective*. Do not highlight or underline everything. If you highlight every other sentence, nothing will stand out for you on the page. Highlight only the key words and ideas or concepts you do not understand.

Taking Notes

Taking notes is a terrific study strategy. It helps you understand, organize, and remember information. The secret to taking good notes is knowing what you should write down. As with highlighting, the key is to be selective. Take notes about the same things you would underline, especially main ideas, rules, and other items you need to learn. Whenever possible, include examples so that you can *see* the concept clearly.

Making Notes

Making notes is often as important as *taking* notes. Making notes means that you *respond* to what you study. There are several ways you can respond ("talk back to") the text:

- **Write questions.** If you come across something you don't understand, write a question. *What does this mean? Why is this word used this way? Why is this the best title?* Then, answer all of your questions.
- **Make connections.** Any time you make connections between ideas, you improve your chances of remembering that material. For example, if you are trying to learn the definition of the word *demographic,* you may know that *dem*-ocracy refers to government by the *people,* while *graphic* refers to *information,* written or drawn. From that you can remember that *demographic* has to do with *information* about *people.*
- **Write your reactions.** Your reactions work much like connections, and they can help you remember information.

Outlining and Mapping Information

Outlines are great tools, especially for sequential learners. They help you focus on what is most important by making it easier to review key ideas and see relationships among those ideas. With an outline, you can see how supporting information is related to main ideas.

The basic outline structure is this:

I.   Topic
    1.   Main idea
        a.   major supporting idea
           i.   minor supporting idea

Mapping information is similar to making an outline. The difference is that maps are less structured. You do not have to organize ideas from top to bottom. Instead, with a map, the ideas can go all over the page. The key is that you still show how the ideas are related.

Making Flashcards

Flashcards are a simple but very effective study tool. First, buy or cut out small pieces of paper (3 × 5 index cards work well). On one side, put a question or word you need to learn. On the back, put the answer. You can use different colors and pictures, especially if you are a visual learner.

Memorizing vs. Remembering

It is true that "repetition is the key to mastery." Try repeating a new phone number over and over, for example. Eventually you will remember it. But it may only stay in your **short-term** memory. In a few days (or maybe even a few hours), you are likely to forget the number. You need to *use it* to really learn it and store the information in your **long-term** memory.

While there are some tricks you can use to help remember things in the short term, your best bet is to *use* what you are learning as much as possible and as soon as possible. This is especially important when you are studying for the ACT because much of the test focuses on your reasoning skills and not simple memorization. This means you really have to understand the material because you will not be given the opportunity to simply recall information. This does not mean that you do not need to know basic information in all the areas covered. If, for example, you do not know common punctuation rules, you will get answers wrong on the ACT English Test. If you find (through the ACT Assessment Test or practice questions) that you do not remember certain grammar rules or math concepts, you will need to study them.

Here are some general strategies to help you remember information as you prepare for the ACT:

- **Learn information in small chunks.** Our brains process small chunks of information better than large ones. If you have a list of 20 grammar rules, break that list into four lists of five rules each.
- **Spread out your memory work.** Do not try to remember too much at one time. For example, if you break up those 20 rules into four lists, do not try to do all four lists, one after another. Instead, try studying one list each day in several short, spaced-out sessions. For example, spend 20 minutes in the morning getting familiar with the new rules. Review the rules again for 15 minutes at lunchtime. Take another 15 minutes while you are on the bus going home. Add another 10-minute review before bed. This kind of **distributed practice** is very effective. It is also a sneaky way to add more study time to your schedule. And, it provides lots of repetition without tiring your brain.
- **Make connections.** You learn best when you make connections to things you already know.
- **Use visual aids,** especially if you are a visual learner. Help yourself "see" in your mind what you need to learn.
- **Use your voice,** especially if you are an auditory learner. Say aloud what you need to learn; you can even sing it if you like, especially if you can make a rhyme. Any time you are learning grammar and structure, say a sample sentence aloud several times. Try different variations, too.

Sleep On It

A rested and relaxed brain learns information best. Whenever possible, study right before you go to sleep or first thing after you wake. Try not to do anything else in between. If you study for an hour and then watch TV for an hour before bed, you will not remember as much as if you studied for an hour and then went right to bed. Right before and after sleep, you are usually in your most relaxed state—and that makes it easier for you to learn.

ACT-Specific Strategies

The amount of material covered in the ACT may seem overwhelming at first. But keep in mind that there should be very little new information for you to learn. The most important thing to do is identify your areas of weakness. Once you do that, you will realize that the few grammar rules and math problems you need to learn are entirely manageable.

LEARN FROM YOUR MISTAKES

Spend time going over your practice questions to determine exactly why you got an answer wrong. Did you misread the question? Are you unfamiliar with comma usage? Only when you pinpoint exactly why you answered something incorrectly can you learn to get it right.

ACCESS YOUR TEACHERS

Talk to your current and past teachers to find out how they can help. They can probably point out the areas they think you need to review and they may be able to give you extra help on subjects that are giving you trouble.

GO THROUGH OLD TESTS AND TEXTS

Some of the material on the ACT will be from subjects you are not currently taking. Go though your old exams (talk to your old teachers if you do not have them) and use your old textbooks to refresh your memory.

▶ Part 3: Test-Taking Strategies

Knowing the material you will be tested on improves your chances of succeeding. But it does not guarantee that you will do your best on the exam. The ACT does not just test your knowledge of English, math, and science. Like all standardized tests, it also measures your test-taking skills. In this section, you will learn strategies for taking standardized tests like the ACT.

Learn about the Test

One sure way to increase your chances of test success is to find out as much as you can about the exam. If you do not know what to expect on the test, you will not know how to study. It is likely that you will be extra anxious about the exam, too. The more you know about the test you are going to take, the better you can prepare—and the more relaxed you will be when the test comes.

You already know what kind of test the ACT is. You know that there are four separate tests that make up the whole ACT Assessment: English, Math, Reading, and Science Reasoning. You know that the test questions for the first three tests are all multiple-choice. You know how much time you have to complete each test. But until you look at actual sample questions, you still do not *really* know what to expect. For example, in the Reading Test, what kind of passages will you be presented with? What kind of questions will you be asked about those passages?

Getting sample tests and working with skill builders like this book can help you in many ways. You will get used to the kind of questions you will be asked and the level of difficulty of those questions. You will also become familiar with the format and get comfortable with the length of the exam.

When you take your practice tests, try to recreate the actual testing conditions as closely as possible. Sit in a chair at a desk or table somewhere free from distractions. Time the test and use only the amount of time you would have on the real test. After you score your test, review your answers carefully. Ask yourself why you got the questions wrong that you did and add those concepts to your study schedule.

Timing

The more practice tests you take, the more comfortable you will be in knowing how long you have to answer each question. You should be able to spend less time answering the easier questions and then come back to the harder ones with the time remaining.

The following list gives you a basic idea of how long you have for each question (remember that some questions will be easier than others and will therefore require less time):

- English: 30 seconds
- Math: 1 minute
- Reading: 30 seconds (with about five minutes to read each passage)
- Science Reasoning: 30 seconds

Multiple-Choice Test Strategies

Multiple-choice is the most popular question format for standardized tests like the ACT. Understandably so: Multiple-choice questions are easy and fast to grade. They are also popular because they are generally considered *objective*. They are questions based solely on information and do not allow the test taker to express opinions.

Multiple-choice questions have three parts:

Stem: the question
Options: the answer choices
Distracters: the incorrect answers

Stem: If $a = 10$, then which of the following represents 803?

Options:

a. $8a + 3$

b. $80a + 3$

c. $8a^2 + 3$

d. $8a^3 + 3$

e. $8a^4 + 3$

In this question, the correct answer is **b**. The other options are all distracters. Here are some strategies to help you answer multiple-choice questions correctly:

1. **Circle or underline key words in the stem.** These are the words that help you search for the correct answer. For example, in the stem:

   The modern bicycle has all of the following safety features except

   the key words are "modern," "safety features," and "except." You need to look in the passage for the safety features of modern bicycles. And you need to find the answer that is *not* specifically mentioned in the passage.

2. **Immediately cross out all answers you know are incorrect.** This will help you find the correct answer. It is an especially important step if you have to guess at the answer.

3. **Beware of distracter techniques.** Test developers will often put in look-alike options, easily confused options, and silly options.

4. **Read stems carefully** to be sure you understand *exactly* what is being asked. Watch for tricky wording such as "All of the following are true *except*." You will find distracters that are accurate and may sound right but do not apply to that stem. For example, if you don't notice the "except" on the bicycle question stem, you might choose a distracter that *is* a safety feature of the modern bicycle. The answer would be accurate but wrong because you did not read the question carefully.

5. **Beware of absolutes.** Read carefully any stem that includes words like *always, never, none,* or *all.* An answer may sound perfectly correct and the general principal may be correct. However, it may not be true in all circumstances.

6. **Work easiest questions first.** Although the questions on the ACT are not in order of difficulty, you should still quickly read through a question, and if it seems too hard, circle it and come back to it later. Remember that easy questions are worth the same as hard questions.

Almost There: Strategies for the Final Days Before the Exam

Your months of preparation will soon pay off. You have worked hard, and the test is just a week or two away. Here are some tips for making sure things go smoothly in the home stretch.

The week before the test:

- Be sure you know exactly where you are taking the test. Get detailed directions. Take a practice drive or mass transit trip so you know exactly how long it will take you to get there.
- Review everything you have learned.
- Get quality sleep each night.
- Practice visualization—see yourself performing well on the ACT.

The day before the test:

- Get to bed early.
- Get light exercise. Do not work out too hard. You do not want to be sore or physically exhausted the day of the exam.
- Get everything you will need ready: pencils/pens, a calculator, admission materials/documentation, and water or any mints or snacks you would like to have along.
- Make a list of everything you need to bring so you don't forget anything in the morning.

The day of the test:

- Get up early. Make sure you set your alarm. Ask a family member to make sure you are up on time.
- Eat a light, healthy breakfast, such as yogurt and granola or a low-fat, low-sugar cereal and fruit.
- Dress comfortably. Wear layers so that you can take off a sweatshirt or sweater if you are too warm in the test room.
- Do not drastically alter your diet. For example, if you drink coffee every morning, do not skip it—you could get a headache. However, do not go for that second cup or super-sized portion. Too much caffeine can make you jittery during the exam, and you can "crash" when the caffeine wears off.

At the test site:

- Chat with others, but *not* about the test. That might only make you more nervous.
- Think positive. Remember, you are prepared.
- Avoid squeezing in a last-minute review. Instead, visualize your success and plan your reward for after the test is over.

After the test:

- Celebrate!

What to Bring to the Test

- Picture ID
- Admission slip
- Calculator
- Water
- A watch
- Three number 2 pencils with erasers
- Sweatshirt or sweater
- A nutritious snack

Handling and Preventing Test Stress

HANDLING TEST STRESS

Test anxiety is like the common cold. Most people suffer from it periodically. It won't kill you, but it can make your life miserable for several days.

Like a cold, test anxiety can be mild or severe. You may just feel an underlying nervousness about the upcoming exam. Or you may be nearly paralyzed with worry, especially if there is a lot riding on the exam. Whatever the case, if you have test anxiety, you need to deal with it. Fortunately, there are many strategies to help prevent and treat test anxiety.

PREVENTION

The best "cure" for test anxiety is to *prevent* it from happening in the first place. Test anxiety is often caused by a lack of preparation. If you learn all you can about the test and create and follow a study plan, you should be in good shape when it comes to exam time. Here are some other, more general strategies:

- **Establish and stick to routine.** Routines help us feel more comfortable and in control. Whenever possible, study at the same time and in the same place. Make your test preparation a habit that is hard to break. Studying for the ACT will become easier as it becomes routine. You will be more likely to avoid distractions, and others will know not to disturb you during your ACT time.
- **Keep your general stress level low.** If there are a lot of other stresses in your life, chances are a big test will make those other stresses seem more difficult to manage. Remember to keep things in perspective. If something is beyond your control, don't waste your energy worrying about it. Instead, think of how you can handle what *is* in your control.
- **Stay confident.** Remind yourself that you are smart and capable. You can take this test—and you can do well on it.
- **Stay healthy.** When your body is run down or ill, your brainpower will suffer, too. And you are much more likely to be overtaken by worries. Take care of yourself throughout the test preparation process. (See more information on page 28).

TREATMENT

If it is too late to prevent test anxiety, don't panic. You can still treat it effectively. Here are some strategies to help reduce test stress:

- **Face your fears.** Admit that you are worried about the test and examine the reasons why. Your fears won't change the fact that you have to take the test, but they can paralyze you and keep you from studying and doing well on the exam. Acknowledge your fears, put them in perspective, and refuse to let your fears hurt you.

   One very helpful strategy is to write your fears down. When you put your worries on paper, they often seem more manageable than when they are bouncing around in your brain and keeping you up at night. Once you write down your fears, you can then brainstorm solutions. For example, imagine you are worried about not being able to find enough time to get your work done and finish studying. Once you put this fear down on paper, you can begin to figure out how to squeeze in the hours you will need to get everything done. And you will feel more in control.

- **Keep things in perspective.** Yes, the ACT is a big deal; it is an important test. But even if you do poorly on the test, is it the end of the world? Will your family stop loving you? Will you be less of a person? Of course not. And if you really blow it, remember that you can take the test again. Perspective is very important to performance. Of course you should be serious about succeeding. But don't lose sight of other important aspects of your life.

- **Be sufficiently prepared.** Anxiety often comes from feeling insecure in a new situation. But if you prepare well, using this and other books, the ACT will not be new to you. And if you follow your study plan, you will know how to answer the questions you will face on the exam. If you have fallen behind, remember that it is not too late to catch up.

- **Stop making excuses.** Excuses may give you some comfort in the short term, but they do not take away test anxiety—and they will not help you do well on the exam. In fact, excuses often make things worse by making you feel guilty and powerless. Do not let yourself feel like a victim. You may have a lot of things going on in your life and many things may interfere with your studies. But you have the power to choose how you deal with your circumstances.

- **Imagine yourself succeeding.** Highly successful people will often tell you that one of their secrets is **visualization**. In their mind's eye, they *see* themselves succeeding. They imagine the situations they will face, and they imagine themselves handling those situations beautifully.

   Visualization is a very powerful tool. It is a way of telling yourself that *you believe you can do it.* The power of this kind of belief is staggering. If you believe you can accomplish something, you are far more likely to accomplish it. Likewise, if you believe you *can't* do something, you are far more likely to *fail* to achieve that goal. Positive visualization will make it easier for you to study and manage your entire test preparation process.

   Anyone can use the power of visualization. Picture yourself sitting calmly through the exam, answering one question after another correctly. See yourself getting excellent test results in the mail. Imagine yourself telling family and friends how well you did on the exam. Picture yourself receiving the college acceptance letter you desire.

■ **Stick to your study plan.** Test anxiety can paralyze you if you let it. And before you know it, you have missed several deadlines on your study plan. Guess what? That will only make your test anxiety worse. As soon as you feel your stomach start to flutter with test anxiety, go back to your study plan. Make an extra effort to stick to your schedule.

A Healthy Mind and a Healthy Body

It is difficult to do your best on a test when you are not feeling well. Your mind *and* body need to be in good shape for the test. If you let your body get run down, you may become ill. That, in turn, will set you back on your study schedule. And that may lead to test anxiety, which can make you feel run down again. This is a downward spiral you need to avoid. If you do feel run down, take a day or two to rest and feel better. Maybe you will be two days behind your study schedule, but when you continue, your studying will be more effective. As long as it is not a constant problem for you and as long as you are not using illness to avoid studying, you will do yourself a favor by resting.

Take good care of yourself throughout the entire test preparation process and especially in the week before the exam. Here are some specific suggestions for staying healthy:

1. **Get enough rest.** Some of us need eight or more hours of sleep each night. Others are happy with just six. You know what your body needs for you to feel clear-headed and energized. Make sleep a priority so that you are able to concentrate the day of the exam. If you have trouble sleeping, try one of the following strategies:

   ■ Get exercise during the day. A tired body will demand more sleep.

   ■ Get up and study. If you study in the night when you can't sleep, you can cut out study time from the next day so you can take a nap or get to bed earlier. (Of course, sometimes studying will help you fall asleep in the first place.)

   ■ Relax with a hot bath, a good book, or sleep-inducing foods. A glass of warm milk, for example, may help you fall back asleep.

   ■ Do some gentle stretching or seated forward bends. Try to touch your toes with your legs outstretched. This is a relaxing posture. Or, practice a few relaxation poses from yoga: child's pose, corpse pose, or cat stretch (see a good website like www.yoga.com for details).

   ■ Spend a few minutes doing deep breathing. Fill your lungs slowly and completely. Hold for a few seconds and then release slowly and completely. You can practice deep breathing any time you need to relax or regain focus.

   ■ Write down your worries. Again, putting your fears on paper can help make them more manageable.

2. **Eat well.** Keeping a healthy diet is often as hard as getting enough rest when you are busy preparing for a test. But how you eat can have a tremendous impact on how you study and how you perform on the exam. You may think you are saving time by eating fast food. But in reality, you are depriving your

body of the nutrition it needs to be at its best. You may think that a couple extra cups of coffee a day are a good thing because you can stay up later and study. But in reality, you are "tricking" your brain into thinking that it's awake and making yourself more dependent on caffeine.

Foods to avoid—especially at test time—include high-sugar, high-calorie, low-nutrition foods, such as donuts, chips, and cookies. Instead, find healthy substitutes such as the following:

INSTEAD OF . . .	EAT . . .
donuts	low-sugar, multi-grain cereal
chips	carrot sticks
cookies	natural granola bar
ice cream	low-fat yogurt
sugary soda	fresh squeezed fruit juice
giant-sized coffee	green tea

3 ▶ ACT English Test Practice

▶ Overview: About the ACT English Test

As a college student, you will do a great deal of writing. From essays to research papers to lab reports, you will have writing assignments in nearly all of your classes, and in many courses, most—perhaps even all—of your grade will be based upon your written work.

Because writing skills are so essential to your academic success, the ACT English Test aims to gauge your knowledge of writing rules and strategies. Your score on this section of the exam provides colleges and universities with a measure of how well you communicate in writing.

On the ACT English Test, you will have 45 minutes to read five prose passages and answer 75 multiple-choice questions. These questions test two types of English skills: your understanding of the conventions of standard written English ("Usage and Mechanics") and your knowledge of rhetorical strategies and techniques ("Rhetorical Skills"). The 40 questions about usage and mechanics cover **punctuation** (13%), **grammar and usage** (16%), and **sentence structure** (24%). The 35 questions about rhetorical skills address general **writing strategies** (16%), **organizational techniques** (15%), and **style** (16%).

▶ Pretest

To make the most of this book, take the following pretest before you begin the English review in this section. The passage and questions are the same type you will find on the ACT. When you are finished, check the answer key on page 34 to assess your results. Your pretest score will help you determine in which areas you need the most careful review and practice.

Batman

Pow! Bam! Zap! Batman triumphs again, foiling evil-doers like the Joker, Penguin, and Catwoman to save the citizens of Gotham City. This superhero created in 1939 and known world wide, continues to be one of the most popular comic strip characters ever created.

        1

Batman was the brainchild of comic book artist Bob Kane. Who was just 22 years old when he was asked

        2

to create a new superhero for DC Comics. Superman was a phenomenal success, and DC Comics wanted another hero, just as powerful, to appeal to its readers. Kane's idea for Batman reportedly came from Leonardo da Vinci's famous sketch of a man flying with bat-like wings and the masked heroes of the *Shadow* and *Zorro*

        3

series.

Kane's Batman was a big success right from the start. The masked hero soon moved from comic books to

        4

its own newspaper strip, and in 1943, Batman episodes were aired on the radio. In 1966, live-action Batman shows hit the TV screen, giving ABC network the ratings boost it badly needed. The series was wildly popular, and the syndicated show still airs today on channels such as the Cartoon Network and Nickelodeon.

Why was Batman so popular? The answer may lie in the background Kane gave his character. Batman is really Bruce Wayne, a millionaire who witnessed the murder of his parents as a child. He vowed to avenge their deaths and the bringing of criminals to justice. He didn't have any supernatural powers. Instead, he devotes

        5   **6**

his life to training his body and mind to fight crime and used his wealth to develop high-tech tools and weapons, like his famous Batmobile, to aid him in his quest. Thus Kane created a superhero who is just as

        7

human as the rest of us, one who suffered and has dedicated himself to righting wrongs. In Batman, Kane

        8

gave us an image of our own superhero potential.

1. a. NO CHANGE
   b. superhero, created in 1939, and known world wide continues
   c. superhero, created in 1939 and known world wide, continues
   d. superhero; created in 1939, and know world wide continues

2. f. NO CHANGE
   g. Kane; who was
   h. Kane, who was
   j. Kane, being

3. a. NO CHANGE
   b. with bat, like wings
   c. with bat like wings
   d. with wings that are like a bat's

4. f. NO CHANGE
   g. was a really successful character whom everyone liked a lot
   h. was liked a lot by a lot of people
   j. was an overwhelming success

5. a. NO CHANGE
   b. bring criminals to justice
   c. criminals being brought to justice
   d. finding justice to bring to criminals

6. f. NO CHANGE
   g. has devoted
   h. did devote
   j. devoted

7. a. NO CHANGE
   b. Accordingly,
   c. For instance,
   d. Furthermore,

8. f. NO CHANGE
   g. one who has
   h. which
   j. OMIT the underlined portion

9. The writer introduces the passage with "Pow! Bam! Zap!" This is most likely done to:
  a. set a light-hearted, silly tone for the essay.
  b. demonstrate the effect of onomatopoeia and exclamation points.
  c. establish a connection to the topic of a comic book hero.
  d. show that in Batman episodes, there was typically a lot of fighting.

10. The author wishes to add the following sentence in order to show why people like Batman and provide readers with more information about the plot of a typical Batman episode:

> *People loved seeing Batman rush in and save the day whenever a villain threatened Gotham City.*

In order to accomplish this goal, it would be most logical and appropriate to place this sentence:
  f. at the end of paragraph 2.
  g. after the first sentence in paragraph 3.
  h. after the second sentence in paragraph 3.
  j. at the end of paragraph 3.

▶ Pretest Answers and Explanations

1. b. The phrase *created in 1939* is relevant but not essential information and should be set off by commas.

2. h. The phrase *who was just 22 years old* must be connected to an independent clause; it is not a complete sentence. A period here makes the sentence a fragment. Semicolons can only go between two independent clauses (two complete thoughts).

3. a. *Bat* and *like* work together to form one modifier, so they should be connected by a hyphen. This is also the most concise choice.

4. j. *Overwhelming* is a more powerful and precise word than *big*. This version is also more concise than versions **g** and **h**.

5. b. This version gives the sentence parallel structure and is the most logical word order.

6. j. This answer gives the sentence consistent verb tense (all verbs in the simple past tense).

7. a. This is the most appropriate transition.

8. g. This version gives the sentence parallel structure and consistent verb tense.

9. c. The introduction uses a comic book convention to make a connection between topic and structure. The tone is light-hearted, but not silly. The introduction does demonstrate the effect of onomatopoeia and exclamation points, but it has a more meaningful purpose. It is not intended to show that there is a lot of fighting in a typical Batman episode, as this is not a theme of the essay.

10. g. In this spot the sentence follows the general statement that Batman was a success; since the sentence provides a reason why the show was successful, this is a logical place to insert it.

▶ Lessons and Practice Questions

As we noted in the overview, there are two main types of multiple-choice questions on the ACT English Test: questions about usage and mechanics, and questions about rhetorical skills. While the exam tests your knowledge of grammar and rhetoric, the test is not about reciting grammar rules or writing techniques. You won't be asked to correct any misspelled words or name five ways to introduce an essay. But you will be asked to identify the correct *use of* words and punctuation and to evaluate or employ writing strategies *in context.* That is, you will apply your knowledge of grammar and rhetoric to written passages, correcting errors within sentences and choosing rhetorical techniques to make passages more effective. So while you don't need to be able to recite grammar rules, you *do* need to know how to apply those rules to write grammatically correct sentences. You also need to know some basic strategies for effective writing. That's what we will review in this chapter.

CONTENT AREA	SPECIFIC SKILLS TESTED	SCORING PERCENTAGE
Usage and Mechanics	Sentence structure	24%
	Punctuation	13%
	Grammar and usage	16%
Rhetorical Skills	General writing strategies	16%
	Organizational techniques	15%
	Style	16%

The passages on the ACT English Test cover general-interest topics such as the life of a famous person or the history of an interesting invention. They are typically four to five short paragraphs in length. As you saw in the pretest, questions about grammar and usage generally refer to specific, underlined words or phrases in the passages while questions about rhetorical skills may refer to one or more sentences or paragraphs or even to the entire passage. The sentences and paragraphs are often numbered to correspond with specific questions.

For each question, you will need to determine which of the four choices is the best answer. You will always have the option of selecting "no change" if you believe the sentence or paragraph is correct or most effective as it stands. Because the questions are contextual, you may need to read several sentences beyond an underlined passage or section to determine the best answer to the question.

▶ Usage/Mechanics

Usage and mechanics questions make up just over half (53%) of your ACT English Test score, and at least 40 of the 75 questions on the exam will fall into this category. To help you do well and feel comfortable during the exam, this section reviews the main punctuation marks and how to use them, basic rules of grammar and usage, and guidelines for effective sentence structure. We will begin with sentence structure, because an understanding of the basics of sentence construction will make it easier to review punctuation and grammar rules.

Sentence Structure

Sentence structure refers to the way we compose sentences: how we string subjects, verbs, objects, and modifiers together in clauses and phrases. Awkward or incorrect placement of phrases and clauses can create confusing or unclear sentences that say things you don't mean. Sentence structure is also important to style. If sentence structure is too simple or repetitive, the writing becomes monotonous for the reader. Sentence variety is an important issue that will be addressed in the rhetorical skills review.

SUBJECTS, PREDICATES, AND OBJECTS

When we write, we express our ideas in sentences. But what *is* a sentence, anyway?

A sentence is the basic unit of written expression in English. It consists of two essential parts—a **subject** and a **predicate**—and it must express a complete thought. The subject of a sentence tells us *who* or *what* the sentence is about—who or what is performing the action of the sentence. The predicate tells us something *about* the subject—what the subject is or does. Thus, in the following sentence:

> *The wind is howling.*

The word *wind* is the subject. It tells us what the sentence is about—who or what performs the action of the sentence. The verb phrase *is howling* is the predicate. It describes the action that is being performed by the subject.

The subject of a sentence can be **singular** or **compound** (plural):

> *I drove for hours.*   *Omar and I drove for hours.*
> singular subject   compound subject (two subjects performing the action)

The predicate can also be singular or compound:

> *I washed the windows.*   *I washed the windows and hung up new curtains.*
> singular predicate   compound predicate (two actions performed by the subject)

In many sentences, someone or something "receives" the action expressed in the predicate. This person or thing is called the **direct object.** In the sentences below, the subject and predicate are separated by a slash (/) and the direct object is underlined:

> *I / washed <u>the windows</u>.* (The windows receive the action of being washed.)
> *Rover / wants <u>food</u>.* (Food receives the action of being wanted by Rover.)

Sentences can also have an **indirect object:** a person or thing which "receives" the direct object. In the sentences below, the direct object is underlined and the indirect object is in bold:

> *I / asked **Vladimir** <u>a question</u>.* (Vladimir receives the question; the question receives the action of being asked.)
> *The guest / gave **the host** <u>a gift</u>.* (The host receives the gift; the gift receives the action of being given.)

Practice 1
For each of the following sentences:

A. Put a slash ("/") between the subject and the predicate.
B. Identify whether the subject is singular or compound.
C. Identify whether the predicate is singular or compound.
D. Underline any direct objects.
E. Circle any indirect objects.

1. Lukas painted a picture.

2. The zookeeper gave the sealions their dinner.

3. Magdalena studied hard and passed the exam easily.

4. Elliott and Evan have been best friends since grade school.

Answers
1. a. Lukas / painted a <u>picture</u>.
  b. Singular subject.
  c. Singular predicate.
  d. <u>picture</u>
  e. No indirect objects.

2. a. The zookeeper / gave the (sealions) their <u>dinner</u>.

    b. Singular subject.

    c. Singular predicate.

    d. See **a.**

    e. See **a.**

3. a. Magdalena / studied hard and passed the <u>exam</u> easily.

    b. Singular subject.

    c. Compound predicate.

    d. See **a.**

    e. No indirect object.

4. a. Elliott and Evan / have been best friends since grade school.

    b. Compound subject.

    c. Singular predicate.

    d. No direct object. (*Best friends* does not receive an action; it is a state of being.)

    e. No indirect object.

INDEPENDENT AND DEPENDENT CLAUSES

A **clause** contains a subject and a predicate and may also have direct and indirect objects. An **independent clause** expresses a complete thought; it can stand on its own as a sentence. A **dependent clause**, on the other hand, cannot stand alone because it expresses an incomplete idea. When a dependent clause stands alone, the result is a **sentence fragment**.

      Independent clause: *He forgot his keys.*

      Dependent clause: *Because he forgot his keys.*

Notice that the dependent clause is incomplete; it requires an additional thought to make a complete sentence, such as:

    <u>*He was late*</u> *because he forgot his keys.*

The independent clause, however, can stand alone. It is a complete thought.

What makes the dependent clause above *dependent* is the word *because*. *Because* is one of many **subordinating conjunctions** like the following:

SUBORDINATING CONJUNCTIONS

after	before	that	when
although	if	though	where
as, as if	once	unless	wherever
because	since	until	while

When a clause begins with a subordinating conjunction, it must be connected to an independent clause to become a complete thought:

He was late	*because he forgot his keys.*
independent clause	dependent clause
I was so tired	*that I left the party.*
independent clause	dependent clause

A sentence with both a dependent clause (DC) and independent clause (IC) is called a **complex sentence.** Both of the sentences above are complex sentences.

When two *independent* clauses are combined, the result is a **compound sentence** like the following:

He was late, so he lost the account.

The most common way to join two independent clauses is with a comma and a **coordinating conjunction**: *and, but, or, nor, for, so, yet.* Independent clauses can also be joined with a semi-colon if the ideas in the sentences are closely related.

I am tall, and he is short.	[IC, coordinating conjunction + IC]
I am tall; he is short.	[IC; IC]
I was late, yet I still got the account.	[IC, coordinating conjunction + IC]

PHRASES AND MODIFIERS

Sentences are often "filled out" by **phrases** and **modifiers.** Phrases are groups of words that *do not* have both a subject and predicate; they might have either a subject or a verb, but not both, and sometimes neither. Modifiers are words and phrases that qualify or describe people, places, things, and actions. The most common phrases are **prepositional phrases,** which consist of a preposition and a noun or pronoun (e.g., *in the barn*). Modifiers include **adjectives** (e.g., *red, exclusive, humid*) and **adverbs** (e.g., *happily, cautiously*). In the following examples, the prepositional phrases are underlined and the modifiers are in bold:

Prepositions: A Short List

Prepositions are extremely important; they help us understand how objects relate to each other in space and time. Recognizing them can help you quickly check for subject-verb agreement and other grammar issues. Here is a list of the most common prepositions. See page 45 for notes about the most common prepositional idioms.

about	behind	down	like	since	up
above	below	during	near	through	upon
across	beneath	except	of	throughout	with
after	beside	for	off	till	without
against	besides	from	on	to	
around	between	in	out	toward	
at	beyond	inside	outside	under	
before	by	into	over	until	

*He was **very** late <u>for an **important**</u> meeting <u>with a **new**</u> client.*
*The **motel** room had a **small** refrigerator <u>in the corner</u> and a **large** table <u>by the door.</u>*
*Sandra was so upset <u>by his **rude** remark</u> that she **immediately** left the **birthday** party.*

Practice 2
For the following sentences:
a. Place brackets "[ ]" around any dependent clauses.
b. Underline any prepositional phrases.
c. Circle any modifiers.

1. Since the research paper is due in just two weeks, I should finish my research over the weekend.

2. Xiu picked Maria up at her house and they drove to the beach in her brand new convertible.

3. After Sean put the entertainment center together, he realized that it wouldn't fit through the door of the TV room.

4. Jenine felt uncomfortable at the party even though she knew almost everyone.

5. High-rise window washing is one of the most dangerous jobs on Earth.

Parts of Speech

A word's **function** and **form** is determined by its **part of speech**. The word *calm,* for example, can be either a verb (*calm* down) or an adjective (a *calm* afternoon); it changes to *calmly* when it is an adverb (They discussed the matter *calmly*). Be sure you know the different parts of speech and the job each part of speech performs in a sentence. The following table offers a quick reference guide for the main parts of speech.

PART OF SPEECH	FUNCTION	EXAMPLES
noun	names a person, place, thing, or concept	*water, Byron, telephone, Main Street, tub, virtue*
pronoun	takes the place of a noun so that the noun does not have to be repeated	*I, you, he, she, us, they, this, that, themselves, somebody, who, which*
verb	describes an action, occurrence, or state of being	*wait, seem, be, visit, renew*
helping verb (also called auxiliary verb)	combines with other verbs (main verbs) to create verb phrases that help indicate tenses	forms of *be, do,* and *have; can, could, may, might, must, shall, should, will, would*
adjective	describes nouns and pronouns; can also identify or quantify	*green, round, old, surprising; that* (e.g., that elephant); *several* (e.g., several elephants)
adverb	describes verbs, adjectives, other adverbs, or entire clauses	*dreamily, quickly, always, very, then*
preposition	expresses the relationship in time or space between words in a sentence	*in, on, around, above, between, underneath, beside, with, upon* (see list on page 40).

Answers

1. [Since the (research) paper is due <u>in just (two) weeks</u>], I should finish my research <u>over the weekend</u>.
2. Xiu picked Maria up <u>at her house</u> and they drove <u>to the beach</u> <u>in her (brand new) convertible</u>.
3. [After Sean put the (entertainment) center together], he realized that it wouldn't fit <u>through the door of the (TV) room</u>.
4. Jenine felt uncomfortable <u>at the party</u> [even though she knew (almost) everyone].
5. (High-rise window) washing is one <u>of the (most dangerous) jobs on Earth</u>.

Sentence Structure for Clarity and Style

Two aspects of sentence structure can make the difference between clear, smooth sentences and sentences that are clunky and confusing: placement of modifiers and parallel structure.

PLACEMENT OF MODIFIERS

As a general rule, words, phrases, or clauses that describe nouns and pronouns should be as close as possible to the words they describe. *The blue wagon,* for example, is a better sentence (clearer, more concise and precise) than *The wagon that is blue.* In the first sentence, the modifier *blue* is right next to the word it modifies (*wagon*).

When modifiers are not next to the words they describe, you not only use extra words, you might also end up with a **misplaced** or **dangling modifier** and a sentence that means something other than what was intended. This is especially true of phrases and clauses that work as modifiers. Take a look at the following sentence, for example:

> *Racing to the car, I watched him trip and drop his bag.*

Who was racing to the car? Because the modifier *racing to the car* is next to *I,* the sentence says that *I* was doing the racing. But the verb *watched* indicates that *he* was the one racing to the car. Here are two corrected versions:

> *I watched as he raced to the car and dropped his bag.*
> *I watched as, racing to the car, he dropped his bag.*

In the first sentence, the phrase *racing to the car* has been revised to *raced to the car* and given the appropriate subject, *he.* In the second sentence, *racing to the car* is right next to the modified element (*he*).
Here's another example:

> *Growling ferociously, I watched as the lions approached each other.*

It's quite obvious that it was the lions, not the speaker, who were growling ferociously. But because the modifier (*growling ferociously*) isn't right next to what it modifies (*the lions*), the sentence actually says that *I* was growling ferociously. Here's the corrected version:

> *I watched as the lions, growling ferociously, approached each other.*

Again, the sentence is clearer now because the modifier is right next to what it modifies.
Sometimes these errors can be corrected simply by moving the modifier to the right place, next to what it modifies. Other times, you may need to add a subject and verb to clarify who or what is modified by the phrase. Here are more examples of misplaced and dangling modifiers and their corrections.

Incorrect:	*Behind the curtain, my doctor told me to put on a gown.*
Correct:	*My doctor told me to put on a gown behind the curtain.*

Incorrect:	*Worn and tattered, Uncle Joe took down the flag.*
Correct:	*Uncle Joe took down the flag, which was worn and tattered.* OR
	Uncle Joe took down the worn, tattered flag.

Incorrect:	*While making breakfast, the smoke alarm went off and woke the baby.*
Correct:	*While I was making breakfast, the smoke alarm went off and woke the baby.* OR
	The smoke alarm went off and woke the baby while I was making breakfast.

PARALLEL STRUCTURE

Parallel structure means that words and phrases in the sentence follow the same grammatical pattern. This makes ideas easier to follow and expresses ideas more gracefully. Notice how parallelism works in the following examples:

Not parallel:	*For weeks, she fretted, worried, and was feeling anxiety.*
	(Two verbs are in the past tense, one is a past participle.)
Parallel:	*For weeks, she <u>fretted</u>, <u>worried</u>, and <u>felt</u> anxious.*
	(All three verbs are in the past tense.)

Not parallel:	*I need a car that gets good gas mileage, has a full warranty, and one that I can depend on.*
	(Two of the characteristics are verb + descriptive phrase; the third is a new clause.)
Parallel:	*I need a car that gets good gas mileage, has a full warranty, and is dependable.*
	(All three characteristics now have the same structure—verb + descriptive word or phrase.)

Parallelism is most often needed in lists, as in the examples above, and in the *not only/but also* sentence pattern.

The error was caused not only <u>by an overworked employee</u> but also by <u>outdated technology</u>.
(Each phrase has a preposition, an adjective, and a noun.)

She is not only the most dependable person I know, but also the friendliest.
(Each phrase uses the superlative form of an adjective. See page 81 for more information on superlatives.)

Practice 3

Choose the best answer to each question below.

1. While waiting for the bus, the bench I sat on was wet.
   a. NO CHANGE
   b. While waiting for the bus, I sat on the bench that was wet.
   c. While waiting for the bus, I sat on a wet bench.
   d. While I sat on a wet bench, I waited for the bus.

2. He told reporters he would quit politics after he lost the election.
   f. NO CHANGE
   g. After he lost the election, he told reporters he would quit politics.
   h. After he lost the election, he would quit politics, he told reporters.
   j. After he quit politics, he told reporters he'd lost the election.

3. Sleeping soundly, I tiptoed through the baby's room.
   a. NO CHANGE
   b. I was sleeping soundly as I tiptoed through the baby's room.
   c. I tiptoed through the baby's room sleeping soundly.
   d. While the baby slept soundly, I tiptoed through the room.

4. Please be sure to throw out your trash, place your silverware in the bin, and your tray should go on the counter.
   f. NO CHANGE
   g. Please be sure to throw out your trash, your silverware should go in the bin, and put your tray on the counter.
   h. Please be sure to throw out your trash and silverware in the bin and tray on the counter.
   j. Please be sure to throw out your trash, place your silverware in the bin, and put your tray on the counter.

5. I am an experienced babysitter, housecleaner, and cook.
   a. NO CHANGE
   b. I am experienced at babysitting, cleaning houses, and a cook.
   c. I am an experienced babysitter, making houses clean, and cooking.
   d. I am an experienced babysitter, housecleaner, and a good cook.

Answers

1. c is the best choice. The subject *I* is right next to the modifier *while waiting for the bus*, and *wet bench* is the most concise phrase.

2. g is the best choice. It most logically and clearly conveys the intended meaning.

3. d is the best choice. The subject *baby* needs to be inserted next to the verb form of *sleep* to make it clear who was sleeping soundly.

4. j is the best choice. Here the sentence maintains parallel structure (verb + object + prepositional phrase).

5. a is the best choice. The sentence maintains parallel structure (noun, noun, noun).

Prepositional Idioms

Another aspect of usage covered on the ACT is prepositional idioms: the specific word or preposition combinations that we use in the English language, such as *take care of* and *according to*. Below is a list of some of the most common prepositional idioms. Review the list carefully to be sure you are using prepositional idioms correctly.

according to	afraid of	anxious about
apologize for (something)	apologize to (someone)	approve of
ashamed of	aware of	blame (someone) for (something)
bored with	capable of	compete with
complain about	composed of	concentrate on
concerned with	congratulate on	conscious of
consist of	depend on/upon	equal to
except for	fond of	from now on
from time to time	frown on/upon	full of
glance at (something)	glance through (something, e.g., a book)	grateful for (something)
grateful to (someone)	in accordance with	in conflict
in the habit of	in the near future	incapable of
inferior to	insist on/upon	interested in
knowledge of	next to	of the opinion

on top of	opposite of	prior to
proud of	regard to	related to
rely on/upon	respect for	responsible for
satisfied with	similar to	sorry for
suspicious of	take care of	thank (someone) for (something)
tired of	with regard to	

Practice 4

Answer the questions below.

1. I am having difficulty <u>concentrating in</u> this assignment.
   a. NO CHANGE
   b. concentrating with
   c. concentrating on
   d. concentrating through

2. I am very <u>satisfied about</u> how things turned out.
   f. NO CHANGE
   g. satisfied with
   h. satisfied by
   j. satisfied of

3. When I <u>glanced at</u> my gas gauge, I realized it was on "empty."
   a. NO CHANGE
   b. glanced on
   c. glanced in
   d. glanced through

4. She has great <u>knowledge about</u> the eighteenth century.
   f. NO CHANGE
   g. knowledge in
   h. knowledge with
   j. knowledge of

5. I plan to remodel this room <u>at the very near future</u>.
    a. NO CHANGE
    b. in the very near future
    c. on the very near future
    d. within the very near future

Answers

1. c.
2. g.
3. a.
4. j.
5. b.

Punctuation

Punctuation marks are the symbols we use to separate sentences, express emotions, and show relationships between objects and ideas. Correct punctuation is essential for clarity; punctuation marks make our meaning clear and add drama and style to our sentences. Poor punctuation, on the other hand, can lead to a great deal of confusion for your readers and can send a message other than what you intended. For example, take a look at the following two versions of the same sentence:

> *Don't call me, stupid!*
> *Don't call me stupid!*

Both use the same words but have two very different meanings because of punctuation. In the first sentence, the comma tells us that the speaker is calling the listener "stupid." In the second sentence, the speaker is angry because the listener has called *him* "stupid."

Punctuation helps to create meaning, and it also has another important function: it enables writers to express a variety of tones and emotions. For example, take a look at these two versions of the same sentence:

> *Wait—I'm coming with you!*
> *Wait, I'm coming with you.*

The first sentence clearly expresses more urgency and excitement thanks to the dash and exclamation point. The second sentence, with its comma and period, does not express emotion; the sentence is neutral.

PUNCTUATION GUIDELINES

There are many rules for punctuation, and the better you know them, the more correctly and effectively you can punctuate your sentences. The table below lists the main punctuation marks and guidelines for when to use them:

IF YOUR PURPOSE IS TO:	USE THIS PUNCTUATION:	EXAMPLE:
End a sentence.	period [.]	This sentence ends in a period.
Connect complete sentences (two independent clauses).	semicolon [;]	A semi-colon can connect two sentences; it is an excellent way to show that two ideas are related.
	comma [,] *and* a conjunction [and, or, nor, for, so, but, yet]	I want pizza, but he wants steak.
	dash [—] (less common, but more dramatic)	I told you he'd be here—here he is!
Connect items in a list.	comma [,] but if one or more items in that list already has a comma, use a semicolon [;]	The table was overturned, the mattress was torn apart, and the dresser drawers were strewn all over the floor.
		The castaways included a professor, who was the group's leader; an actress; and a housewife.
Introduce a list of three or more items.	colon [:]	We need three things: money, money, and more money.
		Colons have three functions: introducing long lists, introducing quotations, and introducing explanations.
Introduce an explanation (what follows "explains" or "answers" what precedes).	colon [:]	There's only one thing to do: go to the police and tell them everything.

IF YOUR PURPOSE IS TO:	USE THIS PUNCTUATION:	EXAMPLE:
Introduce a quotation (words directly spoken).	colon [:] or comma [,]	He said, "This simply won't do."
		The American writer Kate Chopin said this of French short story master Guy de Maupassant: "In a direct, simple way, he told us what he saw."
Indicate a quotation.	quotation marks [" "]	"To be or not to be?" is one of the most famous lines from *Hamlet*.
Indicate a question.	question mark [?]	Why are so many people fascinated by *Star Trek*?
Connect two words that work together as one object or modifier.	hyphen [-]	brother-in-law, well-known author
Separate a word or phrase for emphasis.	dash [—]	I never lie—never.
Separate a word or phrase that is relevant but not essential information.	commas [,]	The group, led by Max, made its way through the forest.
		That restaurant, I heard, is going out of business.
Separate a word or phrase that is relevant but secondary information.	parentheses [( )]	There is an exception to every rule (including this one).
Show possession or contraction.	apostrophe [']	That's Jane's car.

Practice 5

Choose the correctly punctuated version of each sentence below.

1. Where are you going in such a hurry.
   a. NO CHANGE
   b. Where are you going, in such a hurry.
   c. Where are you going in such a hurry?
   d. Where are you going. In such a hurry.

2. Buy these things at the store, bread; lemons; and—milk.
   f. NO CHANGE
   g. Buy these things at the store: bread, lemons, and milk.
   h. Buy these things; at the store, bread, lemons, and milk.
   j. Buy these things at the store—bread, lemons, and milk.

3. She said: Hello.
   a. NO CHANGE
   b. She said, hello.
   c. She said, "Hello."
   d. She said "Hello."

4. "Can you help me?" she asked.
   f. NO CHANGE
   g. Can you help me, she asked?
   h. "Can you help me? she" asked.
   j. "Can you help me;" she asked.

5. There are lot's of accidents on this corner.
   a. NO CHANGE
   b. There are lots of accidents on this corner.
   c. There are lots of accident's on this corner.
   d. There are lots of accidents (on this corner).

6. Watch out thats dangerous.
   f. NO CHANGE
   g. Watch out, that's dangerous.
   h. Watch out—that's dangerous!
   j. Watch out; thats dangerous.

7. That deep-fried dessert is very fattening.

   a. NO CHANGE

   b. That deep, fried dessert is very fattening.

   c. That deep fried dessert; is very fattening.

   d. That deep fried-dessert is very fattening.

8. She is a high priced consultant.

   f. NO CHANGE

   g. She is a high, priced consultant.

   h. She is a high priced, consultant.

   j. She is a high-priced consultant.

9. His kids: who are just the same ages as mine are 2 4 and 6 years old.

   a. NO CHANGE

   b. His kids, who are just the same ages as mine, are 2, 4, and 6 years old.

   c. His kids, who are just the same ages as mine: are 2, 4, and 6 years old.

   d. His kids who are just the same ages as mine are 2, 4, and 6 years old.

10. As the saying goes better late than never.

   f. NO CHANGE

   g. As the saying goes; better late than never.

   h. As the saying goes, "better late than never."

   j. "As the saying goes," better late than never.

Answers

  1. c.

  2. g.

  3. c.

  4. f.

  5. b.

  6. h.

  7. a.

  8. j.

  9. b.

10. h.

COMMA RULES

Many ACT grammar questions deal with commas, the most common punctuation mark within sentences. The presence and placement of commas can dramatically affect meaning and can make the difference between clarity and confusion. The chart on pages 48–49 lists four comma uses, but there are several others. Next is a complete list of comma rules.

Use a comma:

1. With a coordinating conjunction to separate two complete sentences.

> *Let's go home now, and then we can make some dinner.*

> *I'm a little taller, so it will be easier for me to reach that jar.*

2. To set off introductory words, phrases, or clauses.

> *Next Friday, the committee will meet to discuss the proposal.*

> *Once upon a time, there was a brave young girl who lived with her brother in the forest.*

> *Well, it looks like we'll be staying home after all.*

> *Since it's going to rain, we should bring our boots.*

3. To set off a direct address, interjection, or transitional phrase.

> *Sammy, please put your toys away now.*

> *You know, Helen, this is the best apple pie I've ever tasted!*

> *It was, I think, the best movie I've ever seen.*

> *Goodness gracious, that's a fancy car!*

> *There was, however, one catch.*

> *Jonathan, it turns out, will not be joining us for dinner after all.*

> *Sea horses, for example, are unusual in that the males carry the eggs.*

4. Between two modifiers that could be replaced by *and.*

> *The cheetah is a fast, dangerous animal.*
> (Both *fast* and *dangerous* modify *animal.*)

> *The slow, steady rocking of the train put the baby to sleep.*
> (Both *slow* and *steady* modify *rocking.*)

Incorrect: *Denny's old, stamp collection is priceless.*

Correct: *Denny's old stamp collection is priceless.*

(You cannot put "and" between *old* and *stamp*; *old* describes *stamp* and *stamp* modifies *collection*. They do not modify the same noun.)

5. To set off information that is relevant but not essential (non-restrictive).

Essential, not set off:

> *The woman who <u>wrote</u>* <u>Happy Moon</u> *won an award.*
> (We need this information to know which woman we're talking about.)

Non-essential, set off by commas:

> *The children, exhausted by the trip, went to bed early.*
> (The fact that they were exhausted by the trip is not essential to the sentence.)

Essential, not set off:

> *People who smoke too much may get cancer.*

Non-essential, set off by commas:

> *Many people, such as those who smoke, are at a high risk for cancer.*

6. To separate items in a series.

> *The price for the cruise includes breakfast, lunch, dinner, and entertainment.*

> *The recipe calls for fresh cilantro, chopped onions, diced tomatoes, and lemon juice.*

7. To set off most quotations. As a general rule, short quotations are introduced by commas while long quotations (several sentences or more) are introduced by colons. All speech in dialogue should be set off by commas.

> *"Come on," he said.*

> *Emmanuel Kant is famous for the words, "I think, therefore I am."*

> *After he ate a slice, Jerry said, "This is the best pie I've ever tasted."*

8. To set off parts of dates, numbers, titles, and addresses.

> *She was born on April 30, 2002.*

> *Please print 3,000 copies.*

> *Edward Wener, Ph.D. has been contracted to write the book.*

> *Please deliver the package to me at 30 Willow Road, Trenton, NJ.*

Practice 6

Part A: Insert commas where necessary.

1. He said "There's nothing else to say."

2. I want to change majors but I need to get my advisor's approval first.

3. Did you notice by the way that she didn't even say hello?

4. What did you say Louise?

5. There's one thing however that I forgot to mention.

6. I think he went to Woodson which is a Montessori school last year.

7. The Constitution gives us the right to life liberty and the pursuit of happiness.

8. One July 1 1981 I met the woman who would become my wife.

9. We met in Toledo Ohio where she was born.

10. She was a lonely quiet girl.

Part B: A common problem in writing is superfluous (unnecessary) commas. Delete any unnecessary commas in the sentences below.

1. Ken Kesey wrote, *One Flew Over the Cuckoo's Nest,* which is now a classic.

2. Did you know, that Bob Dylan's real name, is Bob Zimmerman?

3. I usually run, before I eat breakfast, if possible.

4. The roses are blooming, in the yard, again.

5. I went back-to-school shopping and got, notebooks, paper, and blank disks, for us.

6. The man, who called you yesterday, is on the phone again.

7. John, please give me the money, that you owe me, by Friday.

8. I said, "Put your money where your mouth is."

9. Give me, that disk, please.

10. Charles, ate the whole pizza himself!

Answers
Part A
1. He said, "There's nothing else to say."
2. I want to change majors, but I need to get my advisor's approval first.
3. Did you notice, by the way, that she didn't even say hello?
4. What did you say, Louise?
5. There's one thing, however, that I forgot to mention.
6. I think he went to Woodson, which is a Montessori school, last year.
7. The Constitution gives us the right to life, liberty, and the pursuit of happiness.
8. On July 1, 1981, I met the woman who would become my wife.
9. We met in Toledo, Ohio, where she was born.
10. She was a lonely, quiet girl.

Part B
1. Ken Kesey wrote *One Flew Over the Cuckoo's Nest,* which is now a classic.
2. Did you know that Bob Dylan's real name is Bob Zimmerman?
3. I usually run before I eat breakfast, if possible.
4. The roses are blooming in the yard again.
5. I went back-to-school shopping and got notebooks, paper, and blank disks for us.
6. The man who called you yesterday is on the phone again.
7. John, please give me the money that you owe me by Friday.
8. I said, "Put your money where your mouth is."
9. Give me that disk, please.
10. Charles ate the whole pizza himself!

PUNCTUATION AND SENTENCE BOUNDARIES

Clearly indicating where sentences begin and end is essential to effective writing. Two of the most common grammatical errors are sentence fragments and run-ons. Because punctuation is essential to separating and connecting sentences, this important grammar review is here in the punctuation section.

Incomplete Sentences (Fragments)

As stated earlier, a complete sentence must: (1) have both a **subject** (who or what performs the action) and a **verb** (a state of being or an action); and (2) express a complete thought. If you do not complete a thought,

Comma Confusion

A common question about commas is whether or not you need a comma after the second to last item in a list (also known as a serial comma):

I bought milk, eggs, bread, and butter.

I bought milk, eggs, bread and butter.

Many grammar books will tell you that this last comma is optional. Our advice is to err on the side of clarity and use the comma. Notice, for example, how not having that last comma can lead to confusion:

I bought milk, eggs, rice and beans.

Did you buy rice and beans separately, or a dish of rice and beans? Without the comma, it's unclear.

In any case, you should definitely *not* put a comma *before* the first item in the list, as in the following sentences:

I bought, milk, eggs, rice, and beans.

Correct:

I bought milk, eggs, rice, and beans.

---

or if you are missing a subject or verb (or both), then you have an incomplete sentence (also called a sentence **fragment**). To correct a fragment, add the missing subject or verb or otherwise change the sentence to complete the thought.

Incomplete:	Which is simply not true. [No subject. (*Which* is not a subject.)]
Complete:	*That* is simply not true.
Incomplete:	For example, the French Revolution. [No verb]
Complete:	The best example is the French Revolution.
Incomplete:	Even though the polar icecaps are melting. [Subject and verb, but not a complete thought.]
Complete:	Some people still don't believe in global warming even though the polar icecaps are melting.

Run-On Sentences

A **run-on** sentence occurs when one sentence "runs" right into the next without proper punctuation between them. Usually, there is either no punctuation at all or just a comma between the two thoughts. But commas alone are not strong enough to separate two complete ideas.

There are five ways to correct run-on sentences:

1. With a period.
2. With a comma *and* a coordinating conjunction: *and, or, nor, for, so, but, yet.*
3. With a semi-colon.
4. With a dash.
5. With a subordinating conjunction to create a dependent clause: *although, because, during, while,* etc.

Here's a run-on sentence corrected with each of the techniques listed above:

Run-on:	The debate was over, now it was time to vote.
Period:	The debate was over. Now it was time to vote.
Comma + conjunction:	The debate was over, and now it was time to vote.
Semi-colon:	The debate was over; now it was time to vote.
Dash:	The debate was over—now it was time to vote.
Subordinating conjunction:	Since the debate was over, it was time to vote.

Practice 7

Rewrite the paragraph below to correct any run-ons or sentence fragments.

I was in the middle of a movie. When the telephone rang. It was my brother, he was calling to tell me he got a new job. Which was really great news. Because he'd been unemployed for five months. He'd been laid off along with thirty others at his company. Fortunately for him. The new job pays better than his old one, and he has more flexible hours, he starts the new job on Monday.

Answer
Your answer may vary slightly.

I was in the middle of a movie when the telephone rang. It was my brother. He was calling to tell me he got a new job, which was really great news because he'd been unemployed for five months. He'd been laid off along with thirty others at his company. Fortunately for him, the new job pays better than his old one, and he has more flexible hours. He starts the new job on Monday.

Basic Grammar and Usage

Grammar and usage refer to the rules that govern the form of the words we use and how we string those words together in sentences. Like punctuation, correct grammar and usage are essential for clear and effective communication. In this section, you will review the following areas of basic grammar and usage:

1. verbs—conjugation and usage
2. consistent verb tense
3. subject-verb agreement
4. gerunds and infinitives
5. pronouns
6. pronoun-antecedent agreement
7. comparative and superlative adjectives and adverbs

   (Sentence fragments and run-ons were reviewed in the previous section.)

Verbs—Conjugation and Usage

Verbs are the "heart" of a sentence. They express the **action** or **state of being** of the subject, telling us what the subject is doing, thinking, or feeling.

> He **raced** to the door. (action)
> She **feels** really lucky to be here. (state of being)
> I **am** absolutely famished. (state of being)
> I **should give** him a call. (action)

Verbs have five basic forms:

1. **Infinitive base:** the base form of the verb plus the word *to.*

   > *to go   to be   to dream   to admire*

   To indicate tenses of regular verbs (when the action of the verb did occur, is occurring, or will occur), we use the base form of the verb and add the appropriate tense endings.

2. **Present tense:** the verb form that expresses what is happening now.

   > I **am** sorry you **are** not coming with us.
   > Jessica **does** yoga every morning.

The present tense of regular verbs is formed as follows:

	SINGULAR	PLURAL
first person (I/we)	base form *(believe)*	base form *(believe)*
second person (you)	base form *(believe)*	base form *(believe)*
third person (he/she/it, they)	base form + *-s/-es (believes)*	base form *(believe)*

3. Present participle: the verb form that describes what is happening now. It ends in *-ing* and is accompanied by a helping verb such as *is*.

> *Jessica <u>is doing</u> a difficult yoga pose.*
> *Stocks <u>are falling</u> again in response to another corporate scandal.*

NOTE: Words that end in *-ing* don't always function as verbs. Sometimes they act as nouns and are called **gerunds**. They can also function as adjectives (called **participial phrases**).

Present participle (verb):	*He <u>is loading</u> the boxes into the car.*
Gerund (noun):	*This parking area is for <u>loading</u> only.*
Participial phrase (adjective):	*The <u>loading</u> dock is littered with paper.*

(You will learn more about gerunds later in this section.)

4. Past tense: the verb form that expresses what happened in the past.

> *It <u>snowed</u> yesterday in the mountains.*
> *I <u>felt</u> better after I <u>stretched</u> and <u>did</u> some deep breathing.*

5. Past participle: the verb form that describes an action that happened in the past and is used with a helping verb, such as *has, have,* or *had.*

> *It <u>has</u> not <u>snowed</u> all winter.*
> *I <u>have waited</u> as long as I can.*

REGULAR VERBS

Most English verbs are "regular"—they follow a standard set of rules for forming the present participle, past tense, and past participle.

- The present participle is formed by adding -*ing*.
- The past and past participle are formed by adding -*ed*.
  - If the verb ends with the letter *e,* just add *d.*
  - If the verb ends with the letter *y,* for the past tense, change the *y* to an *i* and add –*ed.*

Here are some examples:

PRESENT	PRESENT PARTICIPLE	PAST	PAST PARTICIPLE
call	calling	called	called
dream	dreaming	dreamed	dreamed
grasp	grasping	grasped	grasped
manage	managing	managed	managed
promise	promising	promised	promised
select	selecting	selected	selected
try	trying	tried	tried

A handful of English verbs have the same present, past, and past participle form. Here is a partial list of those verbs and several examples:

SAME PRESENT, PAST, AND PAST PARTICIPLE FORM

bet	hit	set
bid	hurt	shut
burst	put	spread
cost	quit	upset
cut	read	

Present: *I **hit** that bump in the road today.*
Past: *I **hit** that bump in the road yesterday, too.*
Past participle: *I've **hit** that bump in the road almost every day this week.*

Present: *Please **set** the table for dinner.*
Past: *He **set** the table for dinner.*
Past participle: *He had already **set** the table for dinner.*

IRREGULAR VERBS

About 150 English verbs are *irregular*; that is, they do not follow the standard rules for changing tense. We can divide these irregular verbs into three categories:

- irregular verbs with the same *past* and *past participle* forms
- irregular verbs with three distinct forms
- irregular verbs with the same *present* and *past participle* forms

The table below lists the most common irregular verbs.

PRESENT	PAST	PAST PARTICIPLE
SAME PAST AND PAST PARTICIPLE FORMS		
bite	bit	bit
dig	dug	dug
bleed	bled	bled
hear	heard	heard
hold	held	held
light	lit	lit
meet	met	met
pay	paid	paid
say	said	said
sell	sold	sold
tell	told	told
shine	shone	shone
shoot	shot	shot
sit	sat	sat
spin	spun	spun

PRESENT	PAST	PAST PARTICIPLE
	SAME PAST AND PAST PARTICIPLE FORMS	
spit	spat	spat
swear	swore	swore
tear	tore	tore
creep	crept	crept
deal	dealt	dealt
keep	kept	kept
kneel	knelt	knelt
leave	left	left
mean	meant	meant
send	sent	sent
sleep	slept	slept
spend	spent	spent
bring	brought	brought
buy	bought	bought
catch	caught	caught
fight	fought	fought
teach	taught	taught
think	thought	thought
feed	fed	fed
flee	fled	fled
find	found	found
grind	ground	ground

PRESENT	PAST	PAST PARTICIPLE
THREE DISTINCT FORMS		
begin	began	begun
ring	rang	rung
sing	sang	sung
spring	sprang	sprung
swim	swam	swum
do	did	done
go	went	gone
am	was	been
is	was	been
see	saw	seen
drink	drank	drunk
shrink	shrank	shrunk
sink	sank	sunk
stink	stank	stunk
swear	swore	sworn
tear	tore	torn
wear	wore	worn
blow	blew	blown
draw	drew	drawn
fly	flew	flown
grow	grew	grown
know	knew	known
throw	threw	thrown
drive	drove	driven

PRESENT	PAST	PAST PARTICIPLE
	THREE DISTINCT FORMS	
strive	strove	striven
choose	chose	chosen
rise	rose	risen
break	broke	broken
speak	spoke	spoken
fall	fell	fallen
shake	shook	shaken
take	took	taken
forget	forgot	forgotten
get	got	gotten
give	gave	given
forgive	forgave	forgiven
forsake	forsook	forsaken
hide	hid	hidden
ride	rode	ridden
write	wrote	written
freeze	froze	frozen
steal	stole	stolen
	SAME PRESENT AND PAST PARTICIPLE FORMS	
come	came	come
overcome	overcame	overcome
run	ran	run

In English, as in many other languages, the essential verb *to be* is highly irregular:

SUBJECT	PRESENT	PAST	PAST PARTICIPLE
I	am	was	have been
you	are	were	have been
he, she, it	is	was	has been
we	are	were	have been
they	are	were	have been

HELPING VERBS

Helping verbs (also called **auxiliary verbs**) are essential to clear communication. They help indicate exactly when an action took place or will take place. They also suggest very specific meanings, such as the subject's ability or intention to do something. The following table lists the helping verbs, their forms, and their meanings.

PRESENT AND FUTURE	PAST	MEANING	EXAMPLES
will	would	intention	*He will send the letter in the morning.*
can	could	ability	*I can make it by 3:00.* *Rose could not believe her luck.*
may, might	might	permission	*May I borrow your car?* *Might we go to the party together?*
should	should + have + past participle	recommendation	*We should leave a good tip.* *They should have offered us a ride home.*
must, have (to)	had (to)	necessity	*I must go to the dentist.* *I had to have two teeth pulled.*
shall	should	obligation	*They said they should call first.*

PRESENT AND FUTURE	PAST	MEANING	EXAMPLES
should	should + have + past participle	expectation	*They <u>should</u> be here any minute.* *They <u>should have been</u> here by now.*
might	might + have + past participle	possibility	*They <u>might</u> be a little late.* *They <u>might have gotten</u> stuck in traffic.*

Practice 8

1. He <u>should have knowed</u> better than to do that.
- **a.** NO CHANGE
- **b.** should had known
- **c.** should have known
- **d.** would have known

2. The blinds <u>were drawed</u> to keep out the sun.
- **f.** NO CHANGE
- **g.** were drawn
- **h.** drew
- **j.** had drawn

3. The key <u>was hidden</u> behind the picture.
- **a.** NO CHANGE
- **b.** was hid
- **c.** did hide
- **d.** had hidden

4. The water <u>creeped</u> up to the bottom of the window.
- **f.** NO CHANGE
- **g.** creep
- **h.** crept
- **j.** had creeped

5. The ship <u>sunk</u> in a matter of minutes.
   a. NO CHANGE
   b. sink
   c. had sank
   d. sank

Answers

1. c.
2. g.
3. a.
4. h.
5. d.

SUBJUNCTIVE MOOD

The **subjunctive mood** is one of the verb forms we often forget to use in conversation, and therefore we often neglect to use it correctly in our writing. Like helping verbs, the subjunctive is used to express a specific meaning, indicating something that is wished for or that is contrary to fact. It is formed by using *were* instead of *was,* as in the following examples:

> *If she <u>were</u> a little older, she could watch the children.* (She is not a little older.)
> *If I <u>were</u> rich, I would travel the world.* (I am not rich.)

TROUBLESOME VERBS

Three verb pairs are particularly troublesome, even for native speakers of English:

> *lie / lay*
> *sit / set*
> *rise / raise*

The key to knowing which verb to use is remembering which verb takes an object. In each pair, one verb is **transitive**—an object "receives" the action—while the other is **intransitive**—the subject itself "receives" or performs the action. For example, *lie* is an action that the subject of the sentence "performs" on itself: *I will <u>lie</u> down.* The transitive verb *lay,* on the other hand, is an action that the subject of the sentence performs upon an object: *He <u>lay</u> the <u>baby</u> down in the crib.* In the following examples, the subjects are in bold and the objects are underlined.

lie: to rest or recline (intransitive—subject only)
lay: to put or place (transitive—needs an object)

I will lie down for a while.
*Will **you** please lay the <u>papers</u> down on the table.*

sit: to rest (intransitive—subject only)
set: to put or place (transitive—needs an object)

*Why don't **we** sit down and talk this over?*
He will set the <u>record</u> straight.

rise: to go up (intransitive—subject only)
raise: to move something up (transitive—needs an object)

*The **sun** will rise at 5:48 A.M. tomorrow.*
He raised the <u>rent</u> to $750 per month.

The basic forms of these verbs can also be a bit tricky. The following table shows how each verb is conjugated.

PRESENT	PRESENT PARTICIPLE (WITH *AM, IS, ARE*)	PAST	PAST PARTICIPLE (WITH *HAVE, HAS, HAD*)
lie, lies	lying	lay	lain
lay, lays	laying	laid	laid
sit, sits	sitting	sat	sat
set, sets	setting	set	set
rise, rises	rising	rose	risen
raise, raises	raising	raised	raised

Practice 9

Choose the correct verb from the italicized pairs in the sentences below.

1. He wished he *was/were* closer to his destination so he could rest.

2. If I *was/were* taller, I might be better at basketball.

3. She *was/were* hoping to get a better offer.

4. He decided to *lay/lie* down because he felt ill.

5. The papers have been *laying/lying* in the driveway for days now.

6. The interest rates have *risen/raised* considerably in the last week.

7. She *sat/set* the keys on the table.

8. I have *lain/laid* here long enough; it's time to get up.

Answers

1. He wished he *were* closer to his destination so he could rest.
2. If I *were* taller, I might be better at basketball.
3. She *was* hoping to get a better offer.
4. He decided to *lie* down because he felt ill.
5. The papers have been *lying* in the driveway for days now.
6. The interest rates have *risen* considerably in the last week.
7. She *set* the keys on the table.
8. I have *lain* here long enough; it's time to get up.

Now that you have reviewed verb conjugation and tense formation, it is time to talk about two key issues with verb usage: consistent tense and subject-verb agreement.

Consistent Verb Tense

One of the quickest ways to confuse readers, especially if you are telling a story or describing an event, is to shift verb tenses. To help readers be clear about *when* actions occur, make sure verbs are consistent in tense. If you begin telling the story in the present tense, for example, stay in the present tense; do not mix tenses as you write. Otherwise, you will leave your readers wondering whether actions are taking place in the present or took place in the past.

> Incorrect: *He <u>got</u> on the bus and <u>realizes</u> he <u>has</u> <u>forgotten</u> his briefcase.*
> Correct: *He <u>got</u> on the bus and <u>realized</u> he <u>had</u> <u>forgotten</u> his briefcase.*
>
> Incorrect: *When we <u>work</u> together, we <u>got</u> better results.*
> Correct: *When we <u>work</u> together, we <u>get</u> better results.*

Subject-Verb Agreement

In English grammar, *agreement* means that sentence elements are balanced. Verbs, for example, should *agree* with their subjects: if the subject is singular, the verb should be singular; if the subject is plural, the verb should be plural.

Incorrect:	*Erik do really good work.*	(singular subject, plural verb)
Correct:	*Erik does really good work.*	(singular subject, singular verb)

Incorrect: *They gets really upset when telemarketers calls at dinnertime.*
(plural subjects, singular verbs)

Correct: *They get really upset when telemarketers call at dinnertime.*
(plural subjects, plural verbs)

Of course, to make sure subjects and verbs agree, you need to be clear about who or what is the subject of the sentence. For example, what is the subject in the following sentence, and which is the correct verb?

Only one of the projects [was/were] completed on time.

In this sentence, the subject is *one*, not *projects*. Though it seems as though *projects* are performing the action of being completed, *projects* cannot be the subject because it is part of a prepositional phrase (*of the projects*), and **subjects are never found in prepositional phrases.** Thus, the verb must be singular (*was*, not *were*) to agree with *one*. In addition, it is only one of the projects—not all—that was completed on time, so again, the verb must be singular.

Here are some other important guidelines for subject-verb agreement:

- If a compound, singular subject is connected by *and*, the verb must be plural.

    Both <u>Dr. Holt and Dr. Weinberg agree</u> that this is an important discovery.

- If a compound, singular subject is connected by *or* or *nor*, the verb must be singular.

    Neither <u>Dr. Holt nor Dr. Weinberg feels</u> that this is an important discovery.

- If one plural and one singular subject are connected by *or* or *nor*, the verb agrees with the closest subject.

    Neither Dr. Holt nor the <u>researchers feel</u> that this is an important discovery.
    Neither the researchers nor <u>Dr. Holt feels</u> that this is an important discovery.

- In an **inverted sentence**, the subject comes *after* the verb, so the first step is to clearly identify the subject. (Sentences that begin with *there is* and *there are*, for example, as well as questions, are inverted sentences.) Once you correctly identify the subject, then you can make sure your verb agrees. The correct subjects and verbs are underlined below.

Incorrect: *There's numerous examples of this phenomenon.*
Correct: *There <u>are</u> numerous <u>examples</u> of this phenomenon.*

Incorrect: *Here is the files you requested.*
Correct: *Here <u>are</u> the <u>files</u> you requested.*

Incorrect: *What is the long-term effects of this decision?*
Correct: *What <u>are</u> the long-term <u>effects</u> of this decision?*

Gerunds and Infinitives

Gerunds and **infinitives** have given many students of English a grammar headache, but they are not so difficult to master. Gerunds, as we noted earlier, *look* like verbs because they end in *-ing,* but they actually function as nouns in sentences:

Tracy loves <u>camping</u>.

Here, the "action" Tracy performs is *loves.* The *thing* (noun) she enjoys is *camping.* In the following sentence, however, *camping* is the *action* Tracy performs, so it is functioning as a verb, not as a gerund:

Tracy <u>is camping</u> in the Pine Barrens next week.

Words ending in *-ing* can also function as adjectives:

Some of our <u>camping</u> gear needs to be replaced before our trip.

Here's another example of how the same word can have three different functions:

Verb: *He is <u>screaming</u> loudly.*
Gerund (noun):   *That <u>screaming</u> is driving me crazy!*
Adjective: *The <u>screaming</u> boy finally stopped.*

What this means is that you cannot count on word endings to determine a word's part of speech. Lots of things that look like verbs may not be—it's how they function in the sentence that counts.

Infinitives are the base (unconjugated) form of the verb preceded by *to: to go, to discover, to challenge.* They are often part of a verb chain, but they are not the main verb (main action) of a sentence:

Alfred likes <u>to run</u> early in the morning.

In this example, *likes* is the main verb; what Alfred likes (the action he likes to take) is *to run* early in the morning.

WHEN TO USE INFINITIVES AND GERUNDS

In many situations, you may be uncertain whether to use an infinitive or a gerund. Which statement is correct: *I like to swim* or *I like swimming*? In this case, both are correct; *like, hate,* and other verbs that express preference can be followed by either an infinitive or gerund. But other verbs can only be followed by one or the other. Here are a few helpful guidelines:

- Always use a **gerund** after a preposition.

    He built the robot by <u>recycling</u> old appliances.
    Renaldo was excited after <u>seeing</u> his test results.

- Always use a **gerund** after the following verbs:

admit	dislike	practice
appreciate	enjoy	put off
avoid	escape	quit
can't help	finish	recall
consider	imagine	resist
delay	keep	risk
deny	miss	suggest
discuss	postpone	tolerate

    I can't help <u>feeling</u> that I should have done more.
    Don't risk <u>losing</u> your money by investing in that company.
    Ralph quit <u>smoking</u> over a year ago.
    The witness recalled <u>hearing</u> the defendant discuss the crime.

- In general, use an **infinitive** after these verbs:

agree	decide	need	refuse
ask	expect	offer	venture
beg	fail	plan	want
bother	hope	pretend	wish
claim	manage	promise	

    I promise <u>to return</u> your car by noon.
    Abby decided <u>to leave</u> before the speech had ended.
    The offer failed <u>to meet</u> my expectations.

- When a noun or pronoun immediately follows these verbs, use an **infinitive**:

advise	command	force	remind	want
allow	convince	need	require	warn
ask	encourage	order	tell	
cause	expect	persuade	urge	

Ian asked his mother <u>to play</u> the video again.

I need you <u>to help</u> me right now.

Wilson reminded his sister <u>to water</u> the plants while he was gone.

Practice 10

1. When I was cleaning the chimney, I find that it needs serious repairs.
   a. NO CHANGE
   b. When I am cleaning the chimney, I find that it needed serious repairs.
   c. When I was cleaning the chimney, I found that it needed serious repairs.
   d. When I cleaned the chimney, I found that it needs seriously to be repaired.

2. After we went to the movies, we come home to find that someone has broken into our house.
   f. After we go to the movies, we come home to find that someone is breaking into our house.
   g. After we went to the movies, we come home to find that someone is breaking into our house.
   h. After we went to the movies, we came home to find that someone has broken into our house.
   j. After we went to the movies, we came home to find that someone had broken into our house.

3. Neither of us feel that this is an effective solution.
   a. NO CHANGE
   b. Neither of us feels that this is an effective solution.
   c. Neither of us felt that this is an effective solution.
   d. Neither of us are feeling that this is an effective solution.

4. We both agree that he should attend this program.
   f. NO CHANGE
   g. We both agrees that he should attend this program.
   h. We both agree that he should attended this program.
   j. We both agreeing that he should attend this program.

5. Only one of the students have finished the book.
   a. NO CHANGE
   b. Only one of the students did finished the book.
   c. Only one of the students have finish the book.
   d. Only one of the students has finished the book.

6. The members of the committee says we should go ahead as planned.

    f. NO CHANGE

    g. The members of the committee say we should go ahead as planned.

    h. The members of the committee have say we should go ahead as planned.

    j. The members of the committee say we should have go ahead as planned.

7. What are the cost of these packages?

    a. NO CHANGE

    b. What cost is of these packages?

    c. What is the cost of these packages?

    d. What are these packages costing?

8. I will not tolerate lying in this house.

    f. NO CHANGE

    g. I will not tolerate to lie in this house.

    h. I will not to tolerate lying in this house.

    j. I will not tolerating lying in this house.

9. Please allow me help you.

    a. NO CHANGE

    b. Please allow me helping you.

    c. Please allow me to helping you.

    d. Please allow me to help you.

10. I always avoid saying things that I might regret.

    f. NO CHANGE

    g. I always avoid to say things that I might regret.

    h. I always avoid saying things that I might to regret.

    j. I always avoid having said things that I might regret.

Answers

1. c.	**6.** g.
2. j.	**7.** c.
3. b.	**8.** f.
4. f.	**9.** d.
5. d.	**10.** f.

Pronouns

Pronouns, as we noted earlier, replace nouns, thus keeping us from having to repeat names and objects over and over. But pronouns can be a bit tricky at times. This section reviews the different kinds of pronouns and the rules they follow.

PERSONAL PRONOUNS

Personal pronouns refer to specific people or things. They can be either singular (*I*) or plural (*we*); they can be subjects (*I*) or objects (*me*).

	SUBJECT	OBJECT
singular	I	me
	you	you
	he	him
	she	her
	it	it
plural	we	us
	they	them

Pronoun mistakes are often made by using the subject form when you really need the object form and vice versa. Here are three guidelines to follow:

- Always use the object pronoun in a prepositional phrase. **Pronouns and nouns in prepositional phrases are always objects.**

    The package was addressed to both my sister and <u>me</u>.
    Between you and <u>me</u>, I don't think she's very talented.

- Always use the subject pronoun when the pronoun is the subject of the sentence.

    I am the man for the job.
    She and I are the same age.

- Always use the subject pronoun in a *than* construction (comparison). When a pronoun follows *than*, it is usually part of a clause that omits the verb in order not to repeat unnecessarily.

    Patty is older than <u>I</u>. [than I am]
    I am more detail-oriented than <u>he</u>. [than he is]

INDEFINITE PRONOUNS

Unlike personal pronouns, **indefinite pronouns**, such as *anybody* and *everyone*, do not refer to a specific person. The following indefinite pronouns are **always singular** and require singular verbs:

anyone, anybody	everyone, everybody	no one, nobody
someone, somebody	either, neither	each
one		

> *I believe <u>someone is</u> trying to get your attention.*
> <u>*Everybody has*</u> *cast his or her vote.*
> <u>*Neither*</u> *doctor* <u>*knows*</u> *what caused the rash.*
> <u>*Does anyone*</u> *know the answer?*
> <u>*Nobody has*</u> *offered a satisfactory explanation.*

The following indefinite pronouns are always plural:

both   few   many   several

> *Both are happy with the terms of the agreement.*
> *Many have tried and failed.*

These indefinite pronouns can be singular or plural, depending upon the noun or pronoun to which they refer:

all   any   most   none   some

> *Some extra <u>time is</u> needed to complete the task.*
> *Some <u>students need</u> extra time to complete the task.*
> *None of the <u>windows work.</u>*
> *None of my <u>money is</u> where I left it.*

Pronoun-Antecedent Agreement

Just as subjects (both nouns and pronouns) must agree with their verbs, pronouns must also agree with their **antecedents**—the words they replace. For example, in the following sentence:

> <u>*Porcupines*</u> *will stay with <u>their</u> mates for <u>their</u> entire adult lives.*

The word *porcupines* is the antecedent and is replaced by *their* twice in the sentence. Because *porcupines* is plural, *their* must also be plural. Indefinite pronouns can also be antecedents. Singular indefinite pronouns require singular pronouns:

> *Everyone* must have *his* or *her* ticket before boarding.
> *Someone* left *his* or *her* book on the table.
> *Neither* of the doctors could find *her* notes from the lecture.

Plural indefinite pronouns, on the other hand, require plural pronouns, just as they need plural verbs:

both   few   many   several

> *Both* of them have done *their* best work so far.
> *Many* have found *their* free time has all but disappeared.
> Only a *few* are still in *their* original cases.

Finally, those pronouns that can be either singular or plural, depending upon the noun or pronoun to which they refer, should take the pronoun that matches their referent. If the antecedent is singular, the pronoun and verb must also be singular. If the antecedent is plural, they must be plural:

all   any   most   none   some

> *All of the chocolate is gone. It was delicious!*
> *All of the cookies are gone. They were delicious!*
>
> *Most of that jewelry collection is worthless; it's mostly fake.*
> *Most of those jewels are worthless; they're fake.*

None of the information is accurate; it's all out of date.
None of the facts are accurate; they're all out of date.

Some of the money looks like counterfeits.
Some of these coins look like counterfeits.

POSSESSIVE PRONOUNS

The **possessive pronouns** *its, your, their,* and *whose* are often confused with the contractions *it's (it is* or *it has), you're (you are), they're (they are),* and *who's (who is).* Because we use apostrophes to show possession in nouns (Ted's car, the dog's bone), many people make the mistake of thinking that pronouns use apostrophes for possession, too. But possessive pronouns *do not* take apostrophes. When a pronoun has an apostrophe, it always shows **contraction**.

POSSESSIVE PRONOUN	MEANING	EXAMPLE
its	belonging to it	The bird left its nest.
your	belonging to you	Your car is blocking the driveway.
their	belonging to them	Their tickets are right behind home plate.
whose	belonging to whom	Whose care is blocking the driveway?

CONTRACTION		
it's	it is	It's time to go.
you're	you are	You're going to have to move your car.
they're	they are	They're going to the Yankees game.
who's	who is	Who's going to the game?

The pronouns *who, that,* and *which* are also often confused. Here are the general guidelines for using these pronouns correctly:

- Use **who** or **whom** when referring to people:

  She is the one who fixed my computer.

- Use **that** when referring to things:

  This is the computer that is having problems.

■ Use **which** when introducing clauses that are not essential to the information in the sentence, *unless* they refer to people. In that case, use **who.**

> *Mark is in Toronto, which is his favorite city.*
> *Rosa, who writes for the school paper, wants to interview me for a story.*

Practice 11

Circle the correct form of the italicized pronouns in the following sentences.

   1. *You're/Your* dog is growling at me.

   2. *He's/His* the one *that/who* won the prize.

   3. Someone left *their/his or her* lights on.

   4. Does anybody know *who's/whose* cell phone this is?

   5. This is Ellen, *which/that/who* reminds me of my mother.

   6. Where are *your/you're* shoes?

   7. Neither of the choices *sound/sounds* good to me.

   8. Most of the stamps in the collection *is/are* gone.

   9. He feels more strongly about it than *me/I.*

 10. To *who/whom* shall I address this letter?

Answers

   1. *Your* dog is growling at me.
   2. *He's* the one *who* won the prize.
   3. Someone left *his or her* lights on.
   4. Does anybody know *whose* cell phone this is?
   5. This is Ellen, *who* reminds me of my mother.
   6. Where are *your* shoes?
   7. Neither of the choices *sounds* good to me.
   8. Most of the stamps in the collection *are* gone.
   9. He feels more strongly about it than *I.*
 10. To *whom* shall I address this letter?

Adjectives and Adverbs

Adjectives and **adverbs** help give our sentences color; they describe things and actions. Adjectives describe nouns and pronouns and tell us *which one, what kind,* and *how many.*

WHICH ONE?	WHAT KIND?	HOW MANY?
that book	*romance* novel	*several* chapters
the *other* class	*steep* expense	*multiple* choices
the *last* song	*jazzy* melody	*six* awards

Adverbs, on the other hand, describe verbs, adjectives, and other adverbs. They tell us *where, when, how,* and *to what extent.*

WHERE?	WHEN?	HOW?	TO WHAT EXTENT?
The plane flew *south*.	Jude arrived *early*.	She sang *beautifully*.	Anthony is *very* talented.
Put the chair *here*.	She registered *late*.	The system is behaving *erratically*.	Eleanor is still *extremely* ill.
I was walking *back* to camp.	Let's meet again *tomorrow*.	They fought *bravely*.	The gas is *dangerously* low.

Remember to keep modifiers as close as possible to what they modify.

FEWER/LESS, NUMBER/AMOUNT

As a rule, use the adjective *fewer* to modify plural nouns or things that can be counted. Use *less* for singular nouns that represent a quantity or a degree. Most nouns to which an -*s* can be added require the adjective *fewer*.

> Use <u>less salt</u> this time.
> Use <u>fewer eggs</u> this time.
> I spent <u>less time</u> on it than I'd planned.
> I spent <u>fewer hours</u> on it than I'd planned.

GOOD/BAD, WELL/BADLY

These pairs of words—*good/well, bad/badly*—are often confused. The key to proper usage is to understand their function in the sentence. *Good* and *bad* are adjectives; they should only be used to modify nouns and pronouns. *Well* and *badly* are adverbs; they should be used to modify verbs.

The <u>coffee</u> is <u>good</u>, but I didn't <u>do</u> so <u>well</u> with the rest of breakfast.
I had a <u>good</u> <u>time</u> and <u>did</u> very <u>well</u> for a beginner.

COMPARISONS

An important function of adjectives and adverbs is comparisons. When you are comparing *two* things, use the **comparative form** (-er) of the modifier. If you are comparing *more than two* things, use the **superlative form** (-est) of the modifier.

To create the **comparative** form, either:

1. add *-er* to the modifier, or
2. place the word *more* or *less* before the modifier.

In general, add *-er* to short modifiers (one or two syllables). Use *more* or *less* with modifiers of more than two syllables.

cheaper   *less expensive*
smarter   *more intelligent*

To create the **superlative** form, either:

1. add *-est* to the modifier, or
2. place the word *most* or *least* before the modifier.

Again, as a general rule, add *-est* to short modifiers (one or two syllables). Use *most* or *least* with modifiers that are more than two syllables.

Wanda is <u>more experienced</u> than I, but I am the <u>most familiar</u> with the software.
Ahmed is clearly the <u>smartest</u> student in the class.
This is the <u>most expensive</u> but also the <u>most practical</u> solution.
He is the <u>wisest</u> man I know.

DOUBLE COMPARISONS AND DOUBLE NEGATIVES

Be sure to **avoid double comparisons.** Don't use both *-er/-est* and *more/less* or *most/least* together.

Incorrect: *This is the most longest I've ever had to wait in line.*
Correct: *This is the <u>longest</u> I've ever had to wait in line.*

Incorrect: *Xavier is more happier now.*
Correct: *Xavier is <u>happier</u> now.*

Likewise, be sure to avoid **double negatives**. When a negative word such as *no* or *not* is added to a statement that is already negative, a double negative—and potential confusion—results. *Hardly* and *barely* are also negative words. Remember, one negative is all you need.

Incorrect: *He doesn't have no idea what she's talking about.*
Correct: *He does<u>n't</u> have any idea what she's talking about.*
He has <u>no</u> idea what she's talking about.

Incorrect: *I can't hardly wait to see you.*
Correct: *I can <u>hardly</u> wait to see you.*
I ca<u>n't</u> wait to see you.

Incorrect: *They don't want no trouble.*
Correct: *They do<u>n't</u> want any trouble.*

Practice 12

Choose the correct word in the italicized pairs below.

1. I have a large *number/amount* of tickets to sell.

2. There are *fewer/less* people outside now.

3. I am feeling *good/well* today.

4. He has been behaving *bad/badly* since his parents got divorced.

5. I can't find *no/any* reason to say no.

6. This is the most *friendly/friendliest* town in America.

Answers

1. I have a large *number* of tickets to sell.
2. There are *fewer* people outside now.
3. I am feeling *well* today.
4. He has been behaving *badly* since his parents got divorced.
5. I can't find *any* reason to say no.
6. This is the *friendliest* town in America.

▶ Rhetorical Skills

Rhetorical skills refers to the series of techniques writers use to create text that is clear, engaging, and appropriate for its audience and purpose. From beginning to end, writing is a process of making decisions about technique. How should you introduce your topic? What is the best way to conclude your essay? What is the most effective way to organize your ideas? What word or image can you use to convey a particular thought?

The rhetorical skills questions on the ACT English Test cover three areas: general writing strategies, organization, and style.

General Writing Strategies

General writing strategies are those basic techniques writers use to develop a readable and engaging text. The strategies covered on the ACT include your ability to:

- write in a way that is appropriate for audience and purpose
- provide appropriate and sufficient support
- craft effective introductions and conclusions
- use effective transitions
- revise for more effective writing

AUDIENCE AND PURPOSE

Effective writing has at its core a constant awareness of and attention to **audience** and **purpose**. Good writers are always thinking about their readers: Who are they? What do they know about the subject? What prejudices or preconceived notions might they have? What will keep their attention?

Good writers are also always thinking about purpose. Is their goal to teach a lesson? Provide information? Entertain? Answer a question? Convince or persuade?

These two core elements—audience and purpose—drive just about every decision a writer makes, beginning with the topic the writer chooses. If your audience is a college admissions officer, for example, then you must write with that reader in mind, and you will choose your topic, style, and approach accordingly. You will follow the directions carefully, keep a tight focus, provide details and specific examples, and write in a formal but not stilted style. On the other hand, if you are writing a letter to a friend to tell her about your latest camping trip, you will likely use an informal style, and you may digress frequently, use slang, use too many exclamation points, and have grammar and usage errors that you would be sure to avoid in your college application essay.

On the ACT English Test, some of the questions will ask you to judge how well a passage responds to its audience and fulfills its purpose. You may be asked, for example, to select text that is most appropriate for the audience or determine what purpose the writer is trying to achieve. To answer these questions correctly, you will need to be able to infer from the clues in the passage both its intended audience and its main purpose.

DETERMINING AUDIENCE

Knowing your audience will help you make a couple of key writing decisions, including choosing appropriate words, level of formality, and level of detail—three matters of style we will discuss in more detail shortly.

If, for example, you are writing about voice recognition software and your audience is composed of speech technology experts, then you will be able to use **jargon** (technical or specialized language) comfortably. If you are writing for a general audience, however, you will need to avoid jargon and write in general terms that all readers will be able to understand.

Level of formality provides another clue to the writer's audience. The degree of formality tells you what kind of relationship the writer has to his or her audience. If the text uses slang, for example, you can infer that the writer has a casual, informal relationship with the reader; he is probably not writing for a general audience.

The **level of detail** and **specificity** in a text also tells you something about the writer's intended audience. It gives you a sense of how much readers know (or are expected to know) about the topic. For example, in the "Batman" passage you read in the pre-test, the writer provides very basic information about the superhero. Clearly, he's not writing for Batman buffs who would already know the history of the Batman character. By opening with "Pow! Bam! Zap!", the writer *is* assuming that most readers have at some point seen the show or read a Batman comic strip, since Batman is such a well-known character in our culture.

On the ACT English Test, you can use this awareness of audience to answer questions about word choice and other stylistic issues. It can also help you answer questions about what kind of information should be added to or deleted from a text. You will see examples of these kinds of questions shortly in the following sections.

DETERMINING PURPOSE

As you read passages on the ACT English Test, it is important to get a clear sense of the writer's purpose. What seems to be the writer's main goal? This will help you answer questions like the following, which refers to a passage about voice recognition technology:

The writer plans to add a fifth paragraph. Which of the following would be her best choice?
a. a paragraph about the history of voice recognition technology
b. a paragraph about the cost of voice recognition software
c. a paragraph comparing features of current voice recognition programs
d. a paragraph with statistics and testimonials about the accuracy of voice recognition programs

The best paragraph to insert depends entirely upon the writer's purpose in the passage. If, based on the content and style of the passage, you conclude that the writer's goal is to convince readers that voice recognition software really works, then **d** is the best choice; it's the paragraph that best supports the writer's purpose. If, on the other hand, the passage aims to help readers pick the best voice recognition software for them, then **c** would be the best choice.

Each writer has a specific purpose behind a given text, but in general, most writers write for one of the following reasons:

Narration: To tell the story of a meaningful experience or event.

Description: To describe in detail a significant person, place, or thing.

Comparison and contrast: To show how two or more things are similar or different.

Process: To explain how something is done or should be done.

Classification/Analysis: To explain how an item fits into a particular category or to analyze its parts.

Definition: To provide a detailed definition of a word or an idea.

Cause and effect: To explain the cause(s) or effect(s) of something.

Education: To teach a lesson or inform readers about a subject.

Evaluation: To judge the effectiveness of something.

Persuasion: To convince readers of something.

Determining purpose is a matter of determining the answer to one key question: What does this text add up to? In other words, what is it all for? Why this information, these words, these details? What main idea do you get from reading the text? (For more information about determining a writer's main idea, see page 208 in the Reading Test review.)

REVISION STRATEGIES

Many questions on the ACT English Test will ask you how an addition, deletion, or other kind of revision would affect the text. **To revise** means to look at something again (to *re-examine*) in order to improve it or amend it. This is quite different from **editing**, which is correcting grammar or usage errors and was covered in the first half of this section. Revising means carefully re-reading a text and then changing it to make it better. Revision is concerned with content and style—what the writer says and how he or she says it. As a general rule, writers revise first, then edit when they are sure their text says what they want to say, in the way that they want to say it.

Revision questions on the ACT English Test focus on two key elements of effective writing:

Support. Does the passage offer sufficient support for its ideas or claims? Support can come in the form of specific examples, facts, reasons, descriptions or anecdotes, or expert opinion and analysis. You may be asked, for example, which of four items would best develop the support in a paragraph.

Focus. Is there a piece of the passage that seems to digress? Would removing a sentence or paragraph improve the focus of the text? Would adding a sentence make it clear how a sentence relates to the main idea of the passage?

For example, notice how the following paragraph loses focus:

(1)Electronic mail (e-mail) has been in widespread use for more than a decade. (2)E-mail simplifies the flow of ideas, connects people from distant offices, eliminates the need for meetings, and often boosts productivity. (3)But e-mail should be carefully managed to avoid unclear and inappropriate communication. (4)E-mail messages should be concise and limited to one topic. (5)It is important to be concise in business. (6)Say what you need to say as succinctly as possible. (7)Avoid wordiness or redundancy. (8)When complex issues need to be addressed, phone calls are still best.

Sentences 5, 6, and 7, while true, do not fit the focus of this paragraph about email. The paragraph would be much stronger if these sentences were omitted.

BEGINNINGS, MIDDLES, AND ENDS

The ACT English Test also assesses your ability to choose effective introductory, transitional, and concluding material. You may be asked, for example, which sentence would best introduce a paragraph or which word is the appropriate transition between two ideas.

Introductions

First impressions count, and that is why introductions are so important in writing. A good introduction:

1. Indicates what the passage is about (its topic) and what the writer is going to say *about* the topic (its main idea).
2. Grabs the reader's attention.
3. Establishes the tone of the passage.

Techniques for grabbing attention include opening with:

- a question
- quotation
- a surprising fact or statement
- an imaginary situation or scenario
- an anecdote
- interesting background information
- a new twist on a familiar phrase

For example, the introduction to the Batman passage in the pretest—"Pow! Bam! Zap!"—is an opening that plays upon a convention of comic strips and the Batman television series.

Transitions

Transitions are the words and phrases used to move from one idea to the next. They help words flow smoothly and show readers how ideas relate to one another. Transitional words and phrases connect ideas within sentences and between sentences, within paragraphs and between paragraphs. They are essential to good writing. Notice, for example, the difference between the two paragraphs below. In the first version, the transitions have been omitted. In the second version, they are underlined.

Most people tend to think of genius as an abnormality—a "good" abnormality, but an abnormality. Psychologists regarded the quirks of genius as too erratic to describe intelligently; Anna Findley's groundbreaking study uncovers predictable patterns in the biographies of geniuses. These do not dispel the common belief that there is a kind of supernatural intervention in the lives of unusually talented men and women. Findley does show that all geniuses experience three intensely productive periods in their lives, one of which always occurs shortly before their deaths. This is true whether the genius lives to be nineteen or ninety.

Most people tend to think of genius as an abnormality—a "good" abnormality, but an abnormality <u>nonetheless</u>. <u>Until recently</u>, psychologists regarded the quirks of genius as too erratic to describe intelligently; <u>however</u>, Anna Findley's groundbreaking study uncovers predictable patterns in the biographies of geniuses. <u>These patterns</u> do not dispel the common belief that there is a kind of supernatural intervention in the lives of unusually talented men and women. <u>However</u>, Findley does show that all geniuses experience three intensely productive periods in their lives, one of which always occurs shortly before their deaths. <u>This fact</u> is true whether the genius lives to be nineteen or ninety.

With the appropriate transitions, the second paragraph reads much more smoothly and makes its ideas more clear.

Certain transitions work best for specific functions. For example, "for example" is a great transition to use when introducing a specific example. Here's a brief list of some of the most common transitional words and phrases:

IF YOU WANT TO:	USE THESE TRANSITIONAL WORDS AND PHRASES:		
introduce an example	for example	for instance	that is
	in other words	in particular	specifically
	in fact	first (second) of all	
show addition	and	in addition	also
	again	moreover	furthermore
show emphasis	indeed	in fact	certainly
acknowledge another	although	though	granted
point of view	despite	even though	

show rank	more importantly	above all	first and foremost
show cause and effect	because	therefore	as a result
	consequently	since	thus
show comparison	likewise	similarly	like
show contrast	unlike	however	on the other hand
	whereas	instead	rather
show the passage of time	then	next	later
	after	before	during
	meanwhile	while	soon

Conclusions

Conclusions, too, should be powerful. After all, people tend to remember most what comes first and last, and the final words have the power to ring in readers' ears for a long time afterwards. A good conclusion will:

1. Restate the main idea.
2. Provide a sense of closure (does not "open a new can of worms" by introducing a new topic).
3. Arouse readers' emotions to make the ending and main idea memorable.

The Batman text, again, provides a good example. The concluding sentence:

> *In Batman, Kane gave us an image of our own superhero potential.*

This sums up what makes Batman so popular, rounding out the passage in a way that makes readers think about their own similarities to Batman and what sort of superheroes they could be.

Many of the same introductory techniques can be used to help make conclusions memorable:

- a quotation
- a question
- an anecdote
- a prediction
- a solution or recommendation
- a call to action

For example, the conclusion to a passage about a healthy diet might end with a call to action:

Take a good, long look in your refrigerator and pantry. What unhealthy foods call your icebox and cabinets their home? Find them, get rid of them, and stock up with foods that will help you live a longer, healthier life.

Practice 13

Read the passage below and answer the questions that correspond to the underlined text.

There are two main theories of punishment: retribution and deterrence. <u>Retribution</u> argues
1
that people who commit crimes deserve to be punished and that the punishment should fit

the crime. <u>An</u> "eye for an eye" philosophy. <u>Deterrence</u> posits that punishing offenders will
2 3
help prevent future crimes.

1. a. NO CHANGE
  b. The first, retribution,
  c. In the beginning, retribution
  d. First and foremost, retribution

2. f. NO CHANGE
  g. However, it is an
  h. Also, an
  j. In other words, it is an

3. a. NO CHANGE
  b. According to deterrence theory,
  c. Deterrence theory, on the other hand,
  d. Meanwhile, deterrence theory

4. Which of the following sentences would most effectively introduce this passage?
  f. Why do we punish those who commit crimes?
  g. Crimes should always be punished.
  h. As they say, crime doesn't pay.
  j. There is a record number of people in American prisons today.

5. Which of the following sentences would most effectively conclude this passage?

    a. Most criminals do not commit crimes again once they are out of jail.

    b. Judges and juries typically combine these two theories when sentencing offenders.

    c. As you can see, crime doesn't pay.

    d. Judges and juries should make sure the punishment is just.

Answers

1. b.

2. j.

3. c.

4. f. This introduction asks a question that will be answered in the passage.

5. b. This conclusion brings the two theories together in a statement that tells us why it is important to know these theories. Choices **a** and **c** are irrelevant; choice **d** is more closely related to the topic but still addresses a different issue.

Organization

The ACT English Test's questions about organization are designed to measure your ability to organize ideas effectively. Questions may ask you the best sequence of sentences or paragraphs, the best place to add a sentence or paragraph, or the best sentence or paragraph to eliminate to improve a paragraph's unity or coherence.

At their core, most non-fiction texts except narratives have the basic underlying structure of main idea → support. That is, they begin with a main idea (sometimes called the **thesis** or **theme** of the text) that controls the whole passage; it is this idea that the text will develop. The rest of the text then provides support for that idea in the form of examples, definitions, reasons, and so on.

On this basic level of main idea → support, everything in the passage must, in fact, support or develop that main idea. When sentences or paragraphs lose relevance, when they digress from that controlling idea, the passage loses its focus.

Beyond this most basic principle of organization, writers typically rely on several main strategies for organizing their support. One of these strategies often serves as the overall organizing principle for the text while individual sections may use other techniques as well. For example, in an essay comparing and contrasting two film versions of *Frankenstein,* the writer will use comparison and contrast as the overall organizing principle, but she may also use order of importance when explaining what makes one version better than the other.

The four most common organizational patterns are:

- chronological order
- order of importance
- comparison and contrast
- cause and effect

CHRONOLOGICAL ORDER

When writers use *time* as their main organization principle, it is called **chronological order**. They describe events in the order in which they did happen, will happen, or should happen. Much of what you read is organized in this way, including historical texts, instructions and procedures, and essays about personal experiences. The third paragraph of the Batman text uses this organizational pattern:

Kane's Batman was a huge success right from the start. The masked hero soon moved from comic books to its own newspaper strip, and in 1943, Batman episodes were aired on the radio. In 1966, live-action Batman shows hit the TV screen, giving ABC network the ratings boost it badly needed. The series was wildly popular, and the syndicated show still airs today on channels such as the Cartoon Network and Nickelodeon.

Passages organized by chronology typically use many transitional words and phrases to help us follow the passage of time. The transitions help us see when things happened and in what order and also help us follow along when the passage shifts from one period of time to another. Transitional words and phrases keep events linked together in the proper order.

Below is a list of some of the most common chronological transitions:

first, second, third, etc.	before	after	next	now
then	when	as soon as	immediately	suddenly
soon	during	while	meanwhile	later
in the meantime	at last	eventually	finally	afterward

Here, the transitions in the Batman paragraph are underlined:

Kane's Batman was a huge success right from the start. The masked hero <u>soon</u> moved from comic books to its own newspaper strip, and <u>in 1943</u>, Batman episodes were aired on the radio. <u>In 1966</u>, live-action Batman shows hit the TV screen, giving ABC network the ratings boost it badly needed. The series was wildly popular, and the syndicated show <u>still</u> airs today on channels such as the Cartoon Network and Nickelodeon.

ORDER OF IMPORTANCE

With this organizational pattern, ideas are arranged by *rank* instead of time. The most important information comes first or last, depending upon the writer's purpose.

Organizing ideas from most important to least important puts the most essential information first. Writers often do this when they are offering advice or when they want to be sure readers get the most important information right away. Newspaper articles, for example, generally use this structure. They begin with the most important information (the *who, what, when, where,* and *why* about the event) so readers don't have to read the whole article to get those facts. Details and background information come later in the article.

When writers move from least to most important, they save their most important idea or piece of information for last. Writers often use this approach when they are presenting an argument because this kind of structure is usually more convincing than the most-to-least organizational pattern. The more controversial the argument, the more important this structure. In an argument, you need to build your case piece-by-piece and win your readers over point by point. If your less important points make sense to the reader, then your more important points will be stronger. And, as the saying goes, writers often "save the best for last" because that's where "the best" often has the most impact. In other words, the writer's **purpose** helps to determine the structure he or she uses.

Transitions are very important for this organizational pattern, too. Here is a list of the most common transitions writers use with the order of importance structure. Most of these work for both the most-to-least important and least-to-most important formats:

first and foremost	most importantly	more importantly	moreover
above all	first, second, third	last but not least	

COMPARISON AND CONTRAST

When you show how two or more things are similar, you are making a **comparison**. When you show how two or more things are different, you are **contrasting** them. As an organizational technique, this pattern allows you to place two (or more) items side by side and see how they measure up against each other. How are they similar or different? And why does it matter? For example, a writer comparing and contrasting the 1931 and 1994 film versions of *Frankenstein* might aim to show that the 1994 version is far truer to the book and rightly depicts Victor Frankenstein as just as much of a monster as the creature he creates.

As with the other organizational patterns, one of the keys to a good comparison and contrast is strong transitions. It's important to let readers know when you are comparing and when you are contrasting. As a reader, it's important to watch for these transitions.

Here are some words and phrases that show similarity:

similarly	in the same way	likewise
like	in a like manner	just as
and	also	both

The following words and phrases, on the other hand, show difference:

but	on the other hand	yet
however	on the contrary	in contrast
conversely	while	unlike

CAUSE AND EFFECT

The fourth most common organizational pattern is **cause** and **effect**. A *cause* is a person or thing that makes something happen (creates an effect). An *effect* is an event or change created by an action (or cause). A passage about cause explains *why* something took place. You might ask, for example, "What caused the Cold War?" A passage about effect, on the other hand, explains *what happened after* something took place. What happened as a result of the Cold War?

Just as certain key words indicate whether you're comparing or contrasting, other key words indicate whether things are causes or effects. Here is a partial list of words and phrases that indicate cause and effect:

WORDS INDICATING CAUSE

because (of)	created (by)
since	caused (by)

WORDS INDICATING EFFECT

therefore	so
hence	consequently
as a result	

To answer questions about organization on the ACT, you need to determine the writer's purpose and be able to recognize organizational patterns on both the essay and paragraph level. In a longer text, all the paragraphs should work together to support the main idea. In a paragraph, all of the sentences should work together to support one controlling idea as well. A **paragraph** is, by definition, a series of sentences about one main idea. If there is more than one main idea, you should have more than one paragraph.

By identifying the organizational pattern, you can determine where to insert sentences or paragraphs; you can also determine whether any sentences or paragraphs are misplaced, such as a sentence that is out of chronological order.

Practice 14

Part A: Divide the following text into at least three paragraphs.

The Cold War was one of the most interesting and troubling times in American history. Several important historical events led to the Cold War. First, in 1939, Albert Einstein wrote a letter to President Franklin D. Roosevelt. In that letter, Einstein told Roosevelt that it was possible to create an atomic weapon, and he asked Roosevelt to fund research and experiments in atomic weapons. Roosevelt agreed, and the government created the Manhattan Project, a massive effort to develop nuclear weapons. Next, the date that will live in infamy: August 6, 1945. The U.S.

dropped an atomic bomb on Hiroshima, Japan—a civilian, not military, target. An estimated 150,000 civilians were killed in the attack. President Harry Truman and others claimed at the time that dropping the bomb was necessary to force Japan to surrender and end World War II. Others argue that we used the bomb largely to show the Soviet Union that we were a superior world power. Though the U.S. and the U.S.S.R. were officially allies, tensions between the two countries were already high. A deep ideological battle between the two countries—one Communist, the other Capitalist—was already in place, and each country was determined to outdo the other. Two years later, in 1947, President Truman established the Truman Doctrine. This important document redefined American foreign policy. It created a "policy of containment" which framed our foreign policy as a battle between "good" and "evil." This dramatically increased the growing tension between the two countries.

Part B: Arrange the following sentences in a logical order.

- Many people are afraid of snakes, but most snakes aren't as dangerous as people think they are.
- There are more than 2,500 different species of snakes around the world.
- Statistically, many other animals are far more dangerous than snakes.
- Only a small percentage of those species are poisonous, and only a few species have venom strong enough to kill a human being.
- In fact, in this country, more people die from dog bites each year than from snakes.
- Furthermore, snakes bite only 1,000–2,000 people in the United States each year, and only ten of those bites (that's less than 1%) result in death.

Answers

Part A

Answers may vary, but this is the most logical way to divide the text into three paragraphs.

The Cold War was one of the most interesting and troubling times in American history. Several important historical events led to the Cold War. First, in 1939, Albert Einstein wrote a letter to President Franklin D. Roosevelt. In that letter, Einstein told Roosevelt that it was possible to create an atomic weapon, and he asked Roosevelt to fund research and experiments in atomic weapons. Roosevelt agreed, and the government created the Manhattan Project, a massive effort to develop nuclear weapons.

Next, the date that will live in infamy: August 6, 1945. The U.S. dropped an atomic bomb on Hiroshima, Japan—a civilian, not military, target. An estimated 150,000 civilians were killed in the attack. President Harry Truman and others claimed at the time that dropping the bomb was necessary to force Japan to surrender and end World War II. Others argue that we used the bomb largely to show the Soviet Union that we were a superior world power. Though the U.S. and the U.S.S.R. were officially allies, tensions between the two countries were already high. A deep ideological battle between the two countries—one Communist, the other Capitalist—was already in place, and each country was determined to outdo the other.

Two years later, in 1947, President Truman established the Truman Doctrine. This important document redefined American foreign policy. It created a "policy of containment" which framed our foreign policy as a battle between "good" and "evil." This dramatically increased the growing tension between the two countries.

Part B

- Many people are afraid of snakes, but most snakes aren't as dangerous as people think they are.
- There are more than 2,500 different species of snakes around the world.
- Only a small percentage of those species are poisonous, and only a few species have venom strong enough to kill a human being.
- Furthermore, snakes bite only 1,000–2,000 people in the United States each year, and only ten of those bites (that's less than 1%) result in death.
- Statistically, many other animals are far more dangerous than snakes.
- In fact, in this country, more people die from dog bites each year than from snakes.

Style

Style refers to the manner in which something is done. For example, we all buy and wear clothes that fit our own personal style—the way we like to look and feel when we are dressed. The same is true of our writing; each of us has his or her own individual style, and the more we understand stylistic techniques, the more effectively we can express ourselves in writing.

Style in writing is created by several different elements. The ACT English Test focuses on four key elements of style:

- word choice (including figurative language and imagery)
- consistency in style and tone
- variety in sentence structure and use of punctuation and other techniques for effect
- avoiding ambiguity, wordiness, and redundancy

WORD CHOICE

One of the most important decisions writers make is a constant one: **word choice**. As you write, you are always, in every sentence, thinking about the right words to express your ideas. The "right" word has four essential characteristics:

1. It expresses the idea you wish to convey.
2. It is exact (precise).
3. It is appropriate for the audience.
4. It is consistent with the style and tone of the text.

Notice how effective word choice cuts back on wordiness and creates much more powerful sentences in the example below:

> She *ate* her lunch *quickly and hungrily.*

> She *devoured* her lunch.
> She *gobbled* her lunch.
> She *inhaled* her lunch.

Each of these italicized verbs has much more impact than the verb *ate* and its two modifiers, *quickly* and *hungrily.* These exact verbs create a vivid picture; they tell us exactly how she ate her lunch.

Exact nouns will improve your sentences, too. Here's an example of a general sentence made more precise:

> The *machine* made a loud *noise* and then stopped.
> The *generator* made a loud *bang* and then stopped.

The second sentence, with its exact nouns, tells us what kind of machine it was and what kind of noise it made, giving us a much clearer picture of what happened.

Adjectives, too, should be precise. Instead of writing:

> I am *very hungry.*

Try an exact adjective:

> I am *famished.*

Famished means *very hungry*—and is a much more powerful word to convey your idea.

LEVEL OF FORMALITY

Word choice determines level of formality, and vice versa. Would you say to your professor, "Yo, wassup?" Probably not. But you certainly might talk that way to your friends. We are usually careful to use the right level of formality when we talk to someone. The same should be true of our writing. Writers must decide how formal or informal they should be when they write, and they make this decision based on their audience and their purpose.

Level of formality can range from the very informal (slang) to the very formal (esoteric, ceremonial) to everything in between. Writers use word choice and sentence structure to manipulate the level of formality. Here's an example:

A: I couldn't believe it. I mean, who would have guessed? I sure didn't! I had no clue, no clue at all. And I was the last person to find out, too. It figures.

B: I was deeply shocked; I had never suspected such a thing. Not surprisingly, I was the last person to become aware of the situation.

These two examples are drastically different in style and in the level of formality. Though they both tell the same story and both use the personal first-person *I,* there's clearly a different relationship to the reader. From the word choice and style—the short sentences, the very casual language—we can tell that the writer of passage A has a more informal, more friendly relationship with the reader than the writer of passage B. The emotion of the writer in passage A is much more transparent, too, because the language is more informal and natural. You get the idea that passage A is addressed to a friend while passage B might be addressed to an official.

On the ACT, you probably won't be asked directly about level of formality. But you can use your awareness of level of formality to draw conclusions about audience and to determine which revisions or additions would best fit the text.

Practice 15

Rank the sentences below according to formality. Put a 1 next to the sentence that is most formal and a 3 next to the sentence that is most casual.

1. _____ Move faster.

_____ Pick up the pace.

_____ Increase your speed.

2. _____ Gimme a hand, would you?

_____ Would you please assist me?

_____ Would you help me out here?

Answers
1. 2 Move faster.
   3 Pick up the pace.
   1 Increase your speed.
2. 3 Gimme a hand, would you?
   1 Would you please assist me?
   2 Would you help me out here?

FIGURATIVE LANGUAGE AND IMAGERY

An important aspect of style is **figurative language** and **imagery**. Figurative language includes **similes** and **metaphors**. A simile compares two things using the words *like* or *as*. A metaphor is stronger than a simile because it makes the comparison without the words *like* or *as*. Here's an example:

No figurative language:	She was running around like crazy.
Simile:	She was running around like the Mad Hatter.
Metaphor:	She was the Mad Hatter.

Figurative language is so effective because it helps readers picture what the writer is describing in an imaginative, original way. ("She was running around like a chicken with its head cut off" is a simile, but it's also a **cliché**—an overused phrase that should be avoided.)

For similes and metaphors to work, the two things being compared must be sufficiently different. For example, it doesn't work to compare a moth to a butterfly. However, it *does* work to compare a butterfly and the way curtains flutter in the wind.

Imagery does not make a comparison, but it does paint a picture for readers by engaging the senses. Here are two examples:

> *The cat lay in a warm circle of sunlight just beneath the window.*
> *The smell of freshly-baked apples and cinnamon drifted across the room to where I sat next to a crackling fire.*

Of course, figurative language and imagery must be appropriate. Figurative language and imagery would be appropriate (even expected) in a narrative essay, but you probably should not include such language in a lab report for your physics class. And in any case, your similes, metaphors, and images should not offend or change the style or tone of your text.

Practice 16

Part A: Create similes and metaphors for the following sentences.

1. He has a quiet manner.
   Simile:
   Metaphor:

2. She was very angry.
   Simile:
   Metaphor:

Part B: Use imagery to describe the following.

1. A body of water

2. A house

Answers

Part A

1. He has a quiet manner.

Simile:　　　He is as quiet as a whisper. (*As quiet as a mouse* is a cliché.)

Metaphor:　　He is a whisper.

2. She was very angry.

Simile:　　　She was as angry as a tornado.

Metaphor:　　She was a tornado.

Part B

1. A body of water

The gentle lapping of the waves lulled me to sleep by the lake.

2. A house

The door to the gray house on the hill slammed shut in the wind, the sound echoing throughout the empty rooms.

CONSISTENCY IN STYLE AND TONE

Appropriate and consistent **tone** is another element of effective writing that will be tested on the ACT English Test. You may be asked to determine whether the writer's tone is appropriate for his or her audience and purpose and to identify whether the writer has shifted tone in the passage.

Tone is *the mood or attitude conveyed by words or speech*. Think, for example, of all the different ways to say *sure* or *hello*. It's how you say the word that conveys so much of its meaning.

When you listen to others, it's usually pretty easy to hear the tone of their voice. But how do you "hear" tone in writing? How can you tell how the words should sound? Say you come across the word *sure* as you are reading. How do you know whether to whisper it or shout it?

When we speak, we create tone by how quickly or slowly we say a word, how loudly or softly we say it, and how we use facial expressions and body language. When we read, though, we can't *hear* how the writer says something. And we certainly can't see the writer's facial expressions or body language. But we can look carefully at word choice, punctuation, and style to help determine tone. For example, recall this pair of sentences from our punctuation review:

> *Wait, I'm coming with you.*
> *Wait—I'm coming with you!*

Here, it is the punctuation that changes the tone. The first sentence is calm, neutral. The second sentence, on the other hand, is emotional, excited.

There are endless varieties of tones when we speak. Likewise, there are endless varieties of tone in writing. Here's a list of some of the more common words used to describe tone:

cheerful	hopeful	sad	gloomy
apologetic	critical	sincere	insincere
sarcastic	ironic	playful	demanding
bossy	indifferent	anxious	respectful
disrespectful	foreboding	uncertain	threatening
matter-of-fact	somber	grateful	annoyed
humorous	mocking	defeated	uplifting
timid	joyful	secure	insecure
hesitant	bold	rude	complimentary
angry	confident	mischievous	proud

Practice 17

Carefully read the sentences below to determine their tone. Read them out loud and listen to how they sound when you read them. With what kind of voice do you read? What is your tone?

1. Um, do you think maybe my pizza will be ready soon?
   a. playful
   b. hesitant
   c. cheerful

2. Where the devil is my pizza?!
   f. gloomy
   g. disrespectful
   h. demanding

3. Alright already, your pizza's coming!
   a. rude
   b. bold
   c. annoyed

4. Just a moment, please. Your pizza will be ready shortly.
   f. respectful
   g. timid
   h. anxious

5. Don't push the yellow button. If you do, the system will shut down.

    a. bossy

    b. matter-of-fact

    c. ironic

6. Don't you dare even go near that yellow button!

    f. threatening

    g. sad

    h. demanding

Answers

1. b.

2. h.

3. c.

4. f.

5. b.

6. f.

VARIETY IN SENTENCE STRUCTURE AND RHETORICAL TECHNIQUES FOR EMPHASIS

Some ACT English Test questions will test your ability to manipulate sentence structure and punctuation for effect. Sentence structure, as we noted earlier, is an important element of style. If all of your sentences have the same pattern, you will end up with writing that is monotonous and dry, like the following passage:

> *He is six feet, three inches tall. He is 34 years old. He loves to play golf. He drives a new convertible. He is a doctor. He works in a hospital. He lives in New Jersey.*

Unsophisticated and quite dull, isn't it? That is because all of the sentences are short and share the same structure; they all start with *he* and a present tense verb. This is quite different from parallel structure. Parallelism means using a repeating sentence pattern to create rhythm within a sentence or paragraph. This kind of repetition, on the other hand, creates monotony and shows a lack of flexibility in creating sentence patterns. Here's the same paragraph revised to show variety in sentence structure:

> *This 34-year-old doctor measures six feet, three inches tall. A New Jersey resident, he is a big fan of golf, and he drives his new convertible to the golf course whenever he can slip away from the hospital.*

Notice how much more interesting this paragraph is now. The seven sentences have been combined into two, and they both start with something other than *he*. Many of the short sentences have been turned into modifiers that make for more varied sentence patterns.

Sentence structure and punctuation can also be used to manipulate emphasis. The best place to put sentence elements that you want to emphasize is at the end (the "save the best for last" approach). What comes last is what lingers longest in the readers' ears.

> *He is tall, dark, and handsome.* [The emphasis is on *handsome*. If *tall* were the most important characteristic, then it should come last.]
> *She is smart, reliable, and experienced.* [The emphasis is on *experienced*; if *smart* is the most important characteristic, then that should be last in the list.]

You can also use a dash to set off part of a sentence for emphasis:

> *He is tall, dark, handsome—and married.*

Here, the stress on the last element is heightened by the dash, which emphasizes the sense of disappointment in the sentence.

Practice 18

Rewrite the following paragraph to create more variety in sentence structure.

> The coast of the State of Maine is one of the most irregular in the world. Draw a straight line from the southernmost city in Maine, Kittery, to the northernmost coastal city, Eastport. This line would measure about 225 miles. Follow the coastline between the same two cities. The distance is more than ten times as far. This irregularity is the result of what is called a *drowned coastline*. The term comes from the glacial activity of the ice age. The glacier descended. It expended enormous force on those mountains. The mountains sank into the sea.

Answer

Answers will vary. Here's one possibility:

> The coast of the State of Maine is one of the most irregular in the world. If you draw a straight line from Kittery, the southernmost city in Maine, to Eastport, the northernmost coastal city, the line would measure about 225 miles. Follow the coastline between the same two cities, however, and the distance is more than ten times as far. This irregularity is the result of what is called a *drowned coastline,* a term that comes from the glacial activity of the ice age. When the glacier descended, it expended enormous force on those mountains, and the mountains sank into the sea.

AVOIDING AMBIGUITY, WORDINESS, AND REDUNDANCY

An **ambiguous** word or phrase is one that has two or more possible meanings. Take a look at this sentence, for example:

That's a big book.

This sentence can be read in two ways: that the book has many pages, or that the cover is large. You can eliminate this ambiguity by revising the sentence in one of the following ways:

That book has many pages.
That book's cover is large.

Another type of ambiguity happens when a phrase is in the wrong place in a sentence (see page 42 for more information on modifier placement). For example, look at the following sentence:

He was standing next to the car on the corner.

Here, the word order, not word choice, creates ambiguity. Was he on the corner, or was the car on the corner? Because the phrase *on the corner* is in the wrong place, the sentence is unclear. It should be revised to read:

He was standing on the corner next to the car.

or

He was standing next to the car parked on the corner.

Unclear Pronoun References

Ambiguity can also result from unclear pronoun references. (For a pronoun review, see pages 75–76.) Here's an example:

Connor told Mark that he needed glasses.

In this sentence, there are two different people *he* could be referring to: Connor and Mark. Clearly, this sentence needs to be revised. But it would be awkward to say *Connor told Mark that Connor needed glasses.* A good way out is to use dialogue:

Connor told Mark, "I need glasses."

Here's another kind of unclear pronoun reference:

I heard <u>they</u> were going to repave our street.

This is an example of a common pronoun error: using a vague "they" when there are specific people behind the action. You may not know exactly who those people are, but you know enough to say something like the following:

I heard <u>the township</u> is going to repave our street.

There are always people behind their actions, and your sentences should say so.

Redundancy and Wordiness

Some ACT English Test questions may ask you to identify or eliminate **redundancy** or **unnecessary wordiness** within sentences. Redundancy is the unnecessary repetition of ideas. Wordiness is the use of several words when a few can express the same idea more clearly and concisely.

On the sentence level, in general, less is more. The fewer words you use to get your point across, the better. Unnecessary words often waste time and cloud meaning. Sentences that don't have any words to waste are clear and have impact.

Wordiness and redundancy typically result from three different causes:

- The use of unnecessary words or phrases.

    Redundant: *Turn left at the <u>green colored</u> house.*
    Correct: *Turn left at the <u>green</u> house.*

- Unnecessary repetition of nouns or pronouns.

    Redundant: *<u>Riva she</u> couldn't believe her ears.*
    Correct: *<u>Riva</u> couldn't believe her ears.*

- The use of wordy phrases instead of adverbs.

    Wordy: *She spoke <u>in a very convincing manner</u>.*
    Concise: *She spoke <u>very convincingly</u>.*

    Wordy: *He had a car <u>that was old and rusty</u>.*
    Concise: *He had an <u>old, rusty</u> car.*

Practice 19

Rewrite the following sentences to correct any ambiguity, wordiness, or redundancy.

1. I returned back to my room after the meeting was over.

2. I heard they are going to put a movie theater on campus.

3. Please repeat again what you said.

4. While barbecuing our steaks, a hungry dog came into our backyard.

5. The servers they really take care of you at this restaurant.

6. The circumstances are very delicate in nature.

7. It was a story that was difficult to tell.

8. Fried in butter, Sylvan likes eggs.

Answers

Answers may vary slightly. Insertions are indicated in italics.

1. I returned ~~back~~ to my room after the meeting was over.

2. I heard ~~they~~ *the trustees* are going to put a movie theater on campus.

3. Please repeat ~~again~~ what you said.

4. While *we were* barbecuing our steaks, a hungry dog came into our backyard.

5. The servers ~~they~~ really take care of you at this restaurant.

6. The circumstances are very delicate ~~in nature~~.

7. It was a *difficult* story ~~that was difficult~~ to tell.

8. ~~Fried in butter,~~ Sylvan likes eggs *fried in butter*.

ce Questions

Directions

Now you have the opportunity to pull together all that you have reviewed and apply it to 80 practice ACT English Test questions. On the following pages, you will find eight passages with questions just like those you will see on the ACT. Read each passage carefully and answer the questions that follow. When you are taking the official ACT, make sure you carefully fill in the appropriate bubble on the answer document.

Bicycles

(1)Today, bicycles are so common that it's hard to believe they haven't always been around. (2)But two hundred years ago, bicycles weren't even existing , and the first bicycle, invented in Germany in 1818, was
<u>1</u>
nothing like our bicycles today—it was made of wood and didn't even have pedals. (3)Since then, however, numerous innovations and improvements in design have made the bicycle one of the most popular means of recreation and transportation around the world.

(4)In 1839, Kirkpatrick Macmillan, a Scottish blacksmith dramatically improved upon the original bicycle
<u>2</u>
design. (5)Macmillan's machine had tires with iron rims to keep them from getting worn down. (6)He also used foot-operated cranks similar to pedals so his bicycle could be ridden at a quick pace. (7)It
<u>3</u>
hadn't looked much like a modern bicycle, though,
<u>4</u>
because its back wheel was substantially larger than its front wheel. (8)In 1861, the French Michaux brothers took the evolution of the bicycle a step further by inventing an improved crank mechanism.

(9)Ten years later, James Starley, an English inventor, revolutionized bicycle design. (10) He made the
<u>5</u>
front wheel many times larger than the back wheel, putting a gear on the pedals to
<u>6</u>
make the bicycle more efficient, and lightened the wheels by using wire spokes. (11)Although this bicycle was much lighter and less tiring to ride, it was still clumsy, extremely top-heavy, and ridden mostly for entertainment.

(12)It wasn't until 1874 that the first truly modern bicycle appeared on the scene. (13) <u>Today there built</u> ,
₇ used, and enjoyed all over the world. (14) <u>H. J. Lawson, invented by another Englishman,</u> the "safety bicy-
₈ cle" would look familiar to today's cyclists. (15)This bicycle had equal sized wheels, which made it less
prone to toppling over. (16)Lawson also attached a chain to the pedals to drive the rear wheel. (17)With
these improvements, the bicycle became extremely popular and useful for transportation.

1. a. NO CHANGE
    b. there was no such thing as a bicycle,
    c. bicycles were uninvented,
    d. whoever heard of a bicycle,

2. f. NO CHANGE
    g. Macmillan was a Scottish blacksmith
    h. Macmillan, a Scottish blacksmith,
    j. Macmillan, he was a Scottish blacksmith,

3. a. NO CHANGE
    b. could be rode quickly
    c. could have been ridden fast
    d. could ride at a quick pace

4. f. NO CHANGE
    g. looked not
    h. didn't look
    j. wasn't looking

5. a. NO CHANGE
    b. He made
    c. He had made
    d. He; made

6. f. NO CHANGE
    g. putted a gear on
    h. put a gear in
    j. put a gear on

7. a. NO CHANGE
   b. Today there are built
   c. Today they, are built
   d. Today, they are built

8. f. NO CHANGE
   g. H. J. Lawson invented by another Englishman
   h. Invented by another Englishman, H.J. Lawson,
   j. Another Englishman inventor, H. J. Lawson,

9. If the writer were trying to convince readers to buy a bicycle, he would:
   a. NO CHANGE
   b. Add a paragraph describing the health and environmental benefits of riding a bike.
   c. Add a paragraph comparing the cost and quality of today's best-selling bicycles.
   d. Add a paragraph about the Tour de France and other bicycle races.

10. Which of the following sequences makes paragraph 4 most logical?
   f. NO CHANGE
   g. 12, 13, 14, 16, 17, 15
   h. 12, 17, 14, 15, 16, 13
   j. 12, 14, 15, 16, 17, 13

Industrial Revolution

The Industrial Revolution was essentially a rapid change <u>in the method of production of material goods.</u>
                                                                                    11
Products once made by hand were now able to be produced by machine or by chemical processes. The

Industrial Revolution transformed Western society, creating an international capitalist economy, urbaniza-

tion, labor reforms, <u>a system to educate the public</u> , and labor specialization.
                         12

(1)In the first century of the Industrial Revolution, the country undergoing the most dramatic change was

England. (2)After 1850, the Industrial Revolution <u>spread rapidly</u> throughout Europe. (3)While the pace
                                                        14
of change during the Industrial Revolution was indeed very rapid, the Industrial Revolution itself

stretched over a rather long period of time— <u>from the middle of the 18th century in the 1700s</u> through
                                                  15
World War I (1914).

Several key discoveries and inventions enabled the Industrial Revolution to take <u>place included</u> machines
                                                                                        16
and tools like the cotton gin, the radio, the circular saw, the cylindrical press, and the steam engine.

Cement, dynamite, and aluminum were invented, as were the bleaching and paper-making processes. At

the same time, there was a tremendous growth in population and urbanization. In fact, the population

growth in England was so dramatic that the country's population *doubled* between 1750–1820. This meant

a great demand for food, clothing, and shelter, demands <u>that became the driving force behind</u> the Indus-
                                                                                       17
trial Revolution.

Mass production of goods was made possible in large part <u>due to</u> the steam engine. The steam engine
                                                                  18
enabled factories to move from the countryside (where they were by bodies of water, their source of

power) into cities and towns, which were becoming increasingly crowded.

11. The writer changed the underlined text to *in how material goods were produced.* The result is a sentence
that is:
   a. more dramatic
   b. more concise
   c. more complex
   d. more accurate

12. f. NO CHANGE
   g. a public education system
   h. systematizing education
   j. public education

13. The most logical sequence for paragraph 2 is:
   a. NO CHANGE
   b. 2, 1, 3
   c. 3, 2, 1
   d. 3, 1, 2

14. f. NO CHANGE
   g. was quickly spreading
   h. spread with great rapidity
   j. spread fast

15. a. NO CHANGE
   b. from the middle of the century eighteen
   c. from the mid-1700s
   d. beginning in the middle of the 1700s, around 1750,

16. f. NO CHANGE
   g. place. These included
   h. place. Thus including
   j. place, including

17. a. NO CHANGE
   b. which had become the driving force of
   c. that forced the driving of
   d. that drove the force behind

18. f. NO CHANGE
   g. by
   h. from
   j. in regard to

19. Which of the following alternatives provides the most logical and effective conclusion for paragraph 4?
   a. Today, we are living in an Information Revolution.
   b. In cities and towns, factories found a ready workforce and large consumer base for their products.
   c. Railroads took goods out of the city back to the countryside.
   d. Overcrowding was a major problem to be dealt with in the cities.

20. The writer wishes to add a fifth paragraph. Which of the following topics would best fit the audience and purpose of this essay?
   f. the work conditions in the factories
   g. child labor
   h. the impact of mass production on the economy
   j. the population explosion and its effects

Annie Smith Peck

Since a hundred years , the highest mountains in South America have lured climbers from all
21

over the world. But until 1908, Peru's Mt. Huascaran resisted the efforts of all those who attempted

to reach its summit. One mountaineer, Annie Smith Peck, vowed to overcome the obstacles and

be the first to the top of Mt. Huascaran. In order to succeed, she would have to organize

expeditions—deal with reluctant companions—survive bad weather, and climb steep cliffs of ice
22

and rock.

Peck was born in the United States in 1850. Although she didn't start mountain climbing until she was in

her thirties, it soon became clear that she had found her life's work. A natural mountaineer, Peck was
23

soon setting records on expeditions in North America and Europe. She traveled to Bolivia in 1903 and

found Mount Huascaran, which had yet to be surmounted, a challenge she simply could not resist .
24

(1)Peck mounted four expeditions and made five attempts before she finally conquered Mt. Huascaran.

(2)Between those expeditions, Peck returned to the United States to raise money. (3)She received help

from many scientific organizations, including the Museum of Natural History. (4)The Museum had also

supported Admiral Peary on his trip to the North Pole. (5)Still, Peck struggled at least as much to raise

money as she did climbing her beloved mountains.
25

In 1908, Peck scraped together the funds for yet another expedition to Mt. Huascaran. This time, she hired

two Swiss guides to assist her with the climb. On their first trip up the mountain's slopes, one of the
26

guides became ill, and the entire team was forced to turn back even though they were very close to the top.

Being so close to success was very frustrating for Peck, who could not even prove how close they had come

because she had accidentally brought the wrong kind of film and was unable to photograph the climb.

The team rested for a few days, the guide recovered, and on August 28th, they set off again. The climb was extremely difficult. Steps had to be <u>cut</u> one by one into the steep ice; snow bridges and crevasses had to be
<u> </u>
27

carefully crossed. The weather was so cold that everyone suffered from frostbite. When Peck and her two guides were just a short distance from the top, they stopped to determine the exact height of the mountain. At that moment, one of the guides took advantage of Peck's distraction and climbed the few remaining feet to the summit so that he was the first to reach the peak. <u>What a jerk!</u> Although Peck was
28

understandably <u>angry, she</u> focused on the triumph of achieving her goal: standing at last on the top of
29

Mt. Huascaran.

21. **a.** NO CHANGE
   b. Through the passing of a hundred years
   c. For over a hundred years
   d. In the time of the last century

22. **f.** NO CHANGE
   g. expeditions, deal with reluctant companions, survive bad weather, and
   h. expeditions; deal with reluctant, companions; survive bad weather; and
   j. expeditions: deal with reluctant companions, survive bad weather, and

23. **a.** NO CHANGE
   b. thirty's, it
   c. thirties. It
   d. thirties, thus it

24. **f.** NO CHANGE
   g. an irresistible challenge
   h. and just had to climb it
   j. the one mountain she just had to climb to the top of

25. **a.** NO CHANGE
   b. climbed
   c. proving she climbed
   d. to climb

26. f. NO CHANGE
  g. assisting
  h. would assist
  j. who had assisted

27. a. NO CHANGE
  b. hacked
  c. put
  d. done

28. f. NO CHANGE
  g. What, a jerk!
  h. He was such a jerk.
  j. OMIT the underlined passage.

29. a. NO CHANGE
  b. angry; she
  c. angry—she
  d. angry. She

30. In revising paragraph 3, the writer would be wise to:
  f. switch sentences 2 and 3
  g. eliminate sentence 4
  h. combine sentences 3 and 4
  j. explain why Peck's previous attempts to climb Mt. Huarascan had failed

The Gateway Arch

The skyline of St. Louis, Missouri, is fairly unremarkable, with one huge <u>exception, the</u> Gateway Arch that
31
stands on the banks of the Mississippi. Part of the Jefferson National Expansion Memorial, the Arch is

<u>a really cool monument</u> built to honor St. Louis' role as the gateway to the West.
32

Construction on the 630-foot high structure <u>began, in 1961</u> , and was completed four years later in 1965.
33
The monument includes an underground visitor center that explores westward expansion through gal-

leries and a theater. Two passenger trams take visitors to the Observation Room and the Museum of West-

ward Expansion at the top.

In 1947, a group of interested citizens known as the Jefferson National Expansion Memorial Association

held a nationwide competition to select a design for a new monument that <u>would celebrate</u> the growth of
                                                                              34

the United States. Other U.S. monuments are spires, statues, or <u>imposed buildings</u>, but the winner of this
                                                                    35

contest was a plan for a completely unique structure. The man <u>that</u> submitted the winning design, Eero
                                                                  36

Saarinen, later became a famous architect. In designing the Arch, Saarinen wanted to "create a monument

which would have lasting significance and would be a landmark of our time."

The Gateway Arch is a masterpiece of engineering, a monument even taller than the Great Pyramid in

Egypt, <u>and on its own way</u>, at least as majestic. The Gateway is an inverted catenary curve, the same shape
        37

that a heavy chain will form if suspended between two points. <u>Covered from top to bottom with a sleek</u>
                                                                 38

<u>stainless steel coating</u>, the Arch often reflects dazzling bursts of sunlight. In a beautiful display of symme-
  38

try, the height of the arch is the same as the distance between the legs at ground level.

31. a. NO CHANGE
   b. exception: the
   c. exception; the
   d. exception. The

32. f. NO CHANGE
   g. a structure that inspires amazement
   h. an amazing structure
   j. OMIT the underlined portion

33. a. NO CHANGE
   b. began (in 1961)
   c. had begun in 1961
   d. began in 1961

34. f. NO CHANGE
   g. should celebrate
   h. did celebrate
   j. would have celebrated

35. a. NO CHANGE
    b. imposing buildings
    c. buildings that imposed
    d. buildings that are imposed

36. f. NO CHANGE
    g. which
    h. who
    j. whom

37. a. NO CHANGE
    b. and, in its own way,
    c. and—in its own way;
    d. and in it's own way

38. f. NO CHANGE
    g. Covered with sleek stainless steel all over its body
    h. Covered with a skin made of steel that is stainless
    j. Covered with a sleek skin of stainless steel

39. The most logical sequence of paragraphs for this essay is:
    a. NO CHANGE
    b. 1, 3, 2, 4
    c. 4, 1, 3, 2
    d. 1, 2, 4, 3

40. The writer has been asked to write a short essay describing in detail a national monument and what the monument honors. Would this essay fulfill that assignment?
    f. Yes, because it focuses on the design of the Arch.
    g. Yes, because the writer describes the Arch and tells why it was commissioned.
    h. No, because the writer does not tell us enough about the designer of the Arch and what he was trying to accomplish.
    j. No, because the writer does not tell us enough about St. Louis' role as a gateway to westward expansion.

Wilma Rudolph

Wilma Rudolph was born a premature child in 1940, in Clarksville, <u>Tennessee. Weighing</u> only four-and-
41

a-half pounds. Wilma's mother did her best to care for her daughter, but the Rudolphs were very poor, and

the local hospital would not care for Wilma. During her childhood, Wilma contracted measles, mumps,

scarlet fever, chicken pox, pneumonia, and later, polio, a crippling disease which at that time had no cure.

At the age of four, she was told she would never walk again.

But Wilma's mother refused to give up. She found an African American medical college fifty miles away

that would give Wilma the care <u>she needs</u> . Although it was difficult to make the trip, Mrs. Rudolph took
42

Wilma to the college twice a week. After two years of treatment, Wilma could walk with a brace. With her

family's help, Wilma was able to walk normally without the aid of a crutch or brace by age twelve.

But simply walking wasn't enough for <u>Wilma, who wanted to be</u> an athlete. She decided to play basket-
43

ball, and for three years, she practiced with the team but didn't play in a single game. Then, in her sopho-

more year of high school, Wilma became a starting guard. <u>For scoring she broke the state records</u> and led
44

her team to the state championship. At the age of sixteen, she traveled to Melbourne, Australia, to run

track events in the 1956 Olympics. She earned a bronze medal as part of a relay team.

<u>After the high school from which she graduated</u> , Wilma was awarded a full scholarship to Tennessee State
45

University, and her track career went into high gear. Before she earned her degree in education, she took a

year off from her studies to compete all over the world. In 1960, Wilma's career as a runner reached its

apex. She set a world record in the 200-meter race at the Olympic <u>trials</u> , at the Olympics in Rome, she
46

won the 100-meters, the 200-meters, and ran the anchor leg on the winning 4×100-meter relay team.

Wilma was proudest of a different kind of victory, <u>in conclusion</u> . When she returned from her triumphs
47

in Rome, she insisted that the homecoming parade held in her honor not be a segregated event. This parade was the first racially integrated event ever held in Clarksville. Wilma continued to participate in

protests until Clarksville's segregation laws were finally <u>changed</u> .
$$\overline{48}$$

41. a. NO CHANGE
   b. Tennessee. She weighed
   c. Tennessee, who weighed
   d. Tennessee, when born weighing

42. f. NO CHANGE
   g. she needed
   h. needed by Wilma
   j. OMIT the underlined portion

43. a. NO CHANGE
   b. Wilma, wanting to be
   c. Wilma who wanted to be
   d. Wilma; who wanted to be

44. f. NO CHANGE
   g. She for scoring broke the state records
   h. She broke the state records for scoring
   j. She breaks the state records of scoring

45. a. NO CHANGE
   b. After graduating from high school,
   c. Since high school graduation,
   d. OMIT the underlined portion.

46. f. NO CHANGE
   g. trials. Then;
   h. trials—then—
   j. trials; then,

47. a. NO CHANGE
   b. however
   c. as a result
   d. therefore

48. f. NO CHANGE
   g. made illegal
   h. struck down
   j. removed

49. While revising, the writer realizes the passage needs an introduction to convey the main idea of the essay. Which of the following sentences should he use as the first sentence to best achieve that purpose?
   a. No one would have guessed that Wilma Rudolph, a crippled child, would someday become an Olympic track star.
   b. Wilma Rudolph owes a great deal to her family, who helped her survive several severe illnesses.
   c. Wilma Rudolph was a famous Olympic athlete who had a lot of health problems as a child.
   d. Wilma Rudolph suffered from diseases that few children contract today.

50. The writer wishes to add the following sentence to highlight how impressive Rudolph's achievements are:

   She was the first American woman ever to win three gold medals at a single Olympics.

   The most logical place to insert this sentence would be:
   f. After the new introductory sentence.
   g. At the end of paragraph 3.
   h. At the end of paragraph 4.
   j. At the beginning of paragraph 5.

Science Fiction

One of the most famous novels of all time, Mary Shelley's *Frankenstein,* marked not only the highpoint of a young woman's literary career. But also the beginning of a brand new genre of literature being science
_____ 51 _____ 52
fiction . In her remarkable tale, Shelley explores what might happen if a scientific possibility—the ability
 52
to restore life to the dead—were to become a reality. This exploration of how what *might* be would affect our world is the essence of science fiction.

What Shelley began, H.G. Wells perfected in dozens of science fiction works including *The Time Machine* and *The War of the Worlds.* While Shelley's Frankenstein created a living creature from the body parts of the dead, Wells' characters traveled through time; created half-animal, half-human creatures; made them-

selves invisible; and <u>having been attacked by Martians</u> . In all of his novels, <u>Wells; like Shelley,</u> used scien-
                      53   **54**
tific possibilities to analyze and often criticize his own society. *War of the Worlds,* for example, is a thinly

disguised attack on the British colonialism of his time.

Science fiction flourished in the United States in the 1920s and 1930s with "pulp" <u>magazines that for the</u>
                                                                                    55
<u>masses churned out science fiction stories</u> . Meanwhile, in Europe, science fiction writers were using
          55
science fiction to help bring about political change. Yevgeny Zamyatin's classic novel *We,* for example,

<u>is against</u> the Soviet Union's Communist agenda.
  56

Today, science fiction writers around the world continue to explore possibilities—possibilities that are fast

becoming realities. Much of what science fiction writers only dreamed of a century ago, such as cloning

and space travel, have already come to pass. What is ahead? How will we handle these and other upcoming

advances? Let us hope that science fiction writers are wrong, for all too often, characters in science fiction

stories, like <u>they're</u> forefather Victor Frankenstein, <u>are unable to handle</u> the responsibility of having so
             57   **58**
much power over nature.

51. a. NO CHANGE
    b. career; but,
    c. career, but
    d. career, and

52. f. NO CHANGE
    g. literature: science fiction
    h. literature, that was, science fiction
    j. literature (science fiction)

53. a. NO CHANGE
    b. are attacked by Martians.
    c. faced attacks from Martians.
    d. being attacked by Martians.

54. f. NO CHANGE
    g. Wells like Shelley,
    h. Wells who was like Shelley
    j. Wells, like Shelley,

55. a. NO CHANGE
    b. magazines that churned out for the masses science fiction stories
    c. magazines, that, churned out science fiction stories, for the masses
    d. magazines that churned out science fiction stories for the masses

56. The writer wishes to use a much stronger word or phrase to convey this idea. Which of the following choices achieves that purpose and maintains the tone of the essay?
    f. criticizes
    g. takes to task
    h. is a scathing indictment of
    j. rips apart

57. a. NO CHANGE
    b. there are
    c. their
    d. whose

58. f. NO CHANGE
    g. handling bad
    h. do not handle well
    j. are badly handling

59. Which of the following revisions would most improve paragraph 4?
    a. Adding a sentence about the issues today's science fiction writers are addressing.
    b. Adding a quotation from *Frankenstein.*
    c. Adding a brief summary of Mary Shelley's life.
    d. Answering the questions in the paragraph.

60. The writer wishes to add a brief summary of the plot of *Frankenstein.* The most logical place for this addition would be:
    f. to add it to the end of paragraph 1
    g. to create a new paragraph between paragraphs 1 and 2
    h. to add it after the third sentence in paragraph 1
    j. to create a new paragraph between paragraphs 2 and 3

Sigmund Freud

The <u>father and originator of</u> psychoanalysis, Sigmund Freud (1856–1939) is largely responsible for the
     61

way we understand <u>ourselves, as creatures, with</u> conflicting "selves" and desires. Freud posited the notion
     62

that the mind is teeming with "psychic energy," and that our personality is shaped largely by the interac-

tions of the levels of the mind. Among Freud's most important contributions to modern psychology and

the contemporary understanding of the self is his theory of the unconscious.

(1)According to Freud, the mind is much like an iceberg. (2)Most of our mind's activities, then, occur

beneath the surface, in the unconscious and beyond our knowing. (3)The *conscious* is the part of the mind

of which we are aware; it is the tip of the iceberg that is visible above the water. (4)The *unconscious,*

<u>on the other hand</u> , is all that is below the surface—the thoughts, feelings, and desires that we are not
     63

aware of but that nonetheless affect our behavior.

Freud believed that the unconscious is *deterministic.* That is, our behaviors are caused (determined) by

thoughts and impulses deep in our unconscious— <u>of which thoughts and impulses we are not aware.</u>
                                          64

<u>This is related to the phenomenon called "Freudian slip."</u> Unless we psychoanalyze ourselves, we may
          65

never be aware of the hidden reasons for our actions. This suggests that the notion of free will

<u>might have been</u> an illusion and that our choices are governed by hidden mental processes over which we
     66

have no control.

Repression is the act of pushing our conflicts to the <u>unconscious. So that</u> we are no longer aware of them.
                                                     67

It is our chief *defense mechanism* (a way to avoid conflict between our true desires and our sense of right

and wrong). Freud believed that too much repression can lead to *neurosis,* a mental disorder resulting in

depression or abnormal behavior, sometimes with physical symptoms but with no evidence of disease.

61. a. NO CHANGE
  b. father (and originator) of
  c. father, and originator of,
  d. father of

62. f. NO CHANGE
  g. ourselves as creatures with
  h. ourselves, being like creatures with
  j. ourselves. As creatures with

63. a. NO CHANGE
  b. likewise
  c. unfortunately
  d. thereby

64. f. NO CHANGE
  g. we are not aware of which thoughts and impulses.
  h. thoughts and impulses of which we are not aware.
  j. which we are not aware of, these thoughts and impulses.

65. Upon revising this essay, the writer would be wise to:
  a. Leave this sentence exactly as it is.
  b. Delete this sentence from the paragraph.
  c. Move this sentence to the end of the paragraph.
  d. Use a better phrase than "related to."

66. f. NO CHANGE
  g. would be
  h. has been
  j. is

67. a. NO CHANGE
  b. unconscious of which
  c. unconscious so that
  d. unconscious, for

68. The most logical sequence of sentences for paragraph 2 is:

    f. NO CHANGE

    g. 1, 3, 4, 2

    h. 3, 4, 1, 2

    j. 2, 1, 3, 4

69. The author's use of italics is designed to do which of the following?

    a. indicate that a foreign language is being used

    b. call attention to Freud's genius

    c. create a more emotional tone

    d. highlight key terms that are defined in the text

70. Which of the following choices provides the most logical and effective transition from the third to the fourth paragraph?

    f. Sometimes the impulses for our behavior come from repressed desires.

    g. Another theory of Freud's is repression.

    h. Freud also believed in repression.

    j. Neurosis can be caused by repression to the unconscious.

Yoga

One of today's hottest fads is also one of the world's oldest practices: the ancient art of yoga. At first, I thought yoga was just another fitness fad, like step aerobics classes or Tae Bo. But after my first class, I understood why yoga has lasted for thousands of years, and why so many people are completely <u>into</u> this
                71
practice.

Yoga is different from other fitness activities because it is not only physical. <u>In the correct form</u>, yoga is a
               72
practice of unification: an emotional, spiritual, *and* physical exercise.

Though it may seem easy to those <u>who</u> have never practiced, yoga poses require great concentration, and
         73
they are surprisingly effective in stretching and strengthening muscles. A simple sitting pose such as *staff pose,* for example, requires you to tighten and lengthen stomach, back, and arm muscles as you stretch <u>you're</u> legs out in front of you and place your hands by your side. More difficult poses, such as *brave war-*
74

rior, require you to balance on one leg and hold a pose that strengthens leg, back, and stomach muscles.

While yoga tones and strengthens the body, it also tones and strengthens the mind. Many poses

<u>can be only held</u> if you are completely focused on the task, and full benefit of the poses comes only
　　　75

through proper breathing. Concentrated, deep breathing during yoga helps you extend more fully into the

poses, thereby gaining greater benefit from the stretch. And the steady circulation of breath through your

body both calms and energizes.

<u>I am still relatively new to yoga. I have only been practicing for one year. I am addicted to yoga</u> unlike any
　　　　　　　　　　　　　　　　　　　　76

other physical activity because it is also a spiritual practice. Through yoga, I am able to release tensions

that lodge in various parts of my body: the tight shoulders, the cramped legs, the <u>belly that is in knots</u> .
　　　　　　　　　　　　　　　　　　　　　　　　　　　　　　　　　77

The physical release is also a spiritual release: I feel calm after doing yoga, reconnected to my body, recon-

nected to my self, more at peace with the world. After a series of *asanas* (poses), I feel the universal life

force within.

71. a. NO CHANGE
　　b. hooked on
　　c. devoted to
　　d. practitioners of

72. f. NO CHANGE
　　g. Done correctly
　　h. To do it correctly
　　j. OMIT the underlined portion

73. a. NO CHANGE
　　b. that
　　c. whom
　　d. which

74. f. NO CHANGE
g. one's
h. your
j. these

75. a. NO CHANGE
b. are only holding
c. can only be holden
d. can only be held

76. The writer wishes to improve the sentence structure here by combining sentences. Which of the following choices is the most effective option?
f. I am still relatively new to yoga. Practicing only for one year, I am addicted to yoga . . .
g. Still relatively new to yoga, I have been practicing for only one year. But I am addicted to yoga . . .
h. I am still relatively new to yoga—I have been practicing for only one year—but I am addicted to yoga . . .
j. Although I am relatively new to yoga, I have been practicing for only one year. Still, I am addicted to yoga . . .

77. a. NO CHANGE
b. knotted belly
c. knots within the belly
d. aching within the stomach area

78. The writer would like to add some figurative language to the essay. Which of the following images would be most effective and appropriate?
f. I feel like a million bucks after doing yoga.
g. Yoga is like a warm blanket.
h. Yoga is like a drug.
j. Yoga is a peaceful journey.

79. If the writer were to combine two paragraphs, which two paragraphs would it be most logical to connect?
a. paragraphs 1 and 2
b. paragraphs 2 and 3
c. paragraphs 3 and 4
d. paragraphs 4 and 5

80. The writer would like readers to do some basic yoga poses after reading this essay. To achieve this goal, the writer should:

    f. list the best yoga videos, so readers can purchase them.

    g. compare and contrast yoga to another fitness activity, such as aerobics.

    h. tell readers how to get into those basic positions.

    j. describe the benefits of deep breathing exercises.

▶ Practice Questions Answers and Explanations

Passage 1: Bicycles

  1. b. This choice has the most appropriate and correct usage and word choice.

  2. h. The phrase *a Scottish blacksmith* is relevant but nonessential information and needs to be set off by commas.

  3. a. This is correct as is.

  4. h. The verb needs to be in the past tense.

  5. b. There should not be a comma between a subject and a verb.

  6. j. This choice gives the sentence parallel structure.

  7. d. Comma after an introductory word or phrase and *they* + *are* contraction.

  8. h. This choice presents the correct word order.

  9. b. This choice gives readers reasons to buy a bicycle for themselves.

10. j. This is the most logical sequence. The sentence about Lawson and naming the safety bicycle must come before the details of the safety bicycle. Sentence 13 is the best conclusion for the paragraph.

Passage 2: Industrial Revolution

11. b. This change would make the sentence more concise.

12. g. This choice makes the sentence parallel.

13. d. This is the most logical sequence: first, the sentence giving the overall timeline of the revolution, then the next two sentences in chronological order.

14. f. This is the most correct and concise choice.

15. c. This is the most concise choice. Choices **a** and **d** are redundant; choice **b** has improper word order.

16. j. This is the best choice. Choice **g** is grammatically correct, but **j** combines the sentences for greater sentence variety.

17. a. This choice presents the correct word order and conveys the correct idea.

18. g. This is the correct prepositional idiom.

19. b. This ties in the issues in the paragraph: mass production, moving into cities and towns, and large populations. Choice **a** is irrelevant, and choices **c** and **d** are related, but off topic.

20. h. All of the topics are related to the Industrial Revolution, but this essay focuses on mass production, so this topic would be the most logical to add.

Passage 3: Annie Smith Peck

21. **c.** This is the most correct and concise choice.

22. **g.** Separate items in a list with commas, unless one or more items already has a comma (then use a semi-colon).

23. **a.** This is correct as it stands. Choice **c** would create a sentence fragment.

24. **g.** This is the most concise and appropriate version.

25. **d.** This gives the sentence parallel structure.

26. **f.** This is correct as it stands.

27. **b.** *Hacked* is the most precise and vivid word choice.

28. **j.** This sentence should be omitted; it does not fit the tone and style of the essay.

29. **a.** This is correct as it stands. Choice **d** would create a sentence fragment.

30. **g.** Sentence 4 is off topic and should be eliminated to maintain the focus of the paragraph.

Passage 4: The Gateway Arch

31. **b.** The colon is the most correct punctuation mark here. Colons introduce explanations.

32. **h.** This choice has the most appropriate and concise word choice. It *could* be omitted without ruining the sentence (choice **j**), but it would take out an idea central to the essay: that the monument is amazing.

33. **d.** There are no commas needed here.

34. **f.** This is the correct helping verb and tense.

35. **b.** *Imposing* should be a modifier, and using the participial form is the most concise.

36. **h.** Use *who* when referring to people.

37. **b.** Put commas around transitional phrases.

38. **j.** This is the most concise and effective version.

39. **b.** This is the most logical choice. The first paragraph introduces the topic and main idea; the third paragraph then describes the background of the Arch and establishes a chronological order; the second paragraph continues the chronology; and the fourth paragraph returns to the idea of the Arch's remarkable design, as established in the introduction.

40. **j.** The writer discusses the design of the monument, but does not describe how the city and monument honor St. Louis's role as a gateway to westward expansion. It simply mentions this fact.

Passage 5: Wilma Rudolph

41. **b.** This choice corrects the sentence fragment.

42. **g.** This choice makes the sentence consistent in tense and is more concise than choice **h**.

43. **a.** This is correct as it stands. The *who* clause is non-essential and should be set off by a comma.

44. **h.** This is the correct word order.

45. **b.** This is the most correct and concise version. The transition here should not be omitted as it makes the passage of time easier to follow.

46. **j.** Choice **f** is a run-on; choice **g** incorrectly uses a semi-colon; and choice **h** incorrectly uses the dash.

47. **b.** *However* is the most appropriate transition here.

48. h. This choice offers the most precise and vivid word choice.

49. a. This choice best conveys the main idea of the passage. Choice **b** focuses only on Rudolph's family; choice **c** understates the physical handicaps she overcame; and choice **d** does not mention her athletic accomplishments.

50. h. The most logical place is after the sentence that lists the three gold medals that Rudolph won.

Passage 6: Science Fiction

51. c. This choice corrects the sentence fragment and keeps the *not only . . . but also* construction intact.

52. g. Choice **f** incorrectly uses *being;* choice **h** includes superfluous commas and uses the past tense, though the genre still exists; and choice **j** sets off what is important in the sentence—the name of the new genre—in parentheses, indicating that it is *not* important.

53. c. This version gives the sentence parallel structure.

54. j. This correctly sets off the transitional phrase with commas.

55. d. This choice presents the correct word order, placing what was churned out immediately after the verb and then the prepositional phrase after, to show who received those stories.

56. h. This is the most strongly worded choice and is consistent with the tone of the essay.

57. c. The possessive pronoun should be used here.

58. f. This version is correct as it stands. The other versions have incorrect or awkward word order or usage.

59. a. This is relevant and would show the current direction of the genre. This is appropriate since the paragraph is about looking ahead to the future of science fiction and humankind. The quotation from *Frankenstein* might or might not be relevant; a summary of Shelley's life would be out of place in this paragraph; and the author is unable to answer the questions in the paragraph—he can only make an educated guess.

60. g. The introduction is too general to include a focus on the plot of *Frankenstein,* and because this novel marked the beginning of science fiction, it is entitled to its own paragraph. It would be out of chronological order to place it anywhere after that.

Passage 7: Sigmund Freud

61. d. This is the most concise choice. The other options are all redundant.

62. g. The commas here are superfluous. Choice **j** would create a sentence fragment.

63. a. This is the most appropriate transitional phrase for this sentence.

64. h. This is the most correct word order.

65. b. This sentence is related, but not within the focus of the paragraph. It is best omitted.

66. j. The simple present tense is correct here.

67. c. This corrects the sentence fragment.

68. g. This should be clear from the transitions and the simile comparing the mind to an iceberg.

69. d. A definition is offered after each italicized term.

70. f. This connects the main ideas in each paragraph: the impulses that control behavior and repression.

Passage 8: Yoga

71. c. This is the most appropriate and precise word choice.

72. g. The introductory phrase is most effective with the verb *do,* and this is the correct form to use.

73. a. The reference is to people, so *who* is correct.

74. h. The possessive pronoun is required here. *One's* is incorrect because that creates a shift in pronoun (from *you* to *one*).

75. d. This is the correct word order.

76. h. This is the most correct and effective combination of sentences. The other versions misuse transitions.

77. b. This choice makes the sentence parallel and is the most concise.

78. j. This is the most appropriate metaphor. Choice **f** is a cliché. Choice **g** is ineffective; it is unclear what emotion the simile is trying to convey. Without further explanation, choice **h** is an inappropriate comparison.

79. a. The second paragraph continues to explain why yoga is different and expresses the main idea of the essay.

80. h. This is the best way to achieve the goal of getting readers to do poses. The writer needs to provide some instruction.

ACT Math Test Practice

▶ Overview: About the ACT Math Test

The 60-minute, 60-question ACT Math Test contains questions from six categories of subjects taught in most high schools up to the start of 12th grade. The categories are listed below with the number of questions from each category:

- Pre-Algebra (14 questions)
- Elementary Algebra (10 questions)
- Intermediate Algebra (9 questions)
- Coordinate Geometry (9 questions)
- Plane Geometry (14 questions)
- Trigonometry (4 questions)

Like the other tests of the ACT, the math test requires you to use your reasoning skills. Believe it or not, this is good news, since it generally means that you do not need to remember every formula you were ever taught in algebra class. You will, however, need a strong foundation in all the subjects listed on the previous page in order to do well on the math test. You may use a calculator, but as you will be shown in the following lessons, many questions can be solved quickly and easily without a calculator.

Essentially, the ACT Math Test is designed to evaluate a student's ability to reason through math problems. Students need to be able to interpret data based on information given and on their existing knowledge of math. The questions are meant to evaluate critical thinking ability by correctly interpreting the problem, analyzing the data, reasoning through possible conclusions, and determining the correct answer—the one supported by the data presented in the question.

Four scores are reported for the ACT Math Test: Pre-Algebra/Elementary Algebra, Intermediate Algebra/Coordinate Geometry, Plane Geometry/Trigonometry, and the total test score.

▶ Pretest

As you did with the English section, take the following pretest before you begin the math review in this chapter. The questions are the same type you will find on the ACT. When you are finished, check the answer key on page 138 to assess your results. Your pretest score will help you determine in which areas you need the most careful review and practice. For a glossary of math terms, refer to page 201 at the end of this chapter.

1. If a student got 95% of the questions on a 60-question test correct, how many questions did the student complete correctly?

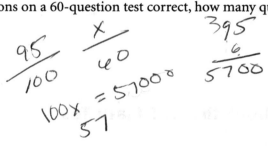

   a. 57
   b. 38
   c. 46
   d. 53
   e. 95

2. What is the smallest possible product for two integers whose sum is 26?
   f. 25
   g. 15
   h. 154
   i. 144
   j. 26

3. What is the value of x in the equation $-2x + 1 = 4(x + 3)$?

   a. $-\frac{6}{11}$

   b. 2

   c. $-\frac{11}{6}$

   d. -9

   e. $-\frac{3}{5}$

(handwritten: $-6x + 11 = 0$ $\frac{4}{6}$)

4. What is the y-intercept of the line $4y + 2x = 12$?

   f. 12

   g. -2

   h. 6

   i. -6

   j. 3

5. The height of the parallelogram below is 4.5 cm and the area is 36 sq cm. Find the length of side QR in centimeters.

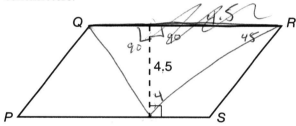

   a. 31.5 cm

   b. 8 cm

   c. 15.75 cm

   d. 9 cm

   e. 6 cm

6. Joey gave away half of his baseball card collection and sold one third of what remained. What fraction of his original collection does he still have?

   f. $\frac{2}{3}$

   g. $\frac{1}{6}$

   h. $\frac{1}{3}$

   i. $\frac{1}{5}$

   j. $\frac{2}{5}$

7. Simplify $\sqrt{40}$.
  a. $2\sqrt{10}$
  b. $4\sqrt{10}$
  c. $10\sqrt{4}$
  d. $5\sqrt{4}$
  e. $2\sqrt{20}$

8. What is the simplified form of $-(3x+5)^2$?
  f. $9x^2 + 30x + 25$
  g. $-9x^2 - 25$
  h. $9x^2 + 25$
  i. $-9x^2 - 30x - 25$
  j. $-39x^2 - 25$

9. Find the measure of $\angle$RST in the triangle below.

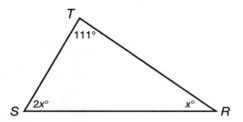

  a. 69
  b. 46
  c. 61
  d. 45
  e. 23

10. The area of a trapezoid is $\frac{1}{2}h(b_1 + b_2)$ where h is the altitude and b_1 and b_2 are the parallel bases. The two parallel bases of a trapezoid are 3 cm and 5 cm and the area of the trapezoid is 28 sq cm. Find the altitude of the trapezoid.
  f. 14 cm
  g. 9 cm
  h. 19 cm
  i. 1.9 cm
  j. 7 cm

11. If $9m - 3 = -318$, then $14m = ?$

    a. -28

    b. -504

    c. -329

    d. -584

    e. -490

12. What is the solution of the following equation? $|x + 7| - 8 = 14$

    f. $\{-14, 14\}$

    g. $\{-22, 22\}$

    h. $\{15\}$

    i. $\{-8, 8\}$

    j. $\{-29, 15\}$

13. Which point lies on the same line as $(2, -3)$ and $(6, 1)$?

    a. $(5, -6)$

    b. $(2, 3)$

    c. $(-1, 8)$

    d. $(7, 2)$

    e. $(4, 0)$

14. In the figure below, $\overline{MN} = 3$ inches and $\overline{PM} = 5$ inches. Find the area of triangle MNP.

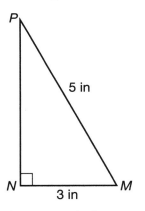

    f. 6 square inches

    g. 15 square inches

    h. 7.5 square inches

    i. 12 square inches

    j. 10 square inches

15. $\overline{AC}$ and $\overline{BC}$ are both radii of circle C and have a length of 6 cm. The measure of $\angle ACB$ is 35°. Find the area of the shaded region.

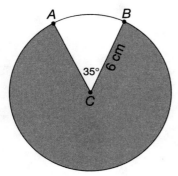

    a. $\frac{79}{2}\pi$

    b. $\frac{7}{2}\pi$

    c. 36π

    d. $\frac{65}{2}\pi$

    e. 4π

16. If $f(x) = 3x + 2$ and $g(x) = -2x - 1$, find $f(g(x))$.

    f. $x + 1$

    g. $-6x - 1$

    h. $5x + 3$

    i. $2x^2 - 4$

    j. $-6x^2 - 7x - 2$

17. What is the value of $\log_4 64$?

    a. 3

    b. 16

    c. 2

    d. -4

    e. 644

18. The equation of line *l* is $y = mx + b$. Which equation is line *m*?

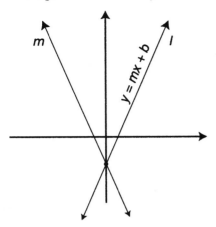

    f. $y = -mx$

    g. $y = -x + b$

    h. $y = 2mx + b$

    i. $y = \frac{1}{2}mx - b$

    j. $y = -mx + b$

19. If Mark can mow the lawn in 40 minutes and Audrey can mow the lawn in 50 minutes, which equation can be used to determine how long it would take the two of them to mow the lawn together?

    a. $\frac{40}{x} + \frac{50}{x} = 1$

    b. $\frac{x}{40} + \frac{x}{50} = 1$

    c. $\frac{1}{x} + \frac{1}{x} = 90$

    d. $50x + 40x = 1$

    e. $90x = \frac{1}{x}$

20. If $\sin\theta = \frac{2}{5}$, find $\cos\theta$.

    f. $\frac{5}{21}$

    g. $\sqrt{\frac{21}{5}}$

    h. $\frac{5}{3}$

    i. $\frac{3}{5}$

    j. $\sqrt{\frac{5}{21}}$

▶ Pretest Answers and Explanations

1. Choice **a** is correct. Multiply 60 by the decimal equivalent of 95% (0.95). $60 \times 0.95 = 57$.

2. Choice **f** is correct. Look at the pattern below.

Sum	Product
1 + 25	25
2 + 24	48
3 + 23	69
4 + 22	88
5 + 21	105

The products continue to get larger as the pattern progresses. The smallest possible product is $1 \times 25 = 25$.

3. Choice **c** is correct. Distribute the 4, then isolate the variable.

$-2x + 1 = 4(x + 3)$

$-2x + 1 = 4x + 12$

$1 = 6x + 12$

$-11 = 6x$

$-\frac{11}{6} = x$

4. Choice **j** is correct. Change the equation into $y = mx + b$ format.

$4y + 2x = 12$

$4y = -2x + 12$

$y = -\frac{1}{2}x + 3$

The y-intercept is 3.

5. Choice **b** is correct. To find the area of a parallelogram, multiply the base times the height.

$A = bh$

Substitute in the given height and area:

$36 = b(4.5)$

$8 = b$

Then, solve for the base.

The base is 8 cm.

6. Choice **h** is correct. After Joey sold half of his collection, he still had half left. He sold one third of the half that he had left ($\frac{1}{3} \times \frac{1}{2} = \frac{1}{6}$), which is $\frac{1}{6}$ of the original collection. In total, he gave away $\frac{1}{2}$ and sold $\frac{1}{6}$, which is a total of $\frac{2}{3}$ of the collection ($\frac{1}{2} + \frac{1}{6} = \frac{3}{6} + \frac{1}{6} = \frac{4}{6} = \frac{2}{3}$). Since he has gotten rid of $\frac{2}{3}$ of the collection, $\frac{1}{3}$ remains.

7. Choice **a** is correct. Break up 40 into a pair of factors, one of which is a perfect square.

$40 = 4 \times 10$.

$\sqrt{40} = \sqrt{4}\sqrt{10} = 2\sqrt{10}$.

8. Choice **i** is correct.

$-(3x + 5)^2 = -(3x + 5)(3x + 5)$

$-(3x + 5)(3x + 5)$

$-(9x^2 + 15x + 15x + 25)$

$-(9x^2 + 30x + 25)$

$-9x^2 - 30x - 25$

9. Choice **b** is correct. Recall that the sum of the angles in a triangle is 180°.

$180 = 111 + 2x + x$

$180 = 111 + 3x$

$69 = 3x$

$23 = x$

The problem asked for the measure of $\angle RST$ which is $2x$. Since x is 23, $2x$ is 46°.

10. Choice **j** is correct. Substitute the given values into the equation and solve for h.

$A = \frac{1}{2}h(b_1 + b_2)$

$28 = \frac{1}{2}h(3 + 5)$

$28 = \frac{1}{2}h(8)$

$28 = 4h$

$h = 7$

The altitude is 7 cm.

11. Choice **e** is correct. Solve the first equation for m.

$9m - 3 = -318$

$9m = -315$

$m = -35$

Then, substitute value of m in $14m$.

$14(-35) = -490$

12. Choice **j** is correct.

$|x + 7| - 8 = 14$

$|x + 7| = 22$

$|22|$ and $|-22|$ both equal 22. Therefore, $x + 7$ can be 22 or -22.

$x + 7 = 22$ $x + 7 = -22$

$x = 15$ $x = -29$

$\{-29, 15\}$

13. Choice **d** is correct. Find the equation of the line containing $(2, -3)$ and $(6, 1)$. First, find the slope.

$\frac{y_2 - y_1}{x_2 - x_1} = \frac{1 - (-3)}{6 - 2} = \frac{4}{4} = 1$

Next, find the equation of the line.

$y - y_1 = m(x - x_1)$

$y - 1 = 1(x - 6)$

$y - 1 = x - 6$

$y = x - 5$

Substitute the ordered pairs into the equations. The pair that makes the equation true is on the line. When $(7, 2)$ is substituted into $y = x - 5$, the equation is true.

$5 = 7 - 2$ is true.

14. Choice **f** is correct. Triangle MNP is a 3-4-5 right triangle. The height of the triangle is 4 and the base is 3. To find the area use the formula $A = \frac{bh}{2}$.

$A = \frac{(3)(4)}{2} = \frac{12}{2} = 6$.

The area of the triangle is 6 square inches.

15. Choice **d** is correct. Find the total area of the circle using the formula $A = \pi r^2$.

$A = \pi(6)^2 = 36\pi$

A circle has a total of 360°. In the circle shown, 35° are NOT shaded, so 325° ARE shaded.

The fraction of the circle that is shaded is $\frac{325}{360}$. Multiply this fraction by the total area to find the shaded area.

$\frac{36\pi}{1} \times \frac{325}{360} = \frac{11,700\pi}{360} = \frac{65\pi}{2}$.

16. Choice **g** is correct.

$f(g(x)) = f(-2x - 1)$

Replace every x in $f(x)$ with $(-2x - 1)$.

$f(g(x)) = 3(-2x - 1) + 2$

$f(g(x)) = -6x - 3 + 2$

$f(g(x)) = -6x - 1$

17. Choice **a** is correct; $\log_4 64$ means $4^? = 64$; $4^3 = 64$. Therefore, $\log_4 64 = 3$.

18. Choice **j** is correct. The lines have the same y-intercept (b). Their slopes are opposites. So, the slope of the first line is m, thus, the slope of the second line is $-m$.

Since the y-intercept is b and the slope is $-m$, the equation of the line is $y = -mx + b$.

19. Choice **b** is correct. Use the table below to organize the information.

	RATE	TIME	WORK DONE
Mark	$\frac{1}{40}$	x	$\frac{x}{40}$
Audrey	$\frac{1}{50}$	x	$\frac{x}{50}$

Mark's rate is 1 job in 40 minutes. Audrey's rate is 1 job in 50 minutes. You don't know how long it will take them together, so time is x. To find the work done, multiply the rate by the time. Add the work done by Mark with the work done by Audrey to get 1 job done.

$\frac{x}{40} + \frac{x}{50} = 1$ is the equation.

20. Choice **g** is correct. Use the identity $\sin^2\theta + \cos^2\theta = 1$ to find $\cos\theta$.

$\sin^2\theta + \cos^2\theta = 1$

$(\frac{2}{5})^2 + \cos^2\theta = 1$

$\frac{4}{25} + \cos^2\theta = 1$

$\cos^2\theta = \frac{21}{25}$

$\cos\theta = \frac{\sqrt{21}}{5}$

▶ Lessons and Practice Questions

Familiarizing yourself with the ACT before taking the test is a great way to improve your score. If you are familiar with the directions, format, types of questions, and the way the test is scored, you will be more comfortable and less anxious. This section contains ACT math test-taking strategies, information, and practice questions and answers to apply what you learn.

The lessons in this chapter are intended to refresh your memory. The 80 practice questions following these lessons contain examples of the topics covered here as well as other various topics you may see on the official ACT Assessment. If in the course of solving the practice questions you find a topic that you are not familiar with or have simply forgotten, you may want to consult a textbook for additional instruction.

▶ Types of Math Questions

Math questions on the ACT are classified by both *topic* and *skill level*. As noted earlier, the six general topics covered are:

Pre-Algebra
Elementary Algebra
Intermediate Algebra

- The math questions start easy and get harder. Pace yourself accordingly.
- Study wisely. The number of questions involving various algebra topics is significantly higher than the number of trigonometry questions. Spend more time studying algebra concepts.
- There is no penalty for wrong answers. Make sure that you answer all of the questions, even if some answers are only a guess.
- If you are not sure of an answer, take your best guess. Try to eliminate a couple of the answer choices.
- If you skip a question, leave that question blank on the answer sheet and return to it when you are done. Often, a question later in the test will spark your memory about the answer to a question that you skipped.
- Read carefully! Make sure you understand what the question is asking.
- Use your calculator wisely. Many questions are answered more quickly and easily without a calculator.
- Most calculators are allowed on the test. However, there are some exceptions. Check the ACT website (ACT.org) for specific models that are not allowed.
- Keep your work organized. Number your work on your scratch paper so that you can refer back to it while checking your answers.
- Look for easy solutions to difficult problems. For example, the answer to a problem that can be solved using a complicated algebraic procedure may also be found by "plugging" the answer choices into the problem.
- Know basic formulas such as the formulas for area of triangles, rectangles, and circles. The Pythagorean theorem and basic trigonometric functions and identities are also useful, and not that complicated to remember.

Coordinate Geometry

Plane Geometry

Trigonometry

In addition to these six topics, there are three skill levels: basic, application, and analysis. Basic problems require simple knowledge of a topic and usually only take a few steps to solve. Application problems require knowledge of a few topics to complete the problem. Analysis problems require the use of several topics to complete a multi-step problem.

The questions appear in order of difficulty on the test, but topics are mixed together throughout the test.

Pre-Algebra

Topics in this section include many concepts you may have learned in middle or elementary school, such as operations on whole numbers, fractions, decimals, and integers; positive powers and square roots; absolute value; factors and multiples; ratio, proportion, and percent; linear equations; simple probability; using charts, tables, and graphs; and mean, median, mode, and range.

NUMBERS

- **Whole numbers** Whole numbers are also known as counting numbers: 0, 1, 2, 3, 4, 5, 6, . . .
- **Integers** Integers are both positive and negative whole numbers including zero: . . . −3, −2, −1, 0, 1, 2, 3 . . .
- **Rational numbers** Rational numbers are all numbers that can be written as fractions ($\frac{2}{3}$), terminating decimals (.75), and repeating decimals (.666 . . .)
- **Irrational numbers** Irrational numbers are numbers that cannot be expressed as terminating or repeating decimals: π or $\sqrt{2}$.

ORDER OF OPERATIONS

Most people remember the order of operations by using a mnemonic device such as PEMDAS or *Please Excuse My Dear Aunt Sally*. These stand for the order in which operations are done:

Parentheses
Exponents
Multiplication
Division
Addition
Subtraction

Multiplication and division are done in the order that they appear from left to right. Addition and subtraction work the same way—left to right.

Parentheses also include any grouping symbol such as brackets [ ], braces { }, or the division bar.

Examples

1. $-5 + 2 \times 8$

2. $9 + (6 + 2 \times 4) - 3^2$

Solutions

1. $-5 + 2 \times 8$
   $-5 + 16$
   11

2. $9 + (6 + 2 \times 4) - 3^2$

$9 + (6 + 8) - 3^2$

$9 + 14 - 9$

$23 - 9$

14

FRACTIONS

Addition of Fractions

To add fractions, they must have a common denominator. The common denominator is a common multiple of the denominators. Usually, the least common multiple is used.

> **Example**
>
> $\frac{1}{3} + \frac{2}{7}$ The least common denominator for 3 and 7 is 21.
>
> $(\frac{1}{3} \times \frac{7}{7}) + (\frac{2}{7} \times \frac{3}{3})$ Multiply the numerator and denominator of each fraction by the same number so that the denominator of each fraction is 21.
>
> $\frac{2}{21} + \frac{6}{21} = \frac{8}{21}$ Add the numerators and keep the denominators the same. Simplify the answer if necessary.

Subtraction of Fractions

Use the same method for multiplying fractions, except subtract the numerators.

Multiplication of Fractions

Multiply numerators and multiply denominators. Simplify the answer if necessary.

> **Example**
>
> $\frac{3}{4} \times \frac{1}{5} = \frac{3}{20}$

Division of Fractions

Take the reciprocal of (flip) the second fraction and multiply.

$$\frac{1}{3} \div \frac{3}{4} = \frac{1}{3} \times \frac{4}{3} = \frac{4}{9}$$

Examples

1. $\frac{1}{3} + \frac{2}{5}$

2. $\frac{9}{10} - \frac{3}{4}$

3. $\frac{4}{5} \times \frac{7}{8}$

4. $\frac{3}{4} \div \frac{6}{7}$

Solutions

1. $\frac{1 \times 5}{3 \times 5} + \frac{2 \times 3}{5 \times 3}$

$\frac{5}{15} + \frac{6}{15} = \frac{11}{15}$

2. $\frac{9 \times 2}{10 \times 2} - \frac{3 \times 5}{4 \times 5}$

$\frac{18}{20} - \frac{15}{20} = \frac{3}{20}$

3. $\frac{4}{5} \times \frac{7}{8} = \frac{28}{40} = \frac{7}{10}$

4. $\frac{3}{4} \times \frac{7}{6} = \frac{21}{24} = \frac{7}{8}$

EXPONENTS AND SQUARE ROOTS

An exponent tells you how many times to the base is used as factor. Any base to the power of zero is one.

Example

$14^0 = 1$

$5^3 = 5 \times 5 \times 5 = 125$

$3^4 = 3 \times 3 \times 3 \times 3 = 81$

$11^2 = 11 \times 11 = 121$

Make sure you know how to work with exponents on the calculator that you bring to the test. Most scientific calculators have a y^x or x^y button that is used to quickly calculate powers.

When finding a square root, you are looking for the number that when multiplied by itself gives you the number under the square root symbol.

$\sqrt{25} = 5$

$\sqrt{64} = 8$

$\sqrt{169} = 13$

ACT MATH TEST PRACTICE

Have the perfect squares of numbers from 1 to 13 memorized since they frequently come up in all types of math problems. The perfect squares (in order) are:

1, 4, 9, 16, 25, 36, 49, 64, 81, 100, 121, 144, 169.

ABSOLUTE VALUE

The absolute value is the distance of a number from zero. For example, $|-5|$ is 5 because -5 is 5 spaces from zero. Most people simply remember that the absolute value of a number is its positive form.

$|-39| = 39$
$|92| = 92$
$|-11| = 11$
$|987| = 987$

FACTORS AND MULTIPLES

Factors are numbers that divide evenly into another number. For example, 3 is a factor of 12 because it divides evenly into 12 four times.

6 is a factor of 66
9 is a factor of 27
-2 is a factor of 98

Multiples are numbers that result from multiplying a given number by another number. For example, 12 is a multiple of 3 because 12 is the result when 3 is multiplied by 4.

66 is a multiple of 6
27 is a multiple of 9
98 is a multiple of -2

RATIO, PROPORTION, AND PERCENT

Ratios are used to compare two numbers and can be written three ways. The ratio 7 to 8 can be written 7:8, $\frac{7}{8}$, or in the words "7 to 8."

Proportions are written in the form $\frac{2}{5} = \frac{x}{25}$. Proportions are generally solved by cross-multiplying (multiply diagonally and set the cross-products equal to each other). For example,

$\frac{2}{5} = \frac{x}{25}$
$(2)(25) = 5x$
$50 = 5x$
$10 = x$

Percents are always "out of 100." 45% means 45 out of 100. It is important to be able to write percents as decimals. This is done by moving the decimal point two places to the left.

45% = 0.45

3% = 0.03

124% = 1.24

0.9% = 0.009

PROBABILITY

The probability of an event is $P(event) = \frac{favorable}{possible}$.

For example, the probability of rolling a 5 when rolling a 6-sided die is $\frac{1}{6}$, because there is one favorable outcome (rolling a 5) and there are 6 possible outcomes (rolling a 1, 2, 3, 4, 5, or 6). If an event is impossible, it cannot happen, the probability is 0. If an event definitely will happen, the probability is 1.

COUNTING PRINCIPLE AND TREE DIAGRAMS

The *sample space* is a list of all possible outcomes. A *tree diagram* is a convenient way of showing the sample space. Below is a tree diagram representing the sample space when a coin is tossed and a die is rolled.

Coin	Die	Outcomes
	1	H1
	2	H2
	3	H3
H	4	H4
	5	H5
	6	H6
	1	T1
	2	T2
	3	T3
T	4	T4
	5	T5
	6	T6

The first column shows that there are two possible outcomes when a coin is tossed, either heads or tails. The second column shows that once the coin is tossed, there are six possible outcomes when the die is rolled, numbers 1 through 6. The outcomes listed indicate that the possible outcomes are: getting a heads, then rolling a 1; getting a heads, then rolling a 2; getting a heads, then rolling a 3; etc. This method allows you to clearly see all possible outcomes.

Another method to find the number of possible outcomes is to use the *counting principle*. An example of this method is on the following page.

Nancy has 4 pairs of shoes, 5 pairs of pants, and 6 shirts. How many different outfits can she make with these clothes?

Shoes	Pants	Shirts
4 choices	5 choices	6 choices

To find the number of possible outfits, multiply the number of choices for each item.

$4 \times 5 \times 6 = 120$

She can make 120 different outfits.

Helpful Hints about Probability

- If an event is certain to occur, the probability is 1.
- If an event is certain NOT to occur, the probability is 0.
- If you know the probability of all other events occurring, you can find the probability of the remaining event by adding the known probabilities together and subtracting that sum from 1.

MEAN, MEDIAN, MODE, AND RANGE

Mean is the average. To find the mean, add up all the numbers and divide by the number of items.

Median is the middle. To find the median, place all the numbers in order from least to greatest. Count to find the middle number in this list. Note that when there is an even number of numbers, there will be two middle numbers. To find the median, find the average of these two numbers.

Mode is the most frequent or the number that shows up the most. If there is no number that appears more than once, there is no mode.

The range is the difference between the highest and lowest number.

Example

Using the data 4, 6, 7, 7, 8, 9, 13, find the mean, median, mode, and range.

Mean: The sum of the numbers is 54. Since there are seven numbers, divide by 7 to find the mean. $54 \div 7 = 7.71$.

Median: The data is already in order from least to greatest, so simply find the middle number. 7 is the middle number.

Mode: 7 appears the most often and is the mode.

Range: $13 - 4 = 9$.

LINEAR EQUATIONS

An equation is solved by finding a number that is equal to an unknown variable.

Simple Rules for Working with Equations

1. The equal sign separates an equation into two sides.

2. Whenever an operation is performed on one side, the same operation must be performed on the other side.

3. Your first goal is to get all of the variables on one side and all of the numbers on the other.

4. The final step often will be to divide each side by the coefficient, leaving the variable equal to a number.

CROSS-MULTIPLYING

You can solve an equation that sets one fraction equal to another by **cross-multiplication**. Cross-multiplication involves setting the products of opposite pairs of terms equal.

> **Example**
>
> $\frac{x}{6} = \frac{x+10}{12}$ becomes $12x = 6(x) + 6(10)$
>
> $$12x = 6x + 60$$
>
> $$\frac{-6x \qquad -6x}{\frac{6x}{6} = \frac{60}{6}}$$
>
> Thus, $\quad x = 10$

Checking Equations

To check an equation, substitute the number equal to the variable in the original equation.

> **Example**
>
> To check the equation from the previous page, substitute the number 10 for the variable x.
>
> $$\frac{x}{6} = \frac{x+10}{12}$$
>
> $$\frac{10}{6} = \frac{10+10}{12}$$
>
> $$\frac{10}{6} = \frac{20}{12}$$
>
> Simplify the fraction on the right by dividing the numerator and denominator by 2.
>
> $$\frac{10}{6} = \frac{10}{6}$$
>
> Because this statement is true, you know the answer $x = 10$ is correct.

Special Tips for Checking Equations

1. If time permits, be sure to check all equations.

2. Be careful to answer the question that is being asked. Sometimes, this involves solving for a variable and than performing an operation.

Example: If the question asks for the value of $x - 2$, and you find $x = 2$, the answer is not 2, but $2 - 2$. Thus, the answer is 0.

CHARTS, TABLES, AND GRAPHS

The ACT Math Test will assess your ability to analyze graphs and tables. It is important to read each graph or table very carefully before reading the question. This will help you to process the information that is presented. It is extremely important to read all of the information presented, paying special attention to headings and units of measure. Here is an overview of the types of graphs you will encounter:

- CIRCLE GRAPHS or PIE CHARTS

  This type of graph is representative of a whole and is usually divided into percentages. Each section of the chart represents a portion of the whole, and all of these sections added together will equal 100% of the whole.

Attendance at a Baseball Game

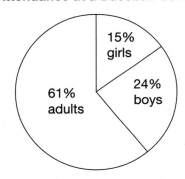

- BAR GRAPHS

  Bar graphs compare similar things with bars of different length, representing different values. These graphs may contain differently shaded bars used to represent different elements. Therefore, it is important to pay attention to both the size and shading of the graph.

Fruit Ordered by Grocer

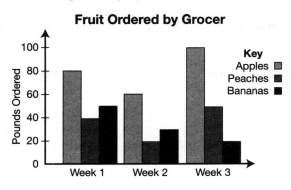

- BROKEN LINE GRAPHS

Broken-line graphs illustrate a measurable change over time. If a line is slanted up, it represents an increase, whereas a line sloping down represents a decrease. A flat line indicates no change.

In the line graph below, Lisa's progress riding her bike is graphed. From 0 to 2 hours, Lisa moves steadily. Between 2 and $2\frac{1}{2}$ hours, Lisa stops (flat line). After her break, she continues again but at a slower pace (line is not as steep as from 0 to 2 hours).

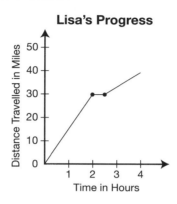

Elementary Algebra

Elementary algebra covers many topics typically covered in an Algebra I course. Topics include operations on polynomials; solving quadratic equations by factoring; linear inequalities; properties of exponents and square roots; using variables to express relationships; and substitution.

OPERATIONS ON POLYNOMIALS

Combining Like Terms: terms with the same variable and exponent can be combined by adding the coefficients and keeping the variable portion the same.

For example,

$$4x^2 + 2x - 5 + 3x^2 - 9x + 10 =$$
$$7x^2 - 7x + 5$$

Distributive Property: multiply all the terms inside the parentheses by the term outside the parentheses.

$$7(2x - 1) = 14x - 7$$

SOLVING QUADRATIC EQUATIONS BY FACTORING

Before factoring a quadratic equation to solve for the variable, you must set the equation equal to zero.

$$x^2 - 7x = 30$$
$$x^2 - 7x - 30 = 0$$

Next, factor.

$(x + 3)(x - 10) = 0$

Set each factor equal to zero and solve.

$x + 3 = 0 \qquad x - 10 = 0$

$x = -3 \qquad \quad x = 10$

The solution set for the equation is $\{-3, 10\}$.

SOLVING INEQUALITIES

Solving inequalities is the same as solving regular equations, with one exception. The exception is that when multiplying or dividing by a negative, you must change the inequality symbol.

For example,

$-3x < 9$

$\dfrac{-3x}{-3} < \dfrac{9}{-3}$

$x > -3$

Notice that the inequality switched from *less than* to *greater than* after division by a negative.

When graphing inequalities on a number line, recall that < and > use open dots and ≤ and ≥ use solid dots.

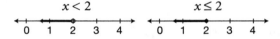

PROPERTIES OF EXPONENTS

When multiplying, add exponents.

$x^3 \cdot x^5 = x^{3+5} = x^8$

When dividing, subtract exponents.

$\dfrac{x^7}{x^2} = x^{7-2} = x^5$

When calculating a power to a power, multiply.

$(x^6)^3 = x^{6 \cdot 3} = x^{18}$

Any number (or variable) to the zero power is 1.

$$5^0 = 1 \qquad m^0 = 1 \qquad 9{,}837{,}475^0 = 1$$

Any number (or variable) to the first power is itself.

$$5^1 = 5 \qquad m^1 = m \qquad 9{,}837{,}475^1 = 9{,}837{,}475$$

Roots

Recall that exponents can be used to write roots. For example, $\sqrt{x} = x^{\frac{1}{2}}$ and $\sqrt[3]{x} = x^{\frac{1}{3}}$. The denominator is the root. The numerator indicates the power. For example, $(\sqrt[3]{x})^4 = x^{\frac{4}{3}}$ and $\sqrt{x^5} = x^{\frac{5}{2}}$. The properties of exponents outlined above apply to fractional exponents as well.

Using Variables to Express Relationships

The most important skill needed for word problems is being able to use variables to express relationships. The following will assist you in this by giving you some common examples of English phrases and their mathematical equivalents.

- "Increase" means add.
  Example
  A number increased by five = $x + 5$.
- "Less than" means subtract.
  Example
  10 less than a number = $x - 10$.
- "Times" or "product" means multiply.
  Example
  Three times a number = $3x$.
- "Times the sum" means to multiply a number by a quantity.
  Example
  Five times the sum of a number and three = $5(x + 3)$.
- Two variables are sometimes used together.
  Example
  A number y exceeds five times a number x by ten.
  $y = 5x + 10$
- Inequality signs are used for "at least" and "at most," as well as "less than" and "more than."
  Examples
  The product of x and 6 is greater than 2.
  $x \times 6 > 2$

When 14 is added to a number x, the sum is less than 21.

$x + 14 < 21$

The sum of a number x and four is at least nine.

$x + 4 \geq 9$

When seven is subtracted from a number x, the difference is at most four.

$x - 7 \leq 4$

ASSIGNING VARIABLES IN WORD PROBLEMS

It may be necessary to create and assign variables in a word problem. To do this, first identify an unknown and a known. You may not actually know the exact value of the "known," but you will know at least something about its value.

Examples

Max is three years older than Ricky.

Unknown = Ricky's age = x

Known = Max's age is three years older

Therefore,

Ricky's age = x and Max's age = $x + 3$

Siobhan made twice as many cookies as Rebecca.

Unknown = number of cookies Rebecca made = x

Known = number of cookies Siobhan made = $2x$

Cordelia has five more than three times the number of books that Becky has.

Unknown = the number of books Becky has = x

Known = the number of books Cordelia has = $3x + 5$

SUBSTITUTION

When asked to substitute a value for a variable, replace the variable with the value.

Example

Find the value of $x^2 + 4x - 1$, for $x = 3$.

Replace each x in the expression with the number 3. Then, simplify.

$= (3)^2 + 4(3) - 1$

$= 9 + 12 - 1$

$= 20$

The answer is 20.

Intermediate Algebra

Intermediate algebra covers many topics typically covered in an Algebra II course such as the quadratic formula; inequalities; absolute value equations; systems of equations; matrices; functions; quadratic inequalities; radical and rational expressions; complex numbers; and sequences.

THE QUADRATIC FORMULA

$x = \frac{-b \pm \sqrt{b^2 - 4ac}}{2a}$ for quadratic equations in the form $ax^2 + bx + c = 0$.

The quadratic formula can be used to solve any quadratic equation. It is most useful for equations that cannot be solved by factoring.

ABSOLUTE VALUE EQUATIONS

Recall that both $|5| = 5$ and $|-5| = 5$. This concept must be used when solving equations where the variable is in the absolute value symbol.

$|x + 4| = 9$

$$x + 4 = 9 \quad \text{or} \quad x + 4 = -9$$
$$x = 5 \qquad\qquad x = -13$$

SYSTEMS OF EQUATIONS

When solving a system of two linear equations with two variables, you are looking for the point on the coordinate plane at which the graphs of the two equations intersect. The elimination or addition method is usually the easiest way to find this point.

Solve the following system of equations:

$y = x + 2$
$2x + y = 17$

First, arrange the two equations so that they are both in the form $Ax + By = C$.

$-x + y = 2$
$2x + y = 17$

Next, multiply one of the equations so that the coefficient of one variable (we will use y) is the opposite of the coefficient of the same variable in the other equation.

$$-1(-x + y = 2)$$
$$\underline{2x + y = 17}$$
$$x - y = -2$$
$$2x + y = 17$$

Add the equations. One of the variables should cancel out.

$3x = 15$

Solve for the first variable.

$x = 5$

Find the value of the other variable by substituting this value into either original equation to find the other variable.

$y = 5 + 2$
$y = 7$

Since the answer is a point on the coordinate plane, write the answer as an ordered pair.

$(5, 7)$

COMPLEX NUMBERS

Any number in the form $a + bi$ is a complex number. $i = \sqrt{-1}$. Operations with i are the same as with any variable, but you must remember the following rules involving exponents.

$i = i$
$i^2 = -1$
$i^3 = -i$
$i^4 = 1$

This pattern repeats every fourth exponent.

RATIONAL EXPRESSIONS

Algebraic fractions (rational expressions) are very similar to fractions in arithmetic.

Example
Write $\frac{x}{5} - \frac{x}{10}$ as a single fraction.

Solution
Just like in arithmetic, you need to find the lowest common denominator (LCD) of 5 and 10, which is 10. Then change each fraction into an equivalent fraction that has 10 as a denominator.

$$\frac{x}{5} - \frac{x}{10} = \frac{x(2)}{5(2)} - \frac{x}{10}$$
$$= \frac{2x}{10} - \frac{x}{10}$$
$$= \frac{x}{10}$$

RADICAL EXPRESSIONS

- Radicals with the same radicand (number under the radical symbol) can be combined the same way "like terms" are combined.

    Example

    $$2\sqrt{3} + 5\sqrt{3} = 7\sqrt{3}$$

    Think of this as similar to:

    $$2x + 5x = 7x$$

- To multiply radical expressions with the same root, multiply the radicands and simplify.

    Example

    $$\sqrt{3} \cdot \sqrt{6} = \sqrt{18}$$

    This can be simplified by breaking 18 into 9×2.

    $$\sqrt{18} = \sqrt{9} \cdot \sqrt{2} = 3\sqrt{2}$$

- Radicals can also be written in exponential form.

    Example

    $$\sqrt[3]{x^5} = x^{\frac{5}{3}}$$

    In the fractional exponent, the numerator (top) is the power and the denominator (bottom) is the root. By representing radical expressions using exponents, you are able to use the rules of exponents to simplify the expression.

INEQUALITIES

The basic solution of linear inequalities was covered in the Elementary Algebra section. Following are some more advanced types of inequalities.

Solving Combined (or Compound) Inequalities

To solve an inequality that has the form $c < ax + b < d$, isolate the letter by performing the same operation on each member of the equation.

Example

If $-10 < -5y - 5 < 15$, find y.

Add five to each member of the inequality.

$$-10 + 5 < -5y - 5 + 5 < 15 + 5$$
$$-5 < -5y < 20$$

Divide each term by −5, changing the direction of both inequality symbols:

$$\frac{-5}{-5} < \frac{-5y}{-5} < \frac{20}{-5} = 1 > y > -4$$

The solution consists of all real numbers less than 1 and greater than −4.

Absolute Value Inequalities

$|x| < a$ is equivalent to $-a < x < a$ and $|x| > a$ is equivalent to $x > a$ or $x < -a$

Example

$|x + 3| > 7$

$$x + 3 > 7 \quad \text{or} \quad x + 3 < -7$$

$$x > 4 \qquad\qquad x < -10$$

Thus, $x > 4$ or $x < -10$.

Quadratic Inequalities

Recall that quadratic equations are equations of the form $ax^2 + bx + c = 0$.

To solve a quadratic inequality, first treat it like a quadratic equation and solve by setting the equation equal to zero and factoring. Next, plot these two points on a number line. This divides the number line into three regions. Choose a test number in each of the three regions and determine the sign of the equation when it is the value of x. Determine which of the three regions makes the inequality true. This region is the answer.

Example

$x^2 + x < 6$

Set the inequality equal to zero.

$x^2 + x - 6 < 0$

Factor the left side.

$(x + 3)(x - 2) < 0$

Set each of the factors equal to zero and solve.

$$x + 3 = 0 \qquad x - 2 = 0$$

$$x = -3 \quad x = 2$$

Plot the numbers on a number line. This divides the number line into three regions.

The number line is divided into the following regions.

numbers less than −3

numbers between −3 and 2

numbers greater than 2

Use a test number in each region to see if $(x + 3)(x - 2)$ is positive or negative in that region.

numbers less than −3	*numbers between −3 and 2*	*numbers greater than 2*
test # = −5	test # = 0	test # = 3
$(-5 + 3)(-5 - 2) = 14$	$(0 + 3)(0 - 2) = -6$	$(3 + 3)(3 - 2) = 6$
positive	negative	positive

The original inequality was $(x + 3)(x - 2) < 0$. If a number is less than zero, it is negative. The only region that is negative is between −3 and 2; $-3 < x < 2$ is the solution.

FUNCTIONS

Functions are often written in the form $f(x) = 5x - 1$. You might be asked to find $f(3)$, in which case you substitute 3 in for x. $f(3) = 5(3) - 1$. Therefore, $f(3) = 14$.

MATRICES

Basics of 2 × 2 Matrices

Addition: $\begin{bmatrix} a_{11} & a_{12} \\ a_{21} & a_{22} \end{bmatrix} + \begin{bmatrix} b_{11} & b_{12} \\ b_{21} & b_{22} \end{bmatrix} = \begin{bmatrix} a_{11} + b_{11} & a_{12} + b_{12} \\ a_{21} + b_{21} & a_{22} + b_{22} \end{bmatrix}$

Subtraction: Same as addition, except subtract the numbers rather than adding.

Scalar Multiplication: $k \begin{bmatrix} a_{11} & a_{12} \\ a_{21} & a_{22} \end{bmatrix} = \begin{bmatrix} ka_{11} & ka_{12} \\ ka_{21} & ka_{22} \end{bmatrix}$

Multiplication of Matrices: $\begin{bmatrix} a_{11} & a_{12} \\ a_{21} & a_{22} \end{bmatrix} \begin{bmatrix} b_{11} & b_{12} \\ b_{21} & b_{22} \end{bmatrix} = \begin{bmatrix} a_{11} b_{11} + a_{12} b_{21} & a_{11} b_{12} + a_{12} b_{22} \\ a_{21} b_{11} + a_{22} b_{21} & a_{21} b_{12} + a_{22} b_{22} \end{bmatrix}$

Coordinate Geometry

This section contains problems dealing with the (x, y) coordinate plane and number lines. Included are slope, distance, midpoint, and conics.

SLOPE

The formula for finding slope, given two points, (x_1, y_1) and (x_2, y_2) is $\frac{y_2 - y_1}{x_2 - x_1}$.

The equation of a line is often written in slope-intercept form which is $y = mx + b$, where m is the slope and b is the y-intercept.

Important Information about Slope

- A line that rises to the right has a positive slope and a line that falls to the right has a negative slope.
- A horizontal line has a slope of 0 and a vertical line does not have a slope at all—it is undefined.
- Parallel lines have equal slopes.
- Perpendicular lines have slopes that are negative reciprocals.

DISTANCE

The distance between two points can be found using the following formula:

$$d = \sqrt{(x_2 - x_1)^2 + (y_2 - y_1)^2}$$

MIDPOINT

The midpoint of two points can be found by taking the average of the x values and the average of the y values.

$$\text{midpoint} = \left(\frac{x_1 + x_2}{2}, \frac{y_1 + y_2}{2}\right)$$

CONICS

Circles, ellipses, parabolas, and hyperbolas are conic sections. The following are the equations for each conic section.

Circle:	$(x - h)^2 + (y - k)^2 = r^2$	where (h, k) is the center and r is the radius.
Ellipse:	$\frac{(x-h)^2}{a^2} + \frac{(y-k)^2}{b^2} = 1$	where (h, k) is the center. If the larger denominator is under y, the y-axis is the major axis. If the larger denominator is under the x-axis, the x-axis is the major axis.
Parabola	$y - k = a(x - h)^2$ or $x - h = a(y - k)^2$	The vertex is (h, k). Parabolas of the first form open up or down. Parabolas of the second form open left or right.
Hyperbola	$\frac{x^2}{a^2} - \frac{y^2}{b^2} = 1$ or $\frac{y^2}{a^2} - \frac{x^2}{b^2} = 1$	

Plane Geometry

Plane geometry covers relationships and properties of plane figures such as triangles, rectangles, circles, trapezoids, and parallelograms. Angle relations, line relations, proof techniques, volume and surface area, and translations, rotations, and reflections are all covered in this section.

To begin this section, it is helpful to become familiar with the vocabulary used in geometry. The list below defines some of the main geometrical terms:

Arc	part of a circumference
Area	the space inside a 2 dimensional figure
Bisect	to cut in 2 equal parts
Circumference	the distance around a circle
Chord	a line segment that goes through a circle, with its endpoint on the circle
Diameter	a chord that goes directly through the center of a circle—the longest line you can draw in a circle
Equidistant	exactly in the middle

Hypotenuse	the longest leg of a right triangle, always opposite the right angle
Parallel	lines in the same plane that will never intersect
Perimeter	the distance around a figure
Perpendicular	2 lines that intersect to form 90-degree angles
Quadrilateral	any four-sided figure
Radius	a line from the center of a circle to a point on the circle (half of the diameter)
Volume	the space inside a 3-dimensional figure

BASIC FORMULAS

Perimeter	the sum of all the sides of a figure
Area of a rectangle	$A = bh$
Area of a triangle	$A = \frac{bh}{2}$
Area of a parallelogram	$A = bh$
Area of a circle	$A = \pi r^2$
Volume of a rectangular solid	$V = lwh$

BASIC GEOMETRIC FACTS

The sum of the angles in a triangle is 180°.

A circle has a total of 360°.

PYTHAGOREAN THEOREM

The **Pythagorean theorem** is an important tool for working with right triangles.

It states: $a^2 + b^2 = c^2$, where a and b represent the legs and c represents the hypotenuse.

This theorem allows you to find the length of any side as along as you know the measure of the other two. So, if leg a = 1 and leg b = 2 in the triangle below, you can find the measure of leg c.

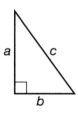

$a^2 + b^2 = c^2$
$1^2 + 2^2 = c^2$
$1 + 4 = c^2$
$5 = c^2$
$\sqrt{5} = c$

PYTHAGOREAN TRIPLES

In a **Pythagorean triple**, the square of the largest number equals the sum of the squares of the other two numbers.

Example

As demonstrated: $1^2 + 2^2 = (\sqrt{5})^2$

1, 2, and $\sqrt{5}$ are also a Pythagorean triple because:

$1^2 + 2^2 = 1 + 4 = 5$ and $(\sqrt{5})^2 = 5$.

Pythagorean triples are useful for helping you identify right triangles. Some common Pythagorean triples are:

3:4:5   8:15:17   5:12:13

MULTIPLES OF PYTHAGOREAN TRIPLES

Any multiple of a Pythagorean triple is also a Pythagorean triple. Therefore, if given 3:4:5, then 9:12:15 is also a Pythagorean triple.

Example

If given a right triangle with sides measuring 6, x, and 10, what is the value of x?

Solution

Because it is a right triangle, use the Pythagorean theorem. Therefore,

$10^2 - 6^2 = x^2$

$100 - 36 = x^2$

$64 = x^2$

$8 = x$

45-45-90 RIGHT TRIANGLES

A right triangle with two angles each measuring 45 degrees is called an **isosceles right triangle**. In an isosceles right triangle:

- The length of the hypotenuse is $\sqrt{2}$ multiplied by the length of one of the legs of the triangle.
- The length of each leg is $\frac{\sqrt{2}}{2}$ multiplied by the length of the hypotenuse.

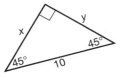

$$x = y = \frac{\sqrt{2}}{2} \times \frac{10}{1} = 10\frac{\sqrt{2}}{2} = 5\sqrt{2}$$

30-60-90 TRIANGLES

In a right triangle with the other angles measuring 30 and 60 degrees:

- The leg opposite the 30-degree angle is half of the length of the hypotenuse. (And, therefore, the hypotenuse is two times the length of the leg opposite the 30-degree angle.)
- The leg opposite the 60-degree angle is $\sqrt{3}$ times the length of the other leg.

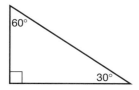

Example

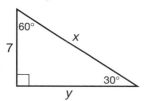

$$x = 2 \cdot 7 = 14 \text{ and } y = 7\sqrt{3}$$

CONGRUENT

Two figures are congruent if they have the same size and shape.

TRANSLATIONS, ROTATIONS, AND REFLECTIONS

Congruent figures can be made to coincide (place one right on top of the other), by using one of the following basic movements.

TRANSLATION (SLIDE)	ROTATION	REFLECTION (FLIP)

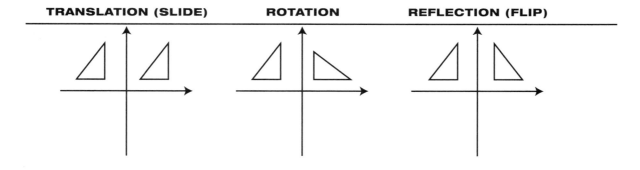

Trigonometry

Basic trigonometric ratios, graphs, identities, and equations are covered in this section.

BASIC TRIGONOMETRIC RATIOS

$\sin A = \frac{opposite}{hypotenuse}$ *opposite* refers to the length of the leg opposite angle *A.*

$\cos A = \frac{adjacent}{hypotenuse}$ *adjacent* refers to the length of the leg adjacent to angle *A.*

$\tan A = \frac{opposite}{adjacent}$

TRIGONOMETRIC IDENTITIES

$$\sin^2 x + \cos^2 x = 1$$

$$\tan x = \frac{\sin x}{\cos x}$$

$$\sin 2x = 2\sin x \cos x$$

$$\cos 2x = \cos^2 x - \sin^2 x$$

$$\tan 2x = \frac{2\tan x}{1 - \tan^2 x}$$

► Practice Questions

Directions

After reading each question, solve each problem, and then choose the best answer from the choices given. (Remember, the ACT Math Test is different from all the other tests in that each math question contains *five* answer choices.) When you are taking the official ACT, make sure you carefully fill in the appropriate bubble on the answer document.

You may use a calculator for any problem, but many problems are done more quickly and easily without one.

Unless directions tell you otherwise, assume the following:

- figures may not be drawn to scale
- geometric figures lie in a plane
- "line" refers to a straight line
- "average" refers to the arithmetic mean

Remember, the questions get harder as the test goes on. You may want to consider this fact as you pace yourself.

1. How is five hundred twelve and sixteen thousandths written in decimal form?

   a. 512.016

   b. 512.16

   c. 512,160

   d. 51.216

   e. 512.0016

2. $4\frac{1}{3} - 1\frac{3}{4} = ?$

   f. $2\frac{7}{12}$

   g. $3\frac{5}{12}$

   h. $3\frac{2}{3}$

   i. $2\frac{5}{12}$

   j. $1\frac{1}{8}$

$$\frac{13}{3} - \frac{7}{4} \implies \frac{52}{12} - \frac{21}{12} = \frac{31}{12}$$

3. Simplify $|3 - 11| + 4 \times 2^3$.

   a. 24

   b. 40

   c. 96

   d. 520

   e. 32

$8 + 4 + 8$

16×8

96

4. The ratio of boys to girls in a kindergarten class is 4 to 5. If there are 18 students in the class, how many are boys?

   f. 9

   g. 8

   h. 10

   i. 7

   j. 12

$4:5 \text{ or } \frac{4}{5} \qquad \frac{x}{18}$

$\frac{5x}{5} \quad \frac{72}{5}$

$x = 12$

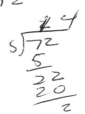

5. What is the median of 0.024, 0.008, 0.1, 0.024, 0.095, and 0.3?

   a. 0.119

   b. 0.095

   c. 0.0595

   d. 0.024

   e. 0.092

$.3, .1, .024, .024, .008$

.095

.3
.1
.095
.024
.024
.008

$6\sqrt{.451}$

$6\sqrt{.451}$ .073
43

21
18

6. Which of the following is NOT the graph of a function?

f.

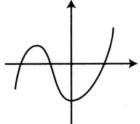

g.

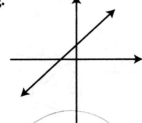

h.

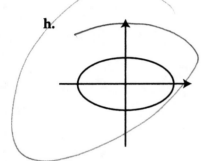

i.

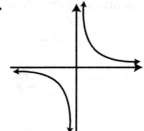

j.

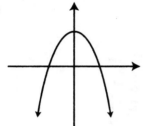

7. $4.6 \times 10^5 = ?$

4,600,000

a. 4.60000

b. 0.000046

c. 4,600,000

d. 460,000

e. 0.0000046

8. What is the value of x^5 for $x = 3$?

f. 15

g. 243

h. 125

i. $\frac{5}{3}$

j. 1.6

9. What is the next number in the pattern below?

0, 3, 8, 15, 24, . . .

a. 35

b. 33

c. 36

d. 41

e. 37

24
+11
35

10. What is the prime factorization of 84?

f. 42×2

g. $7 \times 2 \times 3$

h. $2^2 \times 3 \times 7$

i. $2 \times 6 \times 7$

j. $2^3 \times 7$

84
2 ∧ 42

12
7
84

8 × 1

11. Find the slope of the line $7x = 3y - 9$.

a. 3

b. −9

c. $\frac{7}{3}$

d. −3

e. $\frac{3}{7}$

$y = mx + b$

$\frac{7x + 9}{3} = \frac{3y}{3}$

$\frac{7}{3}x + 3 = y$

12. The perimeter of a rectangle is 20 cm. If the width is 4 cm, find the length of the rectangle.

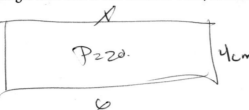

   f. 6 cm
   g. 16 cm
   h. 5 cm
   i. 12 cm
   j. 24 cm

13. Find the area of the figure below.

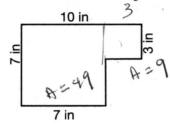

   a. 79 square inches
   b. 91 square inches
   c. 70 square inches
   d. 64 square inches
   e. 58 square inches

14. Five cans of tomatoes cost $6.50. At this rate, how much will 9 cans of tomatoes cost?

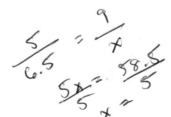 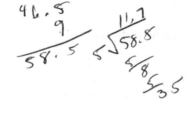

   f. $13.00
   g. $11.70
   h. $1.30
   i. $11.90
   j. $12.40

15. For all $x \neq 0, \frac{2}{3x} + \frac{1}{5} = ?$

   a. $\frac{2}{15x}$

   b. $\frac{10+3x}{15+x}$

   c. $\frac{10+3x}{15x}$

   d. $\frac{2}{15+x}$

   e. $\frac{1}{5x}$

16. Which inequality best represents the graph below?

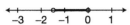

-3   -2   -1   0   1

f. $-1.5 > x > -1$

g. $x \leq 0$

h. $-0.5 > x > 0$

i. $-1.5 < x < 0$

j. $-1.5 \leq x \leq 0$

17. Simplify $-(6x^4y^3)^2$.

a. $-36x^6y^5$

b. $36x^2y$

c. $-36x^8y^6$

d. $36x^8y^4$

e. $-36xy$

18. If $2x + 3y = 55$ and $4x = y + 47$, find $x - y$.

f. 28

g. 16

h. 5

i. 12

j. 24

19. Which inequality represents the graph below?

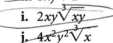

-4   0   4

a. $-4x < 0$

b. $-20x > 5$

c. $x < -4$

d. $-x \leq -4$

e. $-x < 4$

20. Simplify $\sqrt[3]{16x^5y^4}$.

f. $2xy\sqrt[3]{2x^2y}$

g. $8x^2y$

h. $8xy\sqrt[3]{2}$

i. $2xy\sqrt[3]{xy}$

j. $4x^2y^2\sqrt[3]{x}$

21. The formula to convert Celsius to Fahrenheit is $F = \frac{5}{9}C + 32$, where F is degrees Fahrenheit, and C is degrees Celsius. What Fahrenheit temperature is equivalent to 63° Celsius?

   a. 32°
   b. 95°
   c. 67°
   d. 83°
   e. 47°

$$F = \frac{5}{9}C + 32$$
$$F = \left(\frac{5}{9} \cdot \frac{63}{1}\right) + 32$$
$$= \frac{315}{9}$$

$$63 \times 5 = 315$$

$$9\overline{)315} = 35$$

22. What are the solutions to the equation $x^2 + 8x + 15 = 0$?

   f. {8, 15}
   g. {0}
   h. {−5, −3}
   i. no solution
   j. {2, 4}

$$(x+5)(x+3) = 0$$
$$-5 \qquad -3$$

23. If $5k = 9m - 18$, then $m = ?$

   a. $5k + 18$
   b. $\frac{5}{9}k + 2$
   c. $-9 + 5k$
   d. $5k + 9$
   e. $9k + 18$

$$5k = 9m - 18$$
$$\frac{5k + 18}{9} = \frac{9m}{9}$$

24. What is the solution set for $5x - 7 = 5(x + 2)$?

   f. {2}
   g. {7}
   h. no solution
   i. all real numbers
   j. all positive numbers

$$5x - 7 = 5x + 10$$
$$0 \neq 17$$

25. Simplify $\frac{4x^2 + 11x - 3}{x + 3}$ for all $x \neq -3$.

   a. $3x^2 + 11$
   b. $2x + 1$
   c. $4x^2 + 12x$
   d. $4x^2 + 10x - 6$
   e. $4x - 1$

$$\frac{(x \quad)(x \quad)}{x + 3}$$

$$\quad 4 \quad 11$$

26. If $x = \begin{bmatrix} 3 & 4 \\ 5 & 6 \end{bmatrix}$ and $y = \begin{bmatrix} +2 & 4 \\ +1 & 0 \end{bmatrix}$, find $x - y$.

f. $\begin{bmatrix} 5 & 0 \\ 6 & 6 \end{bmatrix}$

g. $\begin{bmatrix} 1 & 8 \\ 4 & 6 \end{bmatrix}$

h. $\begin{bmatrix} -5 & 0 \\ -6 & -6 \end{bmatrix}$

i. $\begin{bmatrix} 4 & 1 \\ 2 & 8 \end{bmatrix}$

j. $\begin{bmatrix} 6 & 1 \\ 2 & 5 \end{bmatrix}$

27. If $\log_3 x = 2$, then $x = ?$

a. 6

b. 9

c. $\frac{2}{3}$

d. 4

e. $\frac{1}{2}$

28. Simplify $\frac{x^2 - 9}{x - 3}$.

f. $x - 12$

g. $x - 6$

h. $x + 3$

i. $-x^2 - 6$

j. $x - 3$

29. The vertices of a triangle are $A(-1, 3)$, $B(3, 0)$, and $C(-2, -1)$. Find the length of side $\overline{AC}$.

a. $\sqrt{15}$

b. $\sqrt{17}$

c. 19

d. 17

e. $3\sqrt{6}$

30. Which of the following equations has a graph that has a y-intercept of 4 and is parallel to $3y - 9x = 24$?

    f. $-12x + 4y = 16$

    g. $9x - 3y = -15$

    h. $2y = 4x + 8$

    i. $7y = 14x + 7$

    j. $3x - 9y = 14$

31. At what point do the lines $x = 9$ and $3x + y = 4$ intersect?

    a. $(3, 9)$

    b. $(\frac{5}{3}, 9)$

    c. $(-20, -9)$

    d. $(9, -23)$

    e. $(9, 4)$

32. Which of the numbers below is the best approximation of $(\sqrt{37})(\sqrt{125})$?

    f. 52

    g. 4,600

    h. 150

    i. 66

    j. 138

33. What is the solution set of the equation $x^2 - 4x - 4 = 2x + 23$?

    a. $\{-4, 4\}$

    b. $\{-4, 23\}$

    c. $\{1, 11.5\}$

    d. $\{-3, 9\}$

    e. $\{5, 6\}$

$x^2 - 6 - 27 = 0$

$(x - 9)(x + 3) = 0$

$+9 \qquad -3$

34. If a fair coin is flipped and a die is rolled, what is the probability of getting tails and a 3?

    f. $\frac{1}{2}$

    g. $\frac{1}{12}$

    h. $\frac{1}{6}$

    i. $\frac{1}{4}$

    j. $\frac{1}{8}$

35. What is $\frac{1}{2}$% of 90?

   a. 45

   b. 0.045

   c. 4.5

   d. 0.45

   e. 450

36. Between which two integers does $\sqrt{41}$ lie?

   f. 5 and 6

   g. 8 and 9

   h. 4 and 5

   i. 7 and 8

   j. 6 and 7

37. Mike has 12 bags of shredded cheese to use to make pizzas. If he uses $\frac{3}{4}$ of a bag of cheese for each pizza, how many pizzas can he make?

   a. 12

   b. 24

   c. 36

   d. 9

   e. 16

38. Greene ran the 100-meter dash in 9.79 seconds. What was his speed in kilometers per hour (round to the nearest kilometer)?

   f. 31 km/h

   g. 37 km/h

   h. 1 km/h

   i. 10 km/h

   j. 25 km/h

39. Larry has 4 blue socks, 6 red socks, and 10 purple socks in his drawer. Without looking, Larry randomly pulled out a red sock from the drawer. If Larry does not put the red sock back in the drawer, what is the probability that the next sock he randomly draws will be red?

   a. $\frac{1}{4}$

   b. $\frac{3}{10}$

   c. $\frac{5}{19}$

   d. $\frac{3}{7}$

   e. $\frac{1}{6}$

40. What is the product of 5×10^{-4} and 6×10^8?

    f. 11×10^4

    g. 3×10^4

    h. 1.1×10^5

    i. 3×10^5

    j. 5.6×10^{-4}

41. What is the sine of angle B in the triangle below?

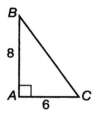

    a. $\frac{3}{4}$

    b. $\frac{3}{5}$

    c. $\frac{4}{3}$

    d. $\frac{4}{5}$

    e. $\frac{5}{4}$

42. Find tan x for the right triangle below.

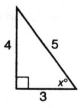

    f. $\frac{5}{4}$

    g. $\frac{3}{4}$

    h. $\frac{4}{3}$

    i. $\frac{6}{3}$

    j. $\frac{5}{3}$

43. The surface area of a box is found by taking the sum of the areas of each of the faces of the box. Find the surface area of a box with dimensions 6 inches by 8 inches by 10 inches.

    a. 480 sq in
    b. 138 sq in
    c. 346 sq in
    d. 376 sq in
    e. 938 sq in

44. Find the area of the shaded region. Recall that the area of a circle is πr^2, where r is the radius of the circle.

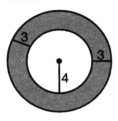

    f. 65π
    g. 6π
    h. 25π
    i. 5π
    j. 33π

45. The area of square WXYZ is 100 square centimeters. Find the length of diagonal WY in centimeters.

    a. $10\sqrt{2}$ cm
    b. 20 cm
    c. 10 cm
    d. $2\sqrt{5}$ cm
    e. $10\sqrt{5}$ cm

46. Find the hypotenuse of the triangle below.

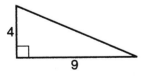

    f. $\sqrt{13}$
    g. $\sqrt{5}$
    h. $\sqrt{65}$
    i. $\sqrt{97}$
    j. 13

47. A circular lid to a jar has a radius of $3\frac{1}{2}$ inches. Find the area of the lid.

    a. $\frac{12}{49}\pi$ sq in

    b. $\frac{49}{12}\pi$ sq in

    c. $\frac{49}{4}\pi$ sq in

    d. $\frac{7}{2}\pi$ sq in

    e. $\frac{4}{49}\pi$ sq in

48. What is the value of x when y is equal to 15 for the equation $y = 4x^2 - 1$?

    f. 2

    g. 16

    h. 64

    i. $\sqrt{5}$

    j. 0

49. The senior class at Roosevelt High has 540 students. Kristen won the election for class president with 60% of the vote. Of that 60%, 75% were female. Assuming that the entire senior class voted, how many females voted for Kristen?

    a. 195

    b. 405

    c. 324

    d. 227

    e. 243

50. If $\cos\theta = \frac{6}{17}$ and $\tan\theta = \frac{5}{6}$, then $\sin\theta = ?$

    f. $\frac{5}{17}$

    g. $\frac{6}{5}$

    h. $\frac{17}{5}$

    i. $\frac{5}{6}$

    j. $\frac{1}{2}$

51. The formula for the volume of a rectangular solid is $V = lwh$. If each dimension is tripled, how many times the original volume will the new volume be?

    a. 3

    b. 9

    c. $\frac{1}{3}$

    d. 27

    e. 81

52. In a right triangle, the two non-right angles measure $7x$ and $8x$. What is the measure of the smaller angle?

    f. 15°

    g. 60°

    h. 30°

    i. 48°

    j. 42°

53. What is the length of the missing leg in the right triangle below?

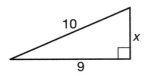

    a. $\sqrt{181}$

    b. 1

    c. $\sqrt{19}$

    d. 4

    e. $\sqrt{21}$

54. The length of a rectangle is twice the width. If the perimeter of the rectangle is 72 feet, what is the length of the rectangle?

    f. 12 feet

    g. 6 feet

    h. 36 feet

    i. 48 feet

    j. 24 feet

55. The area of a triangle is 80 square inches. Find the height if the base is 5 inches more than the height.

    a. $\dfrac{1 + \sqrt{629}}{2}$

    b. $\dfrac{-9 \pm \sqrt{5}}{2}$

    c. $4 \pm \sqrt{85}$

    d. $5 - \sqrt{665}$

    e. $\dfrac{-5 + \sqrt{665}}{2}$

56. Three of the vertices of a square are $(-2, 3)$, $(5, 3)$, and $(-2, -4)$. What is the length of a side of the square?

   f. 5

   g. 4

   h. 3

   i. 7

   j. 8

57. Which of the following lines is perpendicular to $y = 3x + 1$?

   a. $6x + 5 = 2y$

   b. $4 + y = 3x$

   c. $-9y = -3 + 2x$

   d. $2x + y = 4$

   e. $3y + x = 5$

58. Which statement best describes the lines $-2x + 3y = 12$ and $-60 + 15y = 10x$?

   f. the same line

   g. parallel

   h. skew

   i. perpendicular

   j. intersect at one point

59. What is the midpoint of $\overline{XY}$ if X$(-4, -2)$ and Y$(3, 8)$?

   a. $(-7, 6)$

   b. $(-0.5, 3)$

   c. $(-1, 6)$

   d. $(-7, -10)$

   e. $(2, -1.5)$

60. $\frac{4}{3x} + \frac{x-1}{5} = ?$

   f. $\frac{x+3}{15x}$

   g. $\frac{x+3}{8x}$

   h. $\frac{x+3}{3x+5}$

   i. $\frac{3x^2 - 3x + 20}{15x}$

   j. $\frac{x^2 + 4x - 1}{15x}$

61. Simplify $(\frac{1}{2x^2})^{-3}$.

   a. $6x^6$

   b. $8x^6$

   c. $\frac{1}{6x^6}$

   d. $\frac{3}{8x^5}$

   e. $\frac{1}{8x^5}$

62. If $4x = 3y + 15$ and $2y - x = 0$, find x.

   f. 6

   g. 3

   h. 2

   i. -1

   j. 5

63. Simplify $36^{\frac{-3}{2}}$.

   a. -6

   b. -216

   c. -12

   d. $\frac{1}{216}$

   e. $-\frac{1}{216}$

64. If $x^3 = -50$, the value of x is between which two integers?

   f. 3 and 4

   g. 7 and 8

   h. -3 and -4

   i. -2 and -3

   j. -7 and -8

65. Find the value of x.

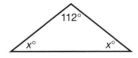

   a. $25°$

   b. $136°$

   c. $112°$

   d. $68°$

   e. $34°$

66. Line *l* is parallel to line *m*. Find the measure of angle *x*.

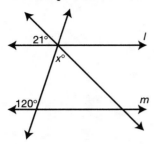

    f. 99°

    g. 39°

    h. 21°

    i. 121°

    j. 106°

67. Find the radius of the circle with center $(4, -2)$ that is tangent to the *y*-axis.

    a. 2

    b. 6

    c. 1

    d. 4

    e. 10

68. Find the area, in square units, of the circle represented by the equation $(x - 5)^2 + (y - 2)^2 = 36$.

    f. 6π

    g. 36π

    h. 25π

    i. -2π

    j. 4π

69. $m\angle ABC = 120°$ and $m\angle CDE = 110°$. Find the measure of $\angle BCD$.

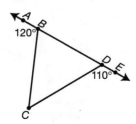

    a. 70°

    b. 50°

    c. 60°

    d. 150°

    e. 40°

70. The ratio of the side lengths of a right triangle is $1:1:\sqrt{2}$. Find the sine of the smallest angle.

    f. $\frac{1}{2}$

    g. $\frac{\sqrt{2}}{2}$

    h. $\sqrt{2}$

    i. 1

    j. 2

71. What is the minimum value of $9\cos x$?

    a. 9

    b. 0

    c. −90

    d. −2

    e. −9

72. A triangle with angles measuring 30°, 60°, and 90° has a smallest side length of 7. Find the length of the hypotenuse.

    f. 14

    g. $7\sqrt{3}$

    h. 2

    i. 12

    j. 18

73. The Abrams' put a cement walkway around their rectangular pool. The pool's dimensions are 12 feet by 24 feet and the width of the walkway is 5 feet in all places. Find the area of the walkway.

    a. 748 square feet

    b. 288 square feet

    c. 460 square feet

    d. 205 square feet

    e. 493 square feet

74. Triangle XYZ is an equilateral triangle. $\overline{YW}$ is an altitude of the triangle. If $\overline{YX}$ is 14 inches, what is the length of the altitude?

    f. $7\sqrt{3}$ inches

    g. 7 inches

    h. $7\sqrt{2}$ inches

    i. $6\sqrt{3}$ inches

    j. 12 inches

75. What is the sum of the solutions to the equation $2x^2 = 2x + 12$?

    a. 4

    b. 7

    c. 1

    d. 9

    e. −1

76. Find the value of $\sin A$ if angle A is acute and $\cos A = \frac{9}{10}$.

    f. $\frac{\sqrt{11}}{10}$

    g. $\frac{5}{4}$

    h. $\frac{10}{9}$

    i. $\frac{19}{100}$

    j. $\frac{\sqrt{19}}{10}$

77. Find the value of x.

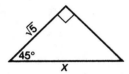

    a. 2

    b. 1

    c. $\sqrt{7}$

    d. $\sqrt{10}$

    e. $2\sqrt{5}$

78. Which equation corresponds to the graph below?

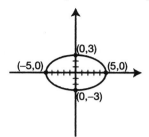

f. $\frac{x^2}{25} + \frac{y^2}{9} = 1$

g. $25x^2 + 9y^2 = 1$

h. $\frac{x^2}{25} - \frac{y^2}{9} = 1$

i. $\frac{y^2}{25} + \frac{x^2}{9} = 1$

j. $5x^2 + 3y^2 = 3$

79. What is the inequality that corresponds to the graph below?

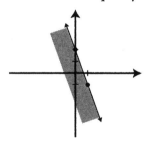

a. $y > 3x + 2$

b. $y \leq -3x + 2$

c. $y \geq -3x + 2$

d. $y < 3x + 2$

e. $y < -3x + 2$

80. What is the domain of the function $f(x) = \frac{4x-5}{x^2+3x-4}$?

    f. $\{x \mid x \neq 0\}$

    g. $\emptyset$

    h. All real numbers

    i. $\{x \mid x \neq 3\}$

    j. $\{x \mid x \neq -4 \text{ and } x \neq 1\}$

► Practice Questions Answers and Explanations

1. Choice **a** is correct. The word *and* indicates a decimal point. Therefore, the decimal point should go after five hundred twelve and before sixteen thousandths. The number 16 must end in the thousandths place, which is three digits to the right of the decimal. The correct answer is 512.016.

   Choice **b** is "five hundred twelve and sixteen hundredths."

   Choice **c** is "five hundred twelve thousand, one hundred sixty."

   Choice **d** is "fifty one and two hundred sixteen thousandths."

   Choice **e** is "five hundred twelve and sixteen ten thousandths."

2. Choice **f** is correct. First, change the fractional parts of the problem to have the common denominator of 12.

   $4\frac{4}{12} - 1\frac{9}{12}$

   Subtract the numerators. Since 4 is less than 9, you must borrow *one whole* from the whole number 4. This means that you are adding $\frac{12}{12}$ to the first fraction.

   $3\frac{16}{12} - 1\frac{9}{12}$.

   Subtract the fractional parts then the whole numbers. The final answer is $2\frac{7}{12}$.

3. Choice **b** is correct. The correct order of operations must be used to simplify the expression. You may remember this as PEMDAS or "Please Excuse My Dear Aunt Sally." The P stands for parentheses or any grouping symbol. Absolute value is a grouping symbol, so it will be done first.

   $|-8| + 4 \times 2^3 =$

   $8 + 4 \times 2^3$

   Next, perform the exponent part.

   $8 + 4 \times 8$

   Then, the multiplication.

   $8 + 32$

   Last, the addition.

   The final answer is 40.

4. Choice **g** is correct. This problem can be approached a couple of different ways. The simplest way might be to look at multiples of 4 and 5 until the multiples add to 18. If both 4 and 5 are multiplied by 2, they become 8 and 10. 8 plus 10 is 18. Therefore, there are 8 boys and 10 girls in the class.

   The problem can also be done with an equation.

   $4x + 5x = 18$

   When solved, $x = 2$. Multiply 4 by 2 to find that there are 8 boys.

5. Choice **c** is correct. To find the median, place the numbers in order from least to greatest and find the middle number. In order, the numbers are:

0.008, 0.024, 0.024, 0.095, 0.1, 0.3

Since there are an even number of numbers, there are two middle numbers (0.024 and 0.095). Take the average of these two middle numbers by adding them and dividing the sum by two. The answer is 0.0595.

6. Choice **h** is correct. Use the vertical line test to see if each graph is a function. A graph is NOT a function if vertical lines drawn through the graph hit the graph more than once.

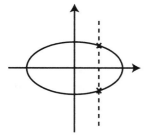

7. Choice **d** is correct. When multiplying by 10^5 you move the decimal point 5 places to the right.

4.60000. = 460,000

The answer is 460,000.

Another way to look at the problem is to recognize that $10^5 = 100,000$ and multiply 4.6 by 100,000. The answer is 460,000.

8. Choice **g** is correct. $3^5 = 3 \times 3 \times 3 \times 3 \times 3 = 243$. The answer is 243.

9. Choice **a** is correct. Consecutive odd integers starting with 3 are being added to find the next number.

0, 3, 8, 15, 24, . . .
+3 +5 +7 +9 +11

Therefore, 11 must be added to 24 to find the next number. The answer is 35.

You may also notice that the numbers can be found using the expression $n^2 - 1$ where n is the place in the pattern. We are looking for the sixth number, so $n = 6$. $6^2 - 1 = 35$. The answer is 35.

10. Choice **h** is correct. First, you can eliminate choices **f** and **i** because they contain numbers that are not prime. Next, use a factor tree to determine the prime factorization.

The prime factorization of 84 is $2 \times 2 \times 3 \times 7$, which can be written in exponential notation as $2^2 \times 3 \times 7$. The answer is $2^2 \times 3 \times 7$.

11. Choice **c** is correct. To easily see the slope, change the equation into the form $y = mx + b$. The equation is then $y = \frac{7}{3}x + 3$. The coefficient of x is the slope. $\frac{7}{3}$ is the answer.

12. Choice **f** is correct. The perimeter is twice the width plus twice the length: $P = 2w + 2l$. Insert 20 for P and 4 for w, then solve for l.

$20 = 2(4) + 2l$

$20 = 8 + 2l$

$20 - 8 = 2l$

$12 = 2l$

$6 = l$

6 is the length.

13. Choice **e** is correct. Find the lengths of the unlabeled sides by comparing them to the given sides. Divide the shape into two rectangles as shown below. Find the area of each of the regions and add together to find the total area.

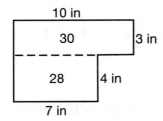

$30 + 28 = 58$ sq in.

14. Choice **g** is correct. Find the cost for one can (unit rate) by dividing the cost of five cans by 5. $\$6.50 \div 5 = \$1.30$ per can. Multiply the cost per can by 9 cans. $\$1.30 \times 9 = \$11.70$. Nine cans cost $\$11.70$.

A proportion can also be used:

$\frac{5}{\$6.50} = \frac{9}{x}$.

To solve the proportion, cross-multiply and divide.

$5x = \$58.50$

$\frac{5x}{5} = \frac{\$58.50}{9}$

$x = \$11.70$

15. Choice **c** is correct. Find a common denominator ($15x$). Multiply the first fraction by $\frac{5}{5}$ and the second fraction by $\frac{3x}{3x}$. The result is $\frac{10}{15x} + \frac{3x}{15x} = \frac{10 + 3x}{15x}$. The answer is $\frac{10 + 3x}{15x}$.

16. Choice **i** is correct. The endpoints are on -1.5 and 0, so the possible choices are **i** and **h**. The endpoints are open dots (not solid) and, therefore, only $<$ or $>$ signs can be used (not $\leq$ or $\geq$). This information narrows the answer choices down to only **i**.

17. Choice **c** is correct. First, raise everything in the parentheses to the second power: $-(6^2(x^4)^2y^3)^2)$. When you have a power to a power you multiply the exponents. Thus, $-(36x^8y^6)$. Apply the negative for the final answer of $-36x^8y^6$.

18. Choice **h** is correct. Use substitution to solve for x and y. First, solve the second equation for y.

$y = 4x - 47$

Next, substitute the above value for y into the first equation and solve for x.

$2x + 3(4x - 47) = 55$

$2x + 12x - 141 = 55$

$14x - 141 = 55$

$14x = 196$

$x = 14$

Now, substitute 14 for x in the second equation and solve for y.

$4(14) = y + 47$

$56 = y + 47$

$y = 9$

The solution to the system of equations is $(14, 9)$. The problem asks you to find $x - y$.

$14 - 9 = 5$.

The answer is 5.

19. Choice **e** is correct. First, eliminate choice **d** because the dot on the graph is open and therefore the inequality sign must be either $<$ or $>$ (*not* $\leq$ or $\geq$). Next, solve each inequality for x remembering that the inequality symbol must be flipped when multiplying or dividing by a negative. The answer choices become:

a. $x > 0$

b. $x < -\frac{1}{4}$

c. $x < -4$

e. $x > -4$

The endpoint is on -4, so the only possibilities are choices **c** and **e**. The arrow points to numbers greater than -4. The answer is choice **e**.

20. Choice **f** is correct. Notice that you are taking the *cube* root, *not* the *square* root. Break up the expression under the radical into perfect cubes.

$\sqrt[3]{(8)(2)x^3x^2y^3y}$

Any exponent divisible by 3 is a cube root. Take out the perfect cubes and leave everything else under the radical.

$2xy\sqrt[3]{2x^2y}$ is the answer.

21. Choice **c** is correct. Substitute the value 63° for C.

$F = \frac{5}{9}(63) + 32$

$F = 35 + 32$

$F = 67$

The answer is 67°F.

22. Choice **h** is correct. The equation is quadratic, so there are two ways to solve it. First, try to factor the left-hand side of the equation. Since it is factorable, solve the equation using factoring.

$x^2 + 8x + 15 = 0$

$(x + 5)(x + 3) = 0$

Set each of the factors equal to zero and solve for x.

$x + 5 = 0 \quad x + 3 = 0$

$x = -5 \quad\quad x = -3$

The solution set is $\{-5, -3\}$.

The quadratic equation can also be used to solve the equation.

$x = \frac{-b \pm \sqrt{b^2 - 4ac}}{2a}$

$x = \frac{-8 \pm \sqrt{(8)^2 - (4)(1)(15)}}{2}$

$x = \frac{-8 \pm \sqrt{64 - 60}}{2}$

$x = \frac{-8 \pm 2}{2}$

$x = \frac{-8 + 2}{2} \quad\quad x = \frac{-8 - 2}{2}$

$x = \frac{-6}{2} = -3 \quad x = \frac{-10}{2} = -5$

The solution set is $\{-5, -3\}$.

23. Choice **b** is correct. Solve the equation for m using inverse operations.

$5k = 9m - 18$

$5k + 18 = 9m$

$\frac{5k + 18}{9} = m$

Since this answer does not appear as one of the choices, you must determine if any of the choices are equivalent to it. If you divide each of the numerator terms by 9 you get $\frac{5}{9}k + 2 = m$, which is choice **b**.

24. Choice **h** is correct. Solve the equation by moving all x terms to one side.

$5x - 5x - 7 = 5x - 5x + 10$

$-7 = 10$

$-7 \neq 10$

$\emptyset$

The x's cancel, leaving $-7 = 10$, which is not true. Since -7 never equals 10, there is no solution.

25. Choice **e** is correct. Factor the numerator.

$\frac{(4x - 1)(x + 3)}{x + 3}$

Use the denominator as a clue when factoring the numerator. Most likely, the denominator will be one of the factors in the numerator.

Cancel the $x + 3$ in the numerator with the $x + 3$ in the denominator. This leaves $4x - 1$.

26. Choice **f** is correct. Subtract the numbers in y from the corresponding numbers in x.

$$\begin{bmatrix} 3-(-2) & 4-4 \\ 5-(-1) & 6-0 \end{bmatrix} = \begin{bmatrix} 5 & 0 \\ 6 & 6 \end{bmatrix}$$

27. Choice **b** is correct. $\log_3 x = 2$ is equivalent to $3^2 = x$. Therefore, $x = 9$.

28. Choice **h** is correct. Factor the numerator. Use the denominator as a clue. Most likely, one of the factors in the numerator will be the same as the denominator. Also, notice that the numerator is the difference of two squares.

$$\frac{(x-3)(x+3)}{x-3}$$

The $x - 3$ in the numerator cancels with the $x - 3$ in the denominator leaving an answer of $x + 3$.

29. Choice **b** is correct. Use the distance formula or the Pythagorean theorem to find the distance. The distance formula is $d = \sqrt{(x_2 - x_1)^2 + (y_2 - y_1)^2}$. Substitute the x and y values for points A and C and solve.

$$d = \sqrt{(-2 - -1)^2 + (-1 - 3)^2}$$
$$d = \sqrt{(-1)^2 + (-4)^2}$$
$$d = \sqrt{1 + 16}$$
$$d = \sqrt{17}$$

To use the Pythagorean theorem (which is what the distance formula is derived from), draw the segment on a coordinate plane and create a right triangle where $\overline{AC}$ is the hypotenuse.

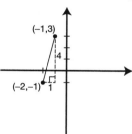

The legs of the right triangle are 1 and 4. Use the Pythagorean theorem to find the length of the hypotenuse.

$$a^2 + b^2 = c^2$$
$$1^2 + 4^2 = c^2$$
$$1 + 16 = c^2$$
$$17 = c^2$$
$$\sqrt{17} = c$$

30. Choice **f** is correct. Since the line is parallel to $3y - 9x = 24$, they have the same slope. Put the equation into $y = mx + b$ form to easily see the slope:

$3y - 9x = 24$

$3y = 9x + 24$

$y = 3x + 8$

The equation above indicates that the slope is 3. The line you are looking for also has a slope of 3. You are looking for the line $y = 3x + 4$. You must put the answer choices in $y = mx + b$ form to compare them to this equation. Equation **f** is correct.

f. $y = 3x + 4$

g. $y = 3x + 5$

h. $y = 2x + 4$

i. $y = 2x + 1$

j. $y = -\frac{1}{3}x - \frac{14}{9}$

31. Choice **d** is correct. You are looking for an x and a y value. The x value must be 9 since one of the equations is $x = 9$. To find y, substitute 9 for x in the second equation.

$3(9) + y = 4$

$27 + y = 4$

$y = -23$

The ordered pair is $(9, -23)$. This point is a solution to both equations.

32. Choice **i** is correct. $\sqrt{37}$ is close to $\sqrt{36}$, which is 6. $\sqrt{125}$ is close to $\sqrt{121}$, which is 11; $(6)(11) = 66$.

33. Choice **d** is correct. The equation is quadratic, so it can be solved by either setting the equation equal to zero and factoring or using the quadratic formula. In this case, factoring is the easiest option. First, set the equation equal to zero:

$x^2 - 6x - 27 = 0$

$(x - 9)(x + 3) = 0$

$x - 9 = 0 \quad x + 3 = 0$

$x = 9 \quad\quad x = -3$

The solution set is $\{-3, 9\}$.

34. g. Find the probability of each event and multiply the answers to find the probability of both events occurring. The probability of getting tails is $\frac{1}{2}$ and the probability of rolling a 3 is $\frac{1}{6}$; $(\frac{1}{2})(\frac{1}{6}) = \frac{1}{12}$. The probability of getting tails *and* rolling a 3 is $\frac{1}{12}$.

35. Choice **d** is correct. Multiply the decimal equivalent of $\frac{1}{2}\%$ by 90. The decimal equivalent of $\frac{1}{2}\%$ is 0.005. $(0.005)(90) = 0.45$.

36. Choice **j** is correct. $\sqrt{41}$ lies between $\sqrt{36}$, which is 6 and $\sqrt{49}$, which is 7. It lies between 6 and 7.

37. Choice **e** is correct. Think about what you would do if he used 2 bags for each pizza.

$12 \div 2 = 6$ pizzas. Follow the same pattern and divide the 12 bags by $\frac{3}{4}$.

$12 \div \frac{3}{4} =$

$\frac{12}{1} \times \frac{4}{3} = \frac{48}{3} = 16$

Mike can make 16 pizzas.

38. Choice **g** is correct. Convert the given rate of meters per second to kilometers per hour.

$\frac{100 \text{m}}{9.79 \text{s}} \times \frac{1 \text{ km}}{1000 \text{m}} \times \frac{60 \text{s}}{1 \text{ min}} \times \frac{60 \text{ min}}{1 \text{h}} = \frac{360,000 \text{ km}}{9.790 \text{h}} = \frac{36.8 \text{ km}}{\text{h}}$

Round the answer to 37 km/h.

39. Choice **c** is correct. Originally, Larry had 20 socks in the drawer. Since he pulled a red one out already, there are only 19 left in the drawer and 5 of them are red.

$P(red) = \frac{\# \, red}{total} = \frac{5}{19}$

40. Choice **i** is correct. Multiply the 5 and 6 to get 30. Then, multiply the powers of 10. $10^{-4} \times 10^8 = 10^4$. Since the bases are the same, you can just add the exponents. So far you have 30×10^4, but this is not an answer choice. Change your answer to scientific notation by moving the decimal in 30 to 3.0. Since the decimal has been moved one place to the left, you must increase the power of 10 by one. Therefore, the answer is 3×10^5.

41. b. $\sin = \frac{opposite}{hypotenuse}$. First, find the hypotenuse by using the Pythagorean theorem, or noticing that it is a 3-4-5 triangle (multiplied by 2). Therefore, the missing side is $5 \times 2 = 10$. $\sin B = \frac{6}{10} = \frac{3}{5}$.

42. Choice **h** is correct. Use the formula $\tan = \frac{opposite}{adjacent}$. $\tan x = \frac{4}{3}$.

43. Choice **d** is correct. There are 3 pairs of sides. The two sides that measure 6×8 each have an area of 48. The two sides that measure 6×10 each have an area of 60. The two sides that measure 8×10 each have an area of 80. Since there are two of each side, multiply the area of each by 2, then add the areas.

$48 \times 2 = 96$

$60 \times 2 = 120 \qquad 96 + 120 + 160 = 376$

$80 \times 2 = 160$

44. Choice **j** is correct. The radius of the large circle is 7 (add the inner radius plus the extra 3 from the ring). Therefore, the area of the large circle is 49π. Subtract the area of the inner circle, which is 16π. $49\pi - 16\pi = 33\pi$.

45. Choice **a** is correct. Take the square root of the area to find the length of one side. $\sqrt{100} = 10$, so the length of the sides of the square is 10 centimeters. When the diagonal is drawn it creates a right triangle with legs of 10 cm each and the diagonal is the hypotenuse.

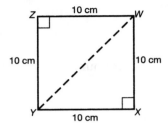

Use the Pythagorean theorem to find the diagonal.

$10^2 + 10^2 = x^2$

$100 + 100 = x^2$

$200 = x^2$

$\sqrt{200} = x$

$10\sqrt{2} = x$

46. Choice **i** is correct. Use the Pythagorean theorem to find the hypotenuse.

$a^2 + b^2 = c^2$

$4^2 + 9^2 = c^2$

$16 + 81 = c^2$

$97 = c^2$

$\sqrt{97} = c$

47. Choice **c** is correct. The formula for area of a circle is $A = \pi r^2$. Change the radius to an improper fraction; $3\frac{1}{2} = \frac{7}{2}$. Use the formula to find the area using the improper fraction. $A = \pi(\frac{7}{2})^2 = \frac{49}{4}\pi$. The area is $\frac{49}{4}\pi$ square inches.

48. Choice **f** is correct. Substitute 15 for y in the equation and solve for x.

$y = 4x^2 - 1$

$15 = 4x^2 - 1$

$16 = 4x^2$

$4 = x^2$

$2 = x$

49. Choice **e** is correct. Find the number of students that voted for Kristen (male and female) by multiplying 540 by the decimal equivalent of 60%. $540 \times 0.60 = 324$. 324 students voted for Kristen. Find 75% of that number. $324 \times 0.75 = 243$. 243 females voted for Kristen.

50. Choice **f** is correct. Use the identity $\tan\theta = \frac{\sin\theta}{\cos\theta}$.

$$\frac{5}{6} = \frac{\sin\theta}{\frac{6}{17}}$$

Multiply both sides by $\frac{6}{17}$ to isolate the $\sin\theta$.

$$\frac{6}{17} \times \frac{5}{6} = \sin\theta$$

$$\frac{5}{17} = \sin\theta$$

51. Choice **d** is correct. The original formula was $V = lwh$. If each dimension is tripled, the length is $3l$, the width is $3w$, and the height is $3h$. When these values are substituted into the equation, the equation becomes $V = (3l)(3w)(3h)$ or $V = 27lwh$. Thus, the new rectangular solid has a volume 27 times the original volume.

52. Choice **j** is correct. The sum of the measures of the angles in a triangle is $180°$. In a right triangle, the right angle is $90°$, so another $90°$ is split between the remaining two angles.

$$7x + 8x = 90$$
$$15x = 90$$
$$x = 6$$

The value of x is 6, but the question asks for the measure of the smaller angle, which is $7x$. Substituting in 6 for x, yields $(7)(6) = 42$. The measure of the angle is $42°$.

53. Choice **c** is correct. Use the Pythagorean theorem to find the missing leg.

$$a^2 + b^2 = c^2$$
$$9^2 + x^2 = 10^2$$
$$81 + x^2 = 100$$
$$x^2 = 19$$
$$x = \sqrt{19}$$

The length of the missing side is $\sqrt{19}$.

54. Choice **j** is correct. Call the width w and the length $2w$. The perimeter is then

$$P = w + w + 2w + 2w$$
$$72 = 6w$$
$$12 = w$$

The width is 12. Since the length is twice the width, the length is 24.

55. Choice **e** is correct. Three of the answer choices can be immediately eliminated because the length of the height cannot be negative. Answer choices **b**, **c**, and **d** all have negative lengths.

Call the height h and the base $h + 5$. The area of a triangle is $\frac{bh}{2}$. Substitute in h and $h + 5$ for the base and height, and set the area equal to 80 since the are of the given triangle is 80; $\frac{h(h + 5)}{2} = 80$

Solve for h. The equation is quadratic, so the quadratic formula will be used; $\frac{h^2 + 5h}{2} = 80$

$h^2 + 5h = 160$

$h^2 + 5h - 160 = h$

Use the quadratic formula to solve.

$\frac{-5 \pm \sqrt{(5)^2 - 4(1)(-160)}}{2(1)}$

$\frac{-5 \pm \sqrt{25 + 640}}{2}$

$\frac{-5 \pm \sqrt{665}}{2}$

The negative value is eliminated from the answer because it does not make sense. The answer is $\frac{-5 + \sqrt{665}}{2}$.

56. Choice **i** is correct. The easiest way to find the length of one side is to draw the square on the coordinate plane and count the spaces. There are 7 spaces between $(-2, 3)$ and $(5, 3)$. Therefore, the length of a side is 7.

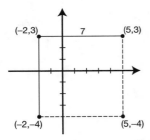

The distance formula can also be used. First, you must decide which points are consecutive vertices of the square. Let's use $(-2, 3)$ and $(5, 3)$. The distance formula is then:

$d = \sqrt{(5 - (-2))^2 + (3 - 3)^2}$

$d = \sqrt{7^2 + 0}$

$d = \sqrt{49}$

$d = 7$

57. Choice **e** is correct. The slope of the given equation is 3. The slope of a line perpendicular to the line is the opposite, reciprocal of 3. This is $-\frac{1}{3}$. Arrange each answer choice in the $y = mx + b$ format to quickly find the slope of each choice.

a. $y = 3x + \frac{5}{2}$

b. $y = 3x - 4$

c. $y = -\frac{2}{9}x + \frac{1}{3}$

d. $y = -2x + 4$

e. $y = -\frac{1}{3}x + \frac{5}{3}$

58. Choice **f** is correct. Arrange the equations of the two lines in $y = mx + b$ format. They both become $y = \frac{2}{3}x + 4$. Therefore, they are the same line.

59. Choice **b** is correct. To find the midpoint, take the average of the x values and the average of the y values.

$(\frac{-4 + 3}{2}, \frac{-2 + 8}{2})$

$(-\frac{1}{2}, \frac{6}{2})$

$(-0.5, 3)$

The midpoint is $(-0.5, 3)$.

60. Choice **i** is correct. Find a common denominator and add the fractions. The common denominator is $15x$.

$\frac{4}{3x} + \frac{x - 1}{5}$

$\frac{20}{15x} + \frac{3x(x - 1)}{15}$

$\frac{20 + 3x(x - 1)}{15x}$

$\frac{20 + 3x^2 - 3x}{15x}$

$\frac{3x^2 - 3x + 20}{15x}$

61. Choice **b** is correct. Since the exponent is negative, take the reciprocal of the fraction, then apply the exponent of 3.

$(\frac{1}{2x^2})^{-3}$

$(\frac{2x^2}{1})^3$

$(2)^3(x^2)^3$

$8x^6$

62. Choice **f** is correct. Use the substitution method to solve for x and y. The second equation can easily be solved for x in terms of y.

$2y - x = 0$

$2y = x$

Substitute this value for x in the first equation and solve for y.

$4x = 3y + 15$

$4(2y) = 3y + 15$

$8y = 3y + 15$

$5y = 15$

$y = 3$

Next, substitute the value 3 for y in the second equation to find x.

$2(3) - x = 0$

$6 - x = 0$

$6 = x$

63. Choice **d** is correct. The negative part of the exponent tells you to take the reciprocal of the number.

$36^{\frac{-3}{2}}$

$(\frac{1}{36})^{\frac{3}{2}}$

The denominator of the fractional exponent is the root and the numerator is the power. Therefore, take the square root and raise that answer to the third power.

$(\sqrt{\frac{1}{36}})^3$

$(\frac{1}{6})^3$

$\frac{1}{216}$

64. Choice **h** is correct. The cube root of a negative number is negative. So, the answer must be negative. $(-3)^3 = -27$ and $(-4)^3 = -64$; -50 falls between -27 and -64. The value of x must be between -3 and -4.

65. Choice **e** is correct. Every triangle has a total of 180°. 112° are used in the top angle, leaving 68° to be shared equally between the bottom two angles. $68 \div 2 = 34°$.

66. Choice **f** is correct. Recall that all triangles have 180°. Next, using the two angle measures given, find the two bottom angles of the triangle. The bottom left angle is supplementary (adds to 180°) with 120°, therefore, it is 60°. The bottom right angle is a corresponding angle to the 21° angle and, therefore, is 21°.

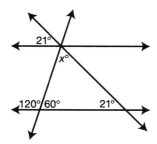

The three angles in the triangle must add to 180°, so x is 99°.

67. Choice **d** is correct. Keeping in mind that a tangent line will only intersect the circle in one place, draw the graph of the circle on the coordinate plane to see that the radius must be 4.

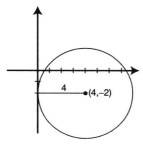

68. Choice **g** is correct. The equation of a circle is in the form $(x - h)^2 + (y - k)^2 = r^2$ where r is the radius. Since the given equation is already in this form, you can find the radius quickly. $r^2 = 36$; therefore, $r = 6$. Use the formula $A = \pi r^2$ to find the area of the circle; $A = \pi(6)^2$ or 36π.

69. Choice **b** is correct. Find the measures of angles DBC and BDC by using the supplements given (remember that supplementary angles add to 180°). $\angle DBC = 60°$ and $\angle BDC = 70°$. The three angles of a triangle must add to 180°. Therefore, $\angle BCD = 50°$.

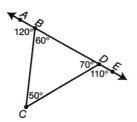

70. Choice **g** is correct. A triangle that has sides in the ratio $1:1:\sqrt{2}$ has angle measures of 45°, 45°, and 90°. The side that measures $\sqrt{2}$ is opposite the 90° angle and is the hypotenuse. See the diagram below.

The smallest angle is one of the 45° angles. To find the sine of 45°, you need to know the side opposite 45°(1) and the hypotenuse ($\sqrt{2}$).

$\sin 45 = \dfrac{1}{\sqrt{2}}$

Rationalize the denominator by multiplying the numerator and denominator by $\sqrt{2}$.

$\dfrac{1}{\sqrt{2}} \times \dfrac{\sqrt{2}}{\sqrt{2}} = \dfrac{\sqrt{2}}{2}$

The sine of 45° is $\dfrac{\sqrt{2}}{2}$.

71. Choice **e** is correct. $-1 \le \cos x \le 1$; therefore, $-9 \le 9\cos x \le 9$. The minimum value is -9.

72. Choice **f** is correct. A 30-60-90 triangle has side lengths in the ratio $1:\sqrt{3}:2$. If the smallest side is 7, the largest side is twice 7, or 14. The hypotenuse is 14.

73. Choice **c** is correct. Refer to the drawing below to see the dimensions of the pool and the walkway. Notice that the walkway is 10 feet longer and 10 feet wider than the pool (NOT 5 feet) because 5 feet is added on EACH side of the pool. To find the area of the walkway, find the area of the large rectangle (walkway and pool combined), and subtract the area of the pool.

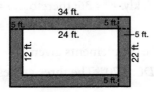

Area of the walkway and pool = $34 \times 22 = 748$ square feet

Area of the pool = $12 \times 24 = 288$ square feet

Area of walkway = $748 - 288 = 460$ square feet

74. Choice **f** is correct. Since $\overline{YW}$ is an altitude in an equilateral triangle, it bisects the opposite side. $\overline{XW}$ and $\overline{WZ}$ are both 7 inches. See the diagram below.

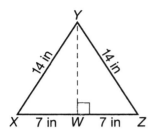

An altitude also makes a right angle and, therefore, the Pythagorean theorem can be used to find the length of the altitude. Refer to triangle *WXY*. The hypotenuse is 14 inches and one leg is 7 inches.

$a^2 + b^2 = c^2$

$7^2 + b^2 = 14^2$

$49 + b^2 = 196$

$b^2 = 147$

$b = \sqrt{147}$

$b = 7\sqrt{3}$

The length of the hypotenuse is $7\sqrt{3}$.

75. Choice **c** is correct. The equation is quadratic. Set it equal to zero and factor.

$2x^2 - 2x - 12 = 0$

$2(x^2 - x - 6) = 0$

$2(x - 3)(x + 2) = 0$

Set each factor equal to zero and solve. (2 can be ignored because $2 \neq 0$).

$x - 3 = 0 \qquad x + 2 = 0$

$x = 3 \qquad\quad x = -2$

The sum of the solutions is $3 + -2 = 1$.

76. Choice **j** is correct. Use the identity $\sin^2 A + \cos^2 A = 1$.

$\sin^2 A + (\frac{9}{10})^2 = 1$

$\sin^2 A + \frac{81}{100} = 1$

$\sin^2 A = \frac{19}{100}$

$\sin A = \sqrt{\frac{19}{100}} = \frac{\sqrt{19}}{10}$

77. Choice **d** is correct. The triangle given is a 45-45-90 triangle so the sides are in the ratio $1:1:\sqrt{2}$. Use a proportion to find *x*.

$\frac{\sqrt{2}}{1} = \frac{x}{\sqrt{5}}$

$x = \sqrt{10}$

78. Choice **f** is correct. An ellipse is defined by an equation such as $\frac{x^2}{a^2} + \frac{y^2}{b^2} = 1$. Therefore, answer choices **f** and **i** are possibilities. Choice **f** is the correct choice because the square root of the number under the x is where the ellipse crosses the x-axis. Another way to check is to substitute the given ordered pairs into the equations to see which one works.

79. Choice **b** is correct. Notice that the y-intercept is 2 and the slope is -3. Thus, the equation must be $y = -3x + 2$. Answer choices **b** and **c** are possibilities. The shading will determine which one. Substitute $(0, 0)$ in for x and y. Since the shading is *over* the point $(0, 0)$, $(0, 0)$ must be a solution to the inequality.

$0 \leq -3(0) + 2$

$0 \leq 2$

TRUE

Therefore, choice **b** is the correct answer.

80. Choice **j** is correct. The only constraint on this function is that the denominator must not be zero. To find which values will yield a denominator of zero, set the denominator equal to zero and solve.

$x^2 + 3x - 4 = 0$

$(x + 4)(x - 1) = 0$

Set each factor equal to zero and solve.

$x + 4 = 0 \qquad x - 1 = 0$

$x = -4 \qquad x = 1$

These are the values of x that do *not* work. All other real numbers *do* work.

The domain is all real numbers, such that $x \neq -4$ and $x \neq 1$.

This is written as $\{x \mid x \neq -4 \text{ and } x \neq 1\}$.

▶ Glossary of Math Terms

This glossary is a tool to prepare you for the ACT Math Test. You will not be asked any vocabulary questions on the ACT Math Test, so there is no need to memorize any of these terms or definitions. However, reading through this list will familiarize you with general math words and concepts, as well as terms you may encounter in the practice questions. These terms come from all the areas of math found on the ACT, but it is not guaranteed that any of the terms below will be included on an official ACT Math Test.

Base—A number used as a repeated factor in an exponential expression. In 8^5, 8 is the base number.

Base 10—see *Decimal numbers.*

Binary System—One of the simplest numbering systems. The base of the binary system is 2, which means that only the digits 0 and 1 can appear in a binary representation of any number.

Circumference—The distance around the outside of a circle.

Composite number—Any integer that can be divided evenly by a number other than itself and 1. All numbers are either prime or composite.

Counting numbers—Include all whole numbers, with the exception of 0.

Decimal—A number in the base 10 number system. Each place value in a decimal number is worth ten times the place value of the digit to its right.

Denominator—The bottom number in a fraction. The denominator of $\frac{1}{2}$ is 2.

Diameter—A chord which passes through the center of the circle and has endpoints on the circle.

Difference—The result of subtracting one number from another.

Divisible by—Capable of being evenly divided by a given number, without a remainder.

Dividend—The number in a division problem that is being divided. In $32 \div 4 = 8$, 32 is the dividend.

Even number—A counting number that is divisible by 2.

Expanded notation—A method of writing numbers as the sum of their units (hundreds, tens, ones, etc.). The expanded notation for 378 is $300 + 70 + 8$.

Exponent—A number that indicates an operation of repeated multiplication. For instance, 3^4 indicates that the number 3 should be multiplied by itself 4 times.

Factor—One of two or more numbers or variables that are being multiplied together.

Fractal—A geometric figure that is self-similar; that is, any smaller piece of the figure will have roughly the same shape as the whole.

Improper fraction—A fraction whose numerator is the same size as or larger than its denominator. Improper fractions are equal to or greater than 1.

Integer—All of the *whole numbers* and negatives too. Examples are $-3, -2, -1, 0, 1, 2,$ and 3. Note that integers *do not* include fractions, or decimals.

Multiple of—A multiple of a number has that number as one of its factors. 35 is a multiple of 7; it is also a multiple of 5.

Negative number—A real number whose value is less than zero.

Numerator—The top number in a fraction. The numerator of $\frac{1}{4}$ is 1.

Odd number—A counting number that is not divisible by 2.

Percent—A ratio or fraction whose denominator is assumed to be 100, expressed using the percent sign; 98% is equal to $\frac{98}{100}$.

Perimeter—The distance around the outside of a polygon.

Polygon—A closed two-dimensional shape made up of several line segments that are joined together.

Positive number—A real number whose value is greater than zero.

Prime number—A real number that is divisible by only 2 positive factors: 1 and itself.

Product—The result when two numbers are multiplied together.

Proper fraction—A fraction whose denominator is larger than its numerator. Proper fractions are equal to less than 1.

Proportion—A relationship between two equivalent sets of fractions in the form $\frac{a}{b} = \frac{c}{d}$.

Quotient—The result when one number is divided into another.

Radical—The symbol used to signify a root operation.

Radius—Any line segment from the center of the circle to a point on the circle. The radius of a circle is equal to half its diameter.

Ratio—The relationship between two things, expressed as a proportion.

Real numbers—Include fractions and decimals in addition to *integers*.

Reciprocal—One of two numbers which, when multiplied together, give a product of 1. For instance, since $\frac{3}{2} \times \frac{2}{3}$ is equal to 1, $\frac{3}{2}$ is the reciprocal of $\frac{2}{3}$.

Remainder—The amount left over after a division problem using whole numbers. Divisible numbers always have a remainder of zero.

Root (square root)—One of two (or more) equal factors of a number. The square root of 36 is 6, because $6 \times 6 = 36$. The cube root of 27 is 3 because $3 \times 3 \times 3 = 27$.

Simplify terms—To combine like terms and reduce an equation to its most basic form.

Variable—A letter, often *x*, used to represent an unknown number value in a problem.

Whole numbers—0, 1, 2, 3, and so on. They do not include negatives, fractions, or decimals.

5 ▶ ACT Reading Test Practice

▶ Overview: About the ACT Reading Test

The ACT Reading Test assesses your ability to read and understand what ACT considers college freshman-level material. The test is 35 minutes long and includes 40 questions. There are four passages on the test, each of which is followed by ten multiple-choice questions. The passages (each around 800 words) are identified by a heading that will tell you what type of text you are about to read (fiction, for example), who the author is, the date it was written, and might also give you more information to help you understand the passage. The lines of the passage are numbered to identify sections of the text in the questions that follow. The passages come directly from original sources in four subject areas or genres: prose fiction, social studies, humanities, and natural science (see page 209 for more information on what these passages include).

The reading test includes different types of passages to test your ability to read and understand many styles of writing. It does not require any outside knowledge of the subjects covered in the passages. In fact, you may be at a slight advantage on the questions that are about subjects that you do not know anything about. All the information you need to answer the questions can and should be gleaned from the passages themselves. In fact, 14 of the 40 questions ask for information that is taken word for word from the passages

(ACT calls these "referring" questions). The rest of the answers must be "inferred" from the information you read in the passages (ACT calls these "reasoning" questions). In order to answer these questions, you need to fully understand the passages as well as be able to infer meaning from them and draw some reasonable conclusions from the passages themselves.

▶ Pretest

Read the following passage and then answer the five questions. These questions are good examples of the types of questions you will find on the ACT Reading Test. As you go through each question, try to anticipate what type of question it is and the best way to go about answering it. Once you have finished all five questions in the pretest, read the explanations on page 206 for details on the best way of finding the answers in the text. How well you do on the pretest will help you determine in which areas you need the most careful review and practice.

SOCIAL STUDIES: This passage is "Of the Origin and Use of Money" from *The Wealth of Nations* by Adam Smith, 1776.

(1)   WHEN the division of labour has been once thoroughly established, it is but a very small part of a man's wants which the produce of his own labour can supply. He supplies the far greater part of them by exchanging that surplus part of the produce of his own labour, which is over and above his own consumption, for such parts of the produce of other men's labour as he has occasion for.

(5) Every man thus lives by exchanging, or becomes in some measure a merchant, and the society itself grows to be what is properly a commercial society.

But when the division of labour first began to take place, this power of exchanging must frequently have been very much clogged and embarrassed in its operations. One man, we shall suppose, has more of a certain commodity than he himself has occasion for, while another has less.

(10) The former consequently would be glad to dispose of, and the latter to purchase, a part of this superfluity. But if this latter should chance to have nothing that the former stands in need of, no exchange can be made between them. The butcher has more meat in his shop than he himself can consume, and the brewer and the baker would each of them be willing to purchase a part of it. But they have nothing to offer in exchange, except the different productions of their respective trades,

(15) and the butcher is already provided with all the bread and beer which he has immediate occasion for. No exchange can, in this case, be made between them. He cannot be their merchant, nor they his customers; and they are all of them thus mutually less serviceable to one another. In order to avoid the inconveniency of such situations, every prudent man in every period of society, after the first establishment of the division of labour, must naturally have endeavoured to manage his affairs

(20) in such a manner, as to have at all times by him, besides the peculiar produce of his own industry, a certain quantity of some one commodity or other, such as he imagined few people would be likely to refuse in exchange for the produce of their industry.

Many different commodities, it is probable, were successively both thought of and employed for this purpose. In the rude ages of society, cattle are said to have been the common instrument

(25) of commerce; and, though they must have been a most inconvenient one, yet in old times we find things were frequently valued according to the number of cattle which had been given in exchange for them. The armour of Diomede, says Homer, cost only nine oxen; but that of Glaucus cost an hundred oxen. Salt is said to be the common instrument of commerce and exchanges in Abyssinia; a species of shells in some parts of the coast of India; dried cod at Newfoundland; tobacco in Vir-

(30) ginia; sugar in some of our West India colonies; hides or dressed leather in some other countries; and there is at this day a village in Scotland where it is not uncommon, I am told, for a workman to carry nails instead of money to the baker's shop or the alehouse.

In all countries, however, men seem at last to have been determined by irresistible reasons to give the preference, for this employment, to metals above every other commodity. Metals can

(35) not only be kept with as little loss as any other commodity, scarce any thing being less perishable than they are, but they can likewise, without any loss, be divided into any number of parts, as by fusion those parts can easily be reunited again; a quality which no other equally durable commodities possess, and which more than any other quality renders them fit to be the instruments of commerce and circulation. The man who wanted to buy salt, for example, and had nothing but

(40) cattle to give in exchange for it, must have been obliged to buy salt to the value of a whole ox, or a whole sheep, at a time. He could seldom buy less than this, because what he was to give for it could seldom be divided without loss; and if he had a mind to buy more, he must, for the same reasons, have been obliged to buy double or triple the quantity, the value, to wit, of two or three oxen, or of two or three sheep. If on the contrary, instead of sheep or oxen, he had metals to give

(45) in exchange for it, he could easily proportion the quantity of the metal to the precise quantity of the commodity which he had immediate occasion for.

1. Which statement best summarizes the main idea of the first paragraph?
   a. Commercial society is based on exploiting the labor of others.
   b. Division of labor is the only way to a truly commercial society.
   c. A person's needs can be best met through the exchange of surplus goods.
   d. Only through hard work will man reach his goals.

2. As it is used in line 11, the word *superfluity* most nearly means:
   f. more than is needed.
   g. material goods.
   h. high quality.
   j. a shortage.

3. One of the main problems with trading goods and services, according to the author is:

    a. goods can spoil before they can be traded.

    b. a common price of goods cannot be met.

    c. trading requires both parties to be honest.

    d. often the goods in trade are not needed by one party.

4. According to the passage, what goods are used in trade in Newfoundland?

    f. dried cod

    g. tobacco

    h. salt

    j. metal

5. It can be inferred from the passage that a reason people originally chose cattle as a form of currency is:

    a. cattle were a valuable commodity.

    b. they chose goods that were readily available.

    c. they had not yet invented a way to melt metal.

    d. cattle were easy to divide.

Pretest Answers and Explanations

1. Question type: main idea

Choice **c** is the correct answer. In this question, you are asked to summarize the basic point of the first paragraph. Often main idea questions will refer to the passage as a whole, but if they refer to only one part, you should find your answer in only the specified section. This means that any information presented in other parts of the passage should be ignored. Also note that the question asks for the "best" answer, meaning that the right answer may not be the perfect summarization of the paragraph, but is the best choice among those given.

The first line of the paragraph presents a point that can be misleading. In this case, the author states that division of labor can only produce a small portion of what a person needs, and was the starting point for a commercial society. Using this information, you can eliminate choice **b** as a possible answer. This point, along with the following lines, which state "he supplies the far greater part of them by exchanging that surplus part of the produce of his own labour . . . for such parts of the produce of other men's labour as he has occasion for," makes it clear that choice **c** is the best answer.

Be wary of answers that make grand statements that may sound good, but have no basis in the test. Choice **a** is a good example of this, since nowhere in the passage is this discussed. Choice **d** is another variation of this. It may be true that to produce a surplus of goods, one would have to work hard, but this is not the point of the passage.

2. Question type: vocabulary

Choice **f** is the correct answer. The vocabulary questions do not test your outside knowledge of any words. Instead you are required to figure out the meaning of the word by the way it is used in the text.

Even if you know the definition of a word, you should still take into account how it is being used. Very often, words are used unconventionally and may have another meaning that you are not aware of.

Often answer choices in the vocabulary questions will sound a lot like the word itself or the meaning of a part of the word. Choice **h** is a good example of this. You may see "super" as meaning high quality, but in fact this is the wrong answer.

In order to come up with the meaning the vocabulary words, you must look not just at the sentence in which the word appears, but also the surrounding sentences. In this case, the sentence where the word is used does not give you much information about its meaning. However, if you read the preceding sentence, the statement "One man . . . has more of a certain commodity than he himself has occasion for" refers directly to "this superfluity." So, choice **f**, "more than is needed" is the best choice.

3. **Question type: generalization**

Choice **d** is the correct answer. Generalization questions force you to absorb a lot of information and then find a more concise or shorter way of saying the same thing. Be aware of answers that are in fact correct statements, but do not answer the question. Choice **a** is a good example of such an answer. The author does say that an advantage to trading metal is that it does not spoil. However, he does not say that a problem that arises when goods are traded is that certain goods will spoil. This can be inferred, but it does not answer the question. Choices **b** and **c** could be argued to be true statements, but they are not mentioned in the passage.

The second paragraph best explains the problems the author associates with trading goods and services. Lines 11–12 sums this up best by saying "But if this latter should chance to have nothing that the former stands in need of, no exchange can be made between them." In other words, one person may not need the goods that are being offered in trade, making **d** the best answer.

4. **Question type: detail**

Choice **f** is the correct answer. Detail questions are generally the most uncomplicated type you will encounter on the test. This does not mean that you should breeze through them. Often a detail will be surrounded by a lot of similar-sounding information that can be easily confused.

If you sift through the list of examples given in paragraph 3, you will see that line 29 states that dried cod was traded in Newfoundland, making choice **f** correct.

5. **Question type: inference**

Choice **b** is the correct answer. When answering an inference question, you must use facts found throughout the passage to make a reasonable conclusion about something that is not directly stated. In this case, the author never explicitly sates the reason cattle were chosen as a form of currency, but there are enough facts given in the passage to make a reasonable assumption about the answer.

The passage states that the "armour of Diomede . . . cost only nine oxen" (line 27). This means that if they could fashion armor, they could most likely melt metal, making choice **c** not the best answer. Choice **a** is not a good answer simply because there is no reference at all to the value of cattle in the passage. Lines 34–41 discuss the difficulty of using cattle in trade, bringing up the point that trading cattle can be a problem because they can not be used to buy things of lesser value (presumably because they cannot be divided into smaller parts). This makes choice **d** incorrect.

One of the best clues as to why cattle were used in trade comes at the end of paragraph 3. In this list of goods used in trade, all the items mentioned were clearly readily available in those areas. Shells would obviously be found in abundance on the coast, dried cod in Newfoundland, etc. This makes choice **b** the best answer.

► Lessons

Types of Reading Questions

As mentioned in the beginning of this section, the questions found on the ACT Reading Test can be broken down into two categories: *referring* and *reasoning*. The *referring* questions can be answered through information that is stated in the text (no interpretation needed). The *reasoning* questions are a little trickier in that they force you to use information that is implied in the test, and not stated outright.

Within these two categories are eight basic types of questions. Examples of these question types can be found in the explanation of the answers in the pretest and the practice questions.

DETAIL QUESTIONS

The passages on the ACT Reading Test are filled with both minor and major pieces of information. Some of the questions will ask you to identify a name or date or some other fact that is stated in the text, but may not be vitally important to the passage as a whole. The detail questions require that you carefully read the passage in order to find the right answer. In a date question, for example, the year may be given for one event and you might be expected to add or subtract years from the actual date stated in the passage in order to come up with the right answer.

MAIN IDEA

Often you will be asked to sum up the events or ideas in a paragraph or in the passage as a whole. These questions may require you to infer authors' opinions or state straight facts from the text.

COMPARISON

Passages that contain many facts (social studies and natural science passages, in particular) are likely candidates for comparison questions. These questions require you to compare sets of information and decide on the main difference between them.

CAUSE AND EFFECT

These questions ask you to deduce the consequence or outcome of a stated event or fact in the passage. In fiction passages, these questions may ask why a character acted or felt a particular way. In some cases, you may be required to figure this out through information not directly stated in the passage.

GENERALIZATION

In this type of question, you will be asked to take a lot of information and choose a more concise way of stating it.

VOCABULARY

The ACT Reading Test does not test your knowledge of specific vocabulary words. It will, however, ask you to figure out the meaning of a word by looking at how it is used within the context of the passage. This means that you can find the definition of the word somewhere in the surrounding sentences. Occasionally, the correct answer is not necessarily the best definition of the word, but rather its meaning when used in the passage.

INFERENCES

The answers to inference questions will not be found directly in the passage itself. In order to get these questions right, you must use information presented in the passage to reach a conclusion about what is asked. In some cases, inference questions ask you to relay a point of view, an overall opinion, or a character's actions that can be deciphered from the text as a whole.

POINT OF VIEW

These questions ask you to state the author's opinion on a subject. Often these questions are found in the fiction passages, but can be asked about any of the subjects in which the author is not remaining objective about his or her subject.

Question Format

The directions at the beginning of the ACT Reading Test ask you to choose the *best answer* from the choices given. This means that more than one answer choice may in fact be a correct statement, but may not answer the specific question. Or the "best" answer may only be the best choice of the choices *given,* not the best possible answer. Some questions ask that you choose the one answer that is incorrect. Another type of question found on the ACT Reading Test presents three statements and you must choose the one statement of the three that is correct. More than any other test on the ACT Assessment Test, question *type* on the reading test is important to keep in mind as you choose your answers.

The Four Types of Reading Passages You Will Encounter

The four passages on the test are divided equally among the four genres listed below. That means you can expect to find one passage from each of the following four categories. All of the passages except the prose fiction are going to be factual in nature.

PROSE FICTION

The passages on the prose fiction section of the test are taken, either whole or in parts, from short stories or novels. The way that you read fiction is different from the way you read any of the other passages on the test. The questions on the fiction passages reflect this difference. You will not be bogged down with lots of facts

Tips and Strategies

In addition to the general test-taking tips discussed in the first part of this book, here are some strategies specific to the ACT Reading Test worth using:

- **Never leave an answer blank.**

ACT does not deduct points for wrong answers. This means there is no penalty for guessing. With this in mind, you should absolutely answer every question, even if it is a total guess. If you do come across a question that completely stumps you, look through the answers and try to find at least one that you know is wrong. The more answers you can eliminate, the better the odds that your guess will end up being the correct answer. (See specific strategies for answering multiple-choice questions on page 23.)

- **Go through the questions before you read the passages.**

Spend a minute or so skimming the questions before you jump into reading the passage. This will give you some idea about what to look for while you are reading.

- **Take notes on the test.**

Mark up the test booklet as you much as you need to as you go through the reading comprehension passages. If you find something that looks important, underline it, make notes in the margins, circle facts. Do not spend too much time studying the details, just make a note and move on. You will have to go back to the text when answering the question anyway.

- **Read all the answers.**

If one answer jumps out at you and you are sure it is right, read all the other answers anyway. Something may seem right just because the ACT has put it there to make you think it is the right answer. This is especially true when it comes to the detail questions. If a date in one of the answers pops out at you because you saw it in the passage, this still may not be the correct answer. Spend the time to at least quickly go through all the answers.

- **Eliminate wrong answers first.**

When you go through the answer options, immediately cross out answers you know are wrong. This will help whittle down your choices if you have to guess, and will keep you from being distracted from the wrong answer choices.

- **Answer questions on the test booklet.**

Circle the answers for all the questions for each passage and then transfer them to the answer sheet. This serves two purposes: first, it allows you to concentrate on choosing the right answer and not filling in ovals. Second, it will keep you from skipping an oval and misnumbering your entire test if you decide to come back to a difficult question later.

- **Do not use what you already know.**

This may seem counterintuitive, but you are expected to answer the questions using only information taken directly from the passage. It is very possible that you will do better on the passages that are about subjects you know nothing about. Often the ACT will include answers that are in fact true, but not according to the passage. To counteract this, ignore anything you already know about the topic and use only the information found in the passage.

- **Check your answers with the text.**

  Even if you are sure the author said he was born in 1943, go back to the actual text and make sure this is right. Many times ACT will add an answer that seems right just to throw you off.

- **Pace yourself.**

  You have a little less than nine minutes to read each of the four passages and answer the questions. You can get a good idea of how long that really is by timing your practice tests. To speed things up, answer the easy questions first. If you find one question is taking too long, circle it in the test book and come back to it later.

---

and theories, but you will need to think about the mood and tone of the story as well as the relationships between the characters.

HUMANITIES

The humanities section is based on a passage taken from a memoir or personal essays about architecture, art, dance, ethics, film, language, literary criticism, music, philosophy, radio, television, or theater. The humanities passages are about real people or events. This means that there will still be many facts that you will need to pay attention to, but these passages can also include the author's opinions.

SOCIAL STUDIES

The questions on the social studies passages are based on writing about anthropology, archaeology, business, economics, education, geography, history, political science, psychology, or sociology. The passages are generally a discussion of research, as opposed to experimentation, and should represent an objective presentation of facts.

NATURAL SCIENCE

The subject covered in the natural sciences passage can come from any of the following areas: anatomy, astronomy, biology, botany, chemistry, ecology, geology, medicine, meteorology, microbiology, natural history, physiology, physics, technology, and zoology. The natural science passage can come from any form of scientific writing: a lab report, article, or textbook. You can expect to see many scientific language, facts, and figures in these types of passages.

▶ Practice Questions

Directions

Each passage in this section is followed by several questions. After reading a passage, choose the best answer from the choices given. When you are taking the official ACT Reading Test, it's a good idea to first mark all of your answer choices on your test booklet, and then transfer them to your bubble answer sheet. This will keep you focused on the test questions (and not on filling in bubbles) and will also reduce your chances of misnumbering your answers.

> **PROSE FICTION:** This passage is taken from **Babbitt,** *by Sinclair Lewis,* *1922.*

(1)　　　There was nothing of the giant in the aspect of the man who was beginning to awaken on the sleeping-porch of a Dutch Colonial house in that residential district of Zenith known as Floral Heights.

　　　His name was George F. Babbitt. He was forty-six years old now, in April, 1920, and he made
(5) nothing in particular, neither butter nor shoes nor poetry, but he was nimble in the calling of selling houses for more than people could afford to pay.

　　　His large head was pink, his brown hair thin and dry. His face was babyish in slumber, despite his wrinkles and the red spectacle-dents on the slopes of his nose. He was not fat but he was exceedingly well fed; his cheeks were pads, and the unroughened hand which lay helpless upon the
(10) khaki-colored blanket was slightly puffy. He seemed prosperous, extremely married and unromantic; and altogether unromantic appeared this sleeping-porch, which looked on one sizable elm, two respectable grass-plots, a cement driveway, and a corrugated iron garage. Yet Babbitt was again dreaming of the fairy child, a dream more romantic than scarlet pagodas by a silver sea.

　　　For years the fairy child had come to him. Where others saw but Georgie Babbitt, she dis-
(15) cerned gallant youth. She waited for him, in the darkness beyond mysterious groves. When at last he could slip away from the crowded house he darted to her. His wife, his clamoring friends, sought to follow, but he escaped, the girl fleet beside him, and they crouched together on a shadowy hillside. She was so slim, so white, so eager! She cried that he was gay and valiant, that she would wait for him, that they would sail—

(20)　　　Rumble and bang of the milk-truck.

　　　Babbitt moaned; turned over; struggled back toward his dream. He could see only her face now, beyond misty waters. The furnace-man slammed the basement door. A dog barked in the next yard. As Babbitt sank blissfully into a dim warm tide, the paper-carrier went by whistling, and the rolled-up *Advocate* thumped the front door. Babbitt roused, his stomach constricted with
(25) alarm. As he relaxed, he was pierced by the familiar and irritating rattle of some one cranking a Ford: snap-ah-ah, snap-ah-ah, snap-ah-ah. Himself a pious motorist, Babbitt cranked with the unseen driver, with him waited through taut hours for the roar of the starting engine, with him agonized as the roar ceased and again began the infernal patient snap-ah-ah—a round, flat sound,

a shivering cold-morning sound, a sound infuriating and inescapable. Not till the rising voice of
(30) the motor told him that the Ford was moving was he released from the panting tension. He glanced
once at his favorite tree, elm twigs against the gold patina of sky, and fumbled for sleep as for a
drug. He who had been a boy very credulous of life was no longer greatly interested in the possible and improbable adventures of each new day.

He escaped from reality till the alarm-clock rang, at seven-twenty.

(35)

III

It was the best of nationally advertised and quantitatively produced alarm-clocks, with all
modern attachments, including cathedral chime, intermittent alarm, and a phosphorescent dial.
(40) Babbitt was proud of being awakened by such a rich device. Socially it was almost as creditable as
buying expensive cord tires.

He sulkily admitted now that there was no more escape, but he lay and detested the grind of
the real-estate business, and disliked his family, and disliked himself for disliking them. The
evening before, he had played poker at Vergil Gunch's till midnight, and after such holidays he was
(45) irritable before breakfast. It may have been the tremendous home-brewed beer of the prohibition-
era and the cigars to which that beer enticed him; it may have been resentment of return from this
fine, bold man-world to a restricted region of wives and stenographers, and of suggestions not to
smoke so much.

From the bedroom beside the sleeping-porch, his wife's detestably cheerful "Time to get up,
(50) Georgie boy," and the itchy sound, the brisk and scratchy sound, of combing hairs out of a stiff
brush.

He grunted; he dragged his thick legs, in faded baby-blue pajamas, from under the khaki
blanket; he sat on the edge of the cot, running his fingers through his wild hair, while his plump
feet mechanically felt for his slippers. He looked regretfully at the blanket—forever a suggestion
(55) to him of freedom and heroism. He had bought it for a camping trip which had never come off.
It symbolized gorgeous loafing, gorgeous cursing, virile flannel shirts.

1. What physical attributes of George Babbitt can be inferred from the passage?
   a. He is overweight.
   b. He is skinny.
   c. He is of average build.
   d. He is very tall.

2. According to the passage, George Babbitt is:
   f. a poet.
   g. a shoemaker.
   h. a real estate broker.
   j. unemployed.

3. It can be inferred from the passage that George Babbitt is:

  a. good at his job.

  b. lazy.

  c. a hard worker.

  d. overworked.

4. What can be inferred from the passage about Babbitt's relationship with his wife?

  f. It is romantic and passionate.

  g. They openly dislike each other.

  h. They have no strong feelings about each other.

  j. Babbitt dislikes his wife and feels guilty about it.

5. As it is used in line 31, the word *patina* most nearly means:

  a. the pattern of clouds in the sky.

  b. the pattern of the elm tree branches.

  c. the shine of the sky.

  d. the color of the sky.

6. Which is the first noise to wake Babbitt from his sleep?

  f. his alarm clock

  g. a milk truck

  h. the paperboy

  j. a car starting

7. The blanket in the last paragraph represents what to Babbitt?

  a. a manly freedom that he has had to abandon

  b. beauty over practicality

  c. warmth and comfort

  d. the sleep to which he wishes to return

8. Which of the following best explains Babbitt's reluctance to get out of bed?

  I.   He dislikes his job.

  II. He has a hangover.

  III. He has had a fight with his wife.

  f. I and II

  g. I only

  h. II only

  j. I, II, and III

9. The young girl in Babbitt's dream best symbolizes what desire?

    a. to return to sleep

    b. to be young and free from his workaday world

    c. the love he once had for his wife

    d. his desire to move out of the suburbs

10. The lines "He who had been a boy very credulous of life was no longer greatly interested in the possible and improbable adventures of each new day" (number 32–33) most closely means:

    f. as a child, Babbitt was optimistic about life, but he now believes they will always be the same.

    g. Babbitt has never seen the possibilities of life.

    h. Babbitt has always looked forward to each new day.

    j. as a boy Babbitt was pessimistic about his life, but now sees its possibilities.

NATURAL SCIENCE: *Diabetes*

(1)   There are two types of diabetes, insulin-dependent and non-insulin-dependent. Between 90 and 95 percent of the estimated 13 to 14 million people in the United States with diabetes have non-insulin-dependent, or Type II, diabetes. Because this form of diabetes usually begins in adults over the age of 40 and is most common after the age of 55, it used to be called adult-onset dia-

(5) betes. Its symptoms often develop gradually and are hard to identify at first; therefore, nearly half of all people with diabetes do not know they have it. Someone who has developed Type II diabetes may feel tired or ill without knowing why, a circumstance which can be particularly dangerous because untreated diabetes can cause damage to the heart, blood vessels, eyes, kidneys, and nerves. While the causes, short-term effects, and treatments of the two types of diabetes differ, both types

(10) can cause the same long-term health problems.

      Most importantly, both types of diabetes affect the body's ability to use digested food for energy. Diabetes does not interfere with digestion, but it does prevent the body from using an important product of digestion, glucose (commonly known as sugar), for energy. After a meal, the normal digestive system extracts glucose from some foods. The blood carries the glucose or sugar

(15) throughout the body, causing blood glucose levels to rise. In response to this rise, the hormone insulin is released into the bloodstream and signals the body tissues to metabolize or burn the glucose for fuel, which causes blood glucose levels to return to normal. The glucose that the body does not use right away is stored in the liver, muscle, or fat.

      In both types of diabetes, this normal process malfunctions. A gland called the *pancreas,*

(20) found just behind the stomach, makes insulin. In patients with insulin-dependent diabetes, the pancreas does not produce insulin at all. This condition usually begins in childhood and is known as Type I (formerly called juvenile-onset) diabetes. These patients must have daily insulin injections to survive. People with non-insulin-dependent diabetes usually produce some insulin in their pancreas, but the body's tissues do not respond very well to the insulin signal and therefore do not

(25) metabolize the glucose properly—a condition known as *insulin resistance.*

Insulin resistance is an important factor in non-insulin-dependent diabetes, and scientists are researching the causes of insulin resistance. They have identified two possibilities. The first is that there could be a defect in the insulin receptors on cells. Like an appliance that needs to be plugged into an electrical outlet, insulin has to bind to a receptor in order to function. Several
(30) things can go wrong with receptors. For example, there may not be enough receptors for insulin to bind to, or a defect in the receptors may prevent insulin from binding. The second possible cause of insulin resistance is that, although insulin may bind to the receptors, the cells may not read the signal to metabolize the glucose. Scientists continue to study these cells to see why this might happen.
(35) There is no cure for diabetes yet. However, there are ways to alleviate its symptoms. In 1986, a National Institutes of Health panel of experts recommended that the best treatment for non-insulin-dependent diabetes is a diet that helps one maintain a normal weight and pays particular attention to a proper balance of the different food groups. Many experts, including those in the American Diabetes Association, recommend that 50 to 60 percent of daily calories come from car-
(40) bohydrates, 12 to 20 percent from protein, and no more than 30 percent from fat. Foods that are rich in carbohydrates, such as breads, cereals, fruits, and vegetables, break down into glucose during digestion, causing blood glucose to rise. Additionally, studies have shown that cooked foods raise blood glucose higher than raw, unpeeled foods. A doctor or nutritionist should always be consulted for more information and for help in planning a diet to offset the effects of this form of
(45) diabetes.

11. According to the passage, the most dangerous aspect of Type II diabetes is:
  a. the daily insulin shots that are needed for treatment of Type II diabetes.
  b. that Type II diabetes may go undetected and, therefore, untreated.
  c. that in Type II diabetes, the pancreas does not produce insulin.
  d. that Type II diabetes interferes with digestion.

12. The author of the passage compares Type I and Type II diabetes and states which of the following are the same for both?
  f. treatments
  g. long-term health risks
  h. short-term effects
  j. causes

13. According to the passage, one place in which excess glucose is stored is the:
  a. stomach.
  b. insulin receptors.
  c. pancreas.
  d. liver.

14. A diet dominated by which of the following is recommended for non-insulin-dependent diabetics?

    f. protein

    g. fat

    h. carbohydrates

    j. raw foods

15. Which of the following is the main function of insulin?

    a. It signals tissues to metabolize sugar.

    b. It breaks down food into glucose.

    c. It carries glucose throughout the body.

    d. It binds to receptors.

16. Which of the following statements best summarizes the main idea of the passage?

    f. Type I and Type II diabetes are best treated by maintaining a high-protein diet.

    g. Type II diabetes is a distinct condition that can be managed by maintaining a healthy diet.

    h. Type I diabetes is an insidious condition most harmful when the patient is not taking daily insulin injections.

    j. Adults who suspect they may have Type II diabetes should immediately adopt a high-carbohydrate diet.

17. Which of the following is mentioned in the passage as a possible problem with insulin receptors in insulin-resistant individuals?

    a. Overeating causes the receptors not to function properly.

    b. There may be an overabundance of receptors.

    c. A defect causes the receptors to bind with glucose.

    d. A defect hinders the receptors from binding with insulin.

18. According to the passage, in normal individuals which of the following processes occur immediately after the digestive system converts some food into glucose?

    f. The glucose is metabolized by body tissues.

    g. Insulin is released into the bloodstream.

    h. Blood sugar levels rise.

    j. The pancreas manufactures increased amounts of insulin.

19. Based on the information in the passage, which of the following best describes people with Type I diabetes?

    a. They do not need to be treated with injections of insulin.

    b. It does not interfere with digestion.

    c. Their pancreases do not produce insulin.

    d. They are usually diagnosed as adults.

20. As it is used in line 44, what is the closest meaning of the word *offset* in the final sentence of the passage?

   f. counteract

   g. cure

   h. move away from

   j. erase

SOCIAL STUDIES: *This passage is adapted from* How the Other Half Lives, *by Jacob A. Riis, 1890. The word* tenement *used throughout the passage refers to rental apartments that are generally of substandard quality.*

(1)   LONG ago it was said that "one half of the world does not know how the other half lives." That was true then. The half that was on top cared little for the struggles, and less for the fate of those who were underneath, so long as it was able to hold them there and keep its own seat. There came a time when the discomfort and crowding below were so great, and the consequent upheavals

(5) so violent, that it was no longer an easy thing to do, and then the upper half fell to wondering what was the matter. Information on the subject has been accumulating rapidly since, and the whole world has had its hands full answering for its old ignorance.

    In New York, the youngest of the world's great cities, that time came later than elsewhere, because the crowding had not been so great. There were those who believed that it would never

(10) come; but their hopes were vain. Greed and reckless selfishness delivered similar results here as in the cities of older lands. "When the great riot occurred in 1863," reads the testimony of the Secretary of the Prison Association of New York before a legislative committee appointed to investigate causes of the increase of crime in the State twenty-five years ago, "every hiding-place and nursery of crime discovered itself by immediate and active participation in the operations of the

(15) mob. Those very places and domiciles, and all that are like them, are today nurseries of crime, and of the vices and disorderly courses which lead to crime. By far the largest part—80% at least—of crimes against property and people are perpetrated by individuals who have either lost connection with home life, or never had any, or whose homes had ceased to afford what are regarded as ordinary wholesome influences of home and family. . . . The younger criminals seem to come

(20) almost exclusively from the worst tenement house districts, that is, when traced back to the very places where they had their homes in the city here." One thing New York was made of sure at that early stage of the inquiry: the boundary line of the Other Half lies through the tenements.

    It is ten years and over, now, since that line divided New York's population evenly. Today three-fourths of New Yorkers live in the tenements, and the nineteenth century drift of the pop-

(25) ulation to the cities is only increasing those numbers. The fifteen thousand tenant houses in the past generation have swelled into thirty-seven thousand, and more than twelve hundred thousand persons call them home. The one way out—rapid transit to the suburbs—has brought no relief. We know now that there is no way out; that the "system" that was the evil offspring of public

neglect and private greed is here to stay, forever a center of our civilization. Nothing is left but to
(30) make the best of a bad bargain.

The story is dark enough, drawn from the plain public records, to send a chill to any heart.
If it shall appear that the sufferings and the sins of the "other half," and the evil they breed, are but
as a fitting punishment upon the community that gave it no other choice, it will be because that
is the truth. The boundary line lies there because, while the forces for good on one side vastly out-
(35) weigh the bad—not otherwise—in the tenements all the influences make for evil; because they are
the hotbeds of the epidemics that carry death to rich and poor alike; the nurseries of poverty and
crime that fill our jails and courts; that throw off forty thousand human wrecks to the island asy-
lums and workhouses year by year; that turned out in the last eight years a round half million beg-
gars to prey upon our charities; that maintain a standing army of ten thousand panhandlers with
(40) all that that implies; because, above all, they touch the family life with deadly moral poison. This
is their worst crime, inseparable from the system. That we have to own it, the child of our own
wrong, does not excuse it, even though it gives it claim upon our utmost patience and tenderest
charity.

21. The main idea of the first paragraph is:
   a. The rich do not care about the poor until their own lives are affected.
   b. The rich know nothing about the lives of the poor.
   c. The rich and the poor lead very different lives.
   d. The poor revolted against the rich.

22. According to the passage, the "other half" refers to:
   f. the rich.
   g. criminals.
   h. children.
   j. the poor.

23. According to the Secretary of the Prison Association, the main reason for increased crime was:
   a. blamed on younger criminals.
   b. a lack of decent housing for the poor.
   c. the wealthy people's indifference to the poor.
   d. a shortage of prisons.

24. At the time the passage was written, how many people lived in tenement housing?
   f. more than 120,000
   g. 37,000
   h. 15,000
   j. more than 1,200,000

25. As it is used in line 15, the word *domicile* most closely means:

   a. dome-shaped

   b. prison

   c. living place

   d. orphanage

26. In the third paragraph, the statement "It is ten years and over, now, since that line divided New York's population evenly" (line 23) best means:

   f. Tenements are no longer located in one area of the city.

   g. The crimes of the poor affect the rich.

   h. More than half of New York's population lives in poverty.

   j. The poor no longer live only in tenements.

27. According to the author, the only way for the poor to successfully escape poverty is:

   a. nothing—there is no escape.

   b. by moving to the suburbs.

   c. through hard work.

   d. through crime.

28. According to the last paragraph, the following statements about tenements are true:

   I.   They foster illegal activity.

   II. They spread disease to the rich.

   II. Rich and poor alike may find themselves living there.

   f. I only

   g. II only

   h. I and II

   j. I, II, and III

29. According to the author, crime committed by the poor:

   a. is not as widespread as the government claims.

   b. is unavoidable, considering their living conditions.

   c. is a problem that should be dealt with harshly.

   d. should be ignored because of their inhumane living conditions.

30. It can be inferred from the passage that the author's opinion of the poor is:

   f. sympathetic.

   g. hostile.

   h. indifferent.

   j. objective.

HUMANITIES: Illuminated Manuscripts

(1)   When I first heard the term "illuminated manuscript" and learned of its association with medieval monasteries, I pictured hand-lettered parchment texts actually lighted from within by a kind of benevolent, supernatural light. I soon discovered, however, that the adjective "illuminated" in this case had nothing to do with light, nor did it always have to do with the Christian

(5)   church or with medieval times. Rather, "to illuminate" simply meant "to adorn" the pages of a manuscript, usually with brilliant colors and sometimes even with precious metals or stones.

Although illuminated manuscripts reached their apogee in the Middle Ages and are best known as a product of the medieval Christian church, they actually had their origins in Egypt, nearly four thousand years ago. The first known illuminated manuscript was the *Egyptian Book*

(10) *of the Dead,* which contained instructions for the ceremonies for burial of the dead and the prayers to be said by those left behind. Originally, those books were commissioned by royalty, nobility, and others of high rank, but eventually even ordinary people could purchase them. Among the scenes commonly contained in the *Egyptian Book of the Dead* were the funeral cortege and the mummification process, as well as depictions of the deceased in the afterlife. Thanks to the dry climate in

(15) Egypt, a number of these ancient manuscripts have survived.

The practice of illuminating manuscripts flourished in Europe. The Vatican Library houses two manuscripts by Virgil, and a copy of the *Iliad* by Homer resides in the Biblioteca Ambrosiana in Milan. A few Bibles and religious storybooks have survived also. Hellenistic and Roman wall painting influenced the illustrations in these texts, and as the age progressed, the artwork came to

(20) be more influenced by classical art with biblical themes. By the seventh century, the most important illuminated manuscripts were the prayer books being produced in monasteries in England and Ireland. The illustrators were greatly influenced by Celtic metalwork from previous centuries, and the works are beautiful and impressive (though they may look slightly primitive to modern eyes as the artists have made no effort to give a sense of perspective).

(25)   By the tenth and eleventh centuries, monasteries in England moved away from their Celtic influence and embraced the Carolingian style. The pictures in these manuscripts, drawn for royals and other wealthy patrons, became more interpretive, actually illustrating passages from the book, with stylized figures looking rather severely out at the reader. By the twelfth century, these English illuminators were integrating illustration and decoration into the text. Bibles made in Eng-

(30) land at this time contained entire scenes. Many of these manuscripts also presented mythical figures, like dragons or part-human, part-animal figures that did not relate directly to the text.

By the Gothic period, the urbanization of Europe led to increasing numbers of illuminated manuscripts. The illustrations became more realistic: The figures wore the clothes of the day and were shown in contemporary settings. The artists also began to be concerned with balance and

(35) perspective. The handwritten books and scrolls were embellished with decorations and illustrations intended to enhance the text, and the paints used were made from natural materials such as minerals and stones. Red, brown, orange, and yellow were derived from ochers and metals; blue came from lapis lazulim azurite, or indigo. In Europe, artists also applied gold leaf.

During the Middle Ages, the illumination of manuscripts was an important art form, and
(40) illuminations employed a variety of decorations and enhancements. Although most of the books
began with an imaginary portrait of the book's author or its patron, in some the first page contained abstract designs that were reminiscent of the Oriental carpet, and thus, the first page later
came to be known as the carpet page. Texts of this time usually had enlarged and embellished initial letters—sometimes shaped like animals, birds, or flowers. Some particularly important texts—
(45) religious, literary, or historical—might have full-page illustrations, which would be placed either
at the appropriate point in the text or grouped together at the beginning.

During the Renaissance, patrons continued to order these hand-illuminated manuscripts—
even though the printing press (c. 1450) made mass production of manuscripts by machine possible. This was not true in the Middle East, however. Consequently, the illuminated manuscript
(50) kept its influential role and many exquisite examples survive to this day. Although the invention
of the printing press could be said to mark the beginning of the end for illuminated manuscripts
in Europe and elsewhere, they performed an invaluable service during their long history. Because
of widespread illiteracy throughout history, pictures have always been an important source of
information. Even people who could not read—whether in ancient Egypt or medieval Europe—
(55) could glean information from the illustrated pages. Perhaps the image of a page lighted from
within is not such a far-fetched description of the illuminated manuscript, after all.

31. The main idea of the passage is:
    a. illuminated manuscripts have played an important role in the artistic and literary lives of a variety
       of cultures.
    b. the artists who illuminated manuscripts became more skilled during the Middle Ages.
    c. the practice of illuminating manuscripts began to die out, for the most part, with the invention of
       the printing press.
    d. illuminating manuscripts are of ancient origin and should be considered sacred works.

32. Which of the following best describes the order of the information as it is presented in the passage?
    f. order of importance
    g. order by quality of the work
    h. hypothesis followed by evidence
    j. chronological order

33. As it is used in line 7, the word *apogee* most nearly means:
    a. beginning.
    b. crises.
    c. rarity.
    d. peak.

34. According to the passage, during what period was the printing press invented?

    f. the Renaissance

    g. the Middle Ages

    h. the Gothic period

    j. the Byzantine era

35. Based on the information in the passage, all of the following are accurate statements about the *Egyptian Book of the Dead* EXCEPT:

    a. The climate in Egypt affected the fate of the *Egyptian Book of the Dead* manuscripts.

    b. The *Egyptian Book of the Dead* describes burial ceremonies.

    c. The *Egyptian Book of the Dead* explains significance of the pyramids.

    d. Eventually, even the common people had access to the *Egyptian Book of the Dead.*

36. A main idea of paragraph 4 is that between the tenth and twelfth centuries in Europe, illumination was used more and more often to:

    f. point toward the religious significance of the text.

    g. further explain the meaning of the text.

    h. infuse traditionally religious texts with fanciful subject matter.

    j. emphasize the seriousness of the text's subject matter.

37. Based on the passage, one can conclude that most illuminated manuscripts pertain to:

    a. the passage from life to death.

    b. religion in some way.

    c. mythical and animal figures.

    d. an even mixture of the sacred and the secular.

38. It can be reasonably inferred that a person who studied history of the illuminated manuscript would also learn the most about which of the following?

    f. the history of the Vatican Library

    g. advancements in biology during the same time period

    h. advancements in art during the same time period

    j. the urbanization of Europe after the Middle Ages

39. It can be inferred from the passage that the printing press "marked the beginning of the end for the illuminated manuscript" because:

    a. mass-produced manuscripts were less expensive than the old illuminated manuscripts.

    b. the less-educated citizenry preferred books that were machine-made.

    c. printed books were less fragile and more portable than illuminated manuscripts.

    d. the printing press for the most part eliminated illiteracy.

40. The main difference between illustrations in illuminated manuscripts made during the seventh century and those created during the Gothic period was that they:

    f. were more realistic in the Gothic period.

    g. were more beautiful in the seventh century.

    h. were more important in the seventh century.

    j. showed more perspective in the seventh century.

> **HUMANITIES:** *This passage is excerpted from "Leonardo da Vinci" from* Knights of Art: Stories of the Italian Painters *by Amy Steedman, 1907.*

(1)   ON the sunny slopes of Monte Albano, between Florence and Pisa, the little town of Vinci lay high among the rocks that crowned the steep hillside. Here in the year 1452 Leonardo, son of Ser Piero da Vinci, was born. It was in the age when people told fortunes by the stars, and when a baby was born they would eagerly look up and decide whether it was a lucky or unlucky star

(5)   which shone upon the child. Surely if it had been possible in this way to tell what fortune awaited the little Leonardo, a strange new star must have shone that night, brighter than the others and unlike the rest in the dazzling light of its strength and beauty.

      Leonardo was always a strange child. Even his beauty was not like that of other children. He had the most wonderful waving hair, falling in regular ripples, like the waters of a fountain, the

(10) color of bright gold, and soft as spun silk. His eyes were blue and clear, with a mysterious light in them, not the warm light of a sunny sky, but rather the blue that glints in the iceberg. They were merry eyes too, when he laughed, but underneath was always that strange cold look. There was a charm about his smile which no one could resist, and he was a favorite with all. Yet people shook their heads sometimes as they looked at him, and they talked in whispers of the old witch who had

(15) lent her goat to nourish the little Leonardo when he was a baby. The woman was a dealer in black magic, and who knew but that the child might be a changeling?

      It was the old grandmother, Mona Lena, who brought Leonardo up and spoilt him not a little. His father, Ser Piero, was a lawyer, and spent most of his time in Florence, but when he returned to the old castle of Vinci, he began to give Leonardo lessons and tried to find out what the boy was

(20) fit for. But Leonardo hated those lessons and would not learn, so when he was seven years old he was sent to school.

      This did not answer any better. The rough play of the boys was not to his liking. When he saw them drag the wings off butterflies, or torture any animal that fell into their hands, his face grew white with pain, and he would take no share in their games. The Latin grammar, too, was a

(25) terrible task, while the many things he longed to know no one taught him.

      So it happened that many a time, instead of going to school, he would slip away and escape up into the hills, as happy as a little wild goat. Here was all the sweet fresh air of heaven, instead of the stuffy schoolroom. Here were no cruel, clumsy boys, but all the wild creatures that he loved. Here he could learn the real things his heart was hungry to know, not merely words which meant

(30) nothing and led to nowhere.

For hours he would lie perfectly still with his heels in the air and his chin resting in his hands, as he watched a spider weaving its web, breathless with interest to see how the delicate threads were turned in and out. The gaily painted butterflies, the fat buzzing bees, the little sharp-tongued green lizards, he loved to watch them all, but above everything he loved the birds. Oh, if only he too had

(35) wings to dart like the swallows, and swoop and sail and dart again! What was the secret power in their wings? Surely by watching he might learn it. Sometimes it seemed as if his heart would burst with the longing to learn that secret. It was always the hidden reason of things that he desired to know. Much as he loved the flowers he must pull their petals off, one by one, to see how each was joined, to wonder at the dusty pollen, and touch the honey-covered stamens. Then when the sun

(40) began to sink he would turn sadly homewards, very hungry, with torn clothes and tired feet, but with a store of sunshine in his heart.

His grandmother shook her head when Leonardo appeared after one of his days of wandering.

'I know thou shouldst be whipped for playing truant,' she said; 'and I should also punish thee

(45) for tearing thy clothes.'

'Ah! But thou wilt not whip me,' answered Leonardo, smiling at her with his curious quiet smile, for he had full confidence in her love.

'Well, I love to see thee happy, and I will not punish thee this time,' said his grandmother; 'but if these tales reach thy father's ears, he will not be so tender as I am towards thee.'

(50) And, sure enough, the very next time that a complaint was made from the school, his father happened to be at home, and then the storm burst.

'Next time I will flog thee,' said Ser Piero sternly, with rising anger at the careless air of the boy. 'Meanwhile we will see what a little imprisonment will do towards making thee a better child.'

Then he took the boy by the shoulders and led him to a little dark cupboard under the stairs,

(55) and there shut him up for three whole days.

There was no kicking or beating at the locked door. Leonardo sat quietly there in the dark, thinking his own thoughts, and wondering why there seemed so little justice in the world. But soon even that wonder passed away, and as usual when he was alone he began to dream dreams of the time when he should have learned the swallows' secrets and should have wings like theirs.

(60) But if there were complaints about Leonardo's dislike of the boys and the Latin grammar, there would be none about the lessons he chose to learn. Indeed, some of the masters began to dread the boy's eager questions, which were sometimes more than they could answer. Scarcely had he begun the study of arithmetic than he made such rapid progress, and wanted to puzzle out so many problems, that the masters were amazed. His mind seemed always eagerly asking for more

(65) light, and was never satisfied.

41. It can reasonably be inferred from the passage that Leonardo's grandmother did not punish him because she:
- **a.** knew his father would punish him.
- **b.** believed it would not do any good.
- **c.** was afraid of Leonardo's magic powers.
- **d.** enjoyed seeing him happy.

42. What can you infer about Leonardo's teachers from the last paragraph of the passage?
- **f.** They were afraid he would ask questions they could not answer.
- **g.** They thought he was unable to learn.
- **h.** They thought he had no desire to learn.
- **j.** They believed he should try to get along with the other students.

43. The person or people who were most responsible for raising Leonardo were his:
- **a.** father.
- **b.** mother.
- **c.** teachers.
- **d.** grandmother.

44. As he is depicted in the passage, Leonardo as a boy can be described as:
- **f.** popular among the other children.
- **g.** insensitive and cruel.
- **h.** a talented artist.
- **j.** eager to learn about what interested him.

45. It can be inferred from the passage that Leonardo:
- I.   did not mind being alone.
- II. was fascinated by flight.
- III. was popular with the other students.
- **a.** I and II only
- **b.** I, II, and III
- **c.** I only
- **a.** II only

46. What year was Leonardo first sent to school?
- **f.** 1452
- **g.** 1455
- **h.** 1459
- **j.** 1461

47. According to the passage, all the following are true EXCEPT:

    a. Leonardo enjoyed learning Latin grammar.

    b. Leonardo enjoyed learning math.

    c. Leonardo enjoyed studying nature.

    d. Leonardo was curious about the way things worked.

48. Which of the following statements best sums up what is meant by lines 33–39 ("Much as he loved the flowers he must pull their petals off, one by one, to see how each was joined, to wonder at the dusty pollen, and touch the honey-covered stamens")?

    f. Leonardo's desire to learn how things worked was stronger than his affection for nature.

    g. Leonardo's love of flowers drove him to destroy them.

    h. Leonardo revered all of nature.

    j. Leonardo's curiosity led him to destructive acts.

49. When Leonardo's father punished him, his reaction could be best described as:

    a. anger.

    b. resignation.

    c. spite.

    d. sadness.

50. According to the passage, one reason Leonardo skipped school was:

    f. he knew his grandmother would not punish him.

    g. the other students taunted him.

    h. Latin grammar bored him.

    j. he had no interest in any school subjects.

    NATURAL SCIENCE: *This passage is taken from a U.S. Fish and Wildlife Service pamphlet entitled "Migration of Birds" by Frederick C. Lincoln, 1935.*

(1)   The changing picture of bird populations throughout the year intrigues those who are observant and who wish to know the source and destination of these birds. While many species of fish, mammals, and even insects undertake amazing migratory journeys, birds as a group are the most mobile creatures on Earth. Even humans with their many vehicles of locomotion do not equal

(5)   some birds in mobility. No human population moves each year as far as from the Arctic to the Antarctic with subsequent return, yet the Arctic Terns do.

    Birds are adapted in their body structure and physiology to life in the air. Their feathered wings and tails, bones, lungs and air sacs, and their metabolic abilities all contribute to this amazing faculty. These adaptations make it possible for birds to seek out environments most favorable

(10) to their needs at different times of the year. This results in the marvelous phenomenon we know

as migration—the regular, recurrent, seasonal movement of populations from one geographic location to another and back again.

Throughout human experience, migratory birds have been important as a source of food after a lean winter and as the harbinger of a change in seasons. The arrival of certain species has (15) been heralded with appropriate ceremonies in many lands. Among the eskimos and other tribes this phenomenon is the accepted sign of the imminence of spring, of warmer weather, and a reprieve from winter food shortages. The European fur traders in Alaska and Canada offered rewards to the Native American who saw the first flight of geese in the spring, and all joined in jubilant welcome to the newcomers.

(20) As North America became more thickly settled, the large flocks of ducks and geese, as well as migratory rails, doves, and woodcock that had been hunted for food became objects of the enthusiastic attention of an increasing army of sportsmen. Most of the nongame species were also found to be valuable as allies of the farmer in his never-ending confrontation against insect pests and weed seeds. And in more recent years, all species have been of ever-increasing recreational and (25) esthetic value for untold numbers of people who enjoy watching birds. We soon realized that our migratory bird resource was an international legacy that could not be managed alone by one state or country and that all nations were responsible for its well being. The need for laws protecting game and nongame birds, as well as the necessity to regulate the hunting of diminishing game species, followed as a natural consequence. In the management of this wildlife resource, it has (30) become obvious that studies must be made of the species' habits, environmental needs, and travels. In the United States, the Department of the Interior recognized the value of this resource and is devoted to programs that will ensure sustainability for these populations as they are faced with the impacts of alteration in land use, loss of habitat, and contaminants from our technological society. Hence bird investigations are made by the U.S. Fish and Wildlife Service, the arm of the (35) Department of Interior charged by Congress under the Migratory Bird Treaty Act with the duty of protecting those avian species that in their yearly journeys pass back and forth between United States and other countries. In addition, the federal government through the activities of the Biological Resources Division of the U.S. Geological Survey also promotes basic research on migration. Federal agencies cooperate with their counterparts in other countries as well as with state (40) agencies, academic institutions, and non-governmental groups to gain understanding and for the protection of migratory species through such endeavors as Partners in Flight, a broadly based international cooperative effort in the Western Hemisphere.

For almost a century the Fish and Wildlife Service and its predecessor, the Biological Survey, have been collecting data on the important details of bird migration. Scientists have gathered (45) information concerning the distribution and seasonal movements of many species throughout the Western Hemisphere, from the Arctic Archipelago south to Tierra del Fuego. Supplementing these investigations is the work of hundreds of United States, Latin American, and Canadian university personnel and volunteer birdwatchers, who report on the migrations and status of birds as observed in their respective localities. This data, stored in field notes, computer files, and scien-

(50) tific journals, constitutes an enormous reservoir of information pertaining to the distribution and movements of North American birds.

The purpose of this publication is to summarize this data and additional information from other parts of the world to present the more important facts about our current understanding of the fascinating subject of bird migration. The U.S. Fish and Wildlife Service is grateful to the many

(55) people who have contributed their knowledge so that others, whether in biology or ornithology classes, members of conservation organizations, or just individuals interested in the welfare of the birds, may understand and enjoy this precious resource as well as preserve it for generations to come.

51. The migratory path of the Arctic Tern:
   a. varies depending on the year.
   b. is from the Arctic to the Antarctic and back to the Arctic.
   c. is from the Arctic to the Antarctic.
   d. is to the North in the summer and South in the winter.

52. According to the author, the main reason birds migrate is:
   f. because their body structure and physiology is best suited for migration.
   g. to find the best climate at different times during the year.
   h. because birds enjoy flying great distances.
   j. because birds are an important source of food in different parts of the worlds.

53. It can be inferred from the passage that the relationship between the European fur traders and the Native Americans was:
   a. friendly.
   b. hostile.
   c. based on commerce.
   d. nonexistent.

54. Which governmental agency is responsible for investigating threats to migratory birds?
   f. U.S. Fish and Wildlife Service
   g. The Department of the Interior
   h. Congress
   j. The Migratory Bird Act

55. Which best describes the role of the Biological Survey?
  a. the agency responsible for collecting data on bird migration
  b. the agency, in connection with the U.S. Fish and Wildlife Service that is responsible for collecting data on bird migration
  c. the agency responsible for collecting data on bird migration before the U.S. Fish and Wildlife Service
  d. the agency responsible for investigating threats to migratory birds

56. The passage states that all of the following are threats to migratory bird populations EXCEPT:
  f. pollution.
  g. hunting.
  h. loss of habitat.
  j. insect pests.

57. As it is used in line 16 of the passage, the word *imminence* most nearly means:
  a. importance.
  b. celebration.
  c. close arrival.
  d. warmth.

58. According to the passage, with the increasing population in North America, migratory birds no longer hunted for food were appreciated by all of the following EXCEPT:
  f. sportsmen.
  g. bird watchers.
  h. European fur traders.
  j. farmers.

59. According to the passage, the need for laws to protect migratory birds was brought about by:
  a. a realization of their value as something other than a source of food.
  b. the increase in sport hunting.
  c. the devastating effects of pollution.
  d. the creation of the Migratory Bird Act.

60. According to the passage, which group or groups keep data on the migration and status of birds?
  f. university personnel and volunteer birdwatchers
  g. Fish and Wildlife Service
  h. Biological Survey
  j. Fish and Wildlife Service along with university personnel and volunteer birdwatchers

PROSE FICTION: Sylvia

(1)   For perhaps the tenth time since the clock struck two, Sylvia crosses to the front-facing window of her apartment, pulls back the blue curtain, and looks down at the street. People hurry along
the sidewalk; although she watches for several long moments, she sees no one enter her building.

       She walks back to the center of the high-ceilinged living room, where she stands frowning
(5)   and twisting a silver bracelet around and around on her wrist. She is an attractive young woman,
although perhaps too thin and with a look that is faintly ascetic; her face is narrow and delicate,
her fine, light-brown hair caught back by a tortoiseshell comb. She is restless now, because she is
being kept waiting. It is nearly two-thirty—a woman named Lola Parrish was to come at two
o'clock to look at the apartment.

(10)   She considers leaving a note and going out. The woman is late, and besides, Sylvia is certain
that Lola Parrish will not be a suitable person with whom to share the apartment. On the phone
she had sounded too old, for one thing—her voice oddly flat and as deep as a man's. However, the
moment for saying the apartment was no longer available slipped past, and Sylvia found herself
agreeing to the two o'clock appointment. If she leaves now, as she has a perfect right to do, she can
(15) avoid the awkwardness of turning the woman away.

       Looking past the blue curtain, however, she sees the sky is not clear but veiled by a white haze,
and the air is oppressively still. She knows that the haze, the stillness, and the heat are conditions
that often precede a summer thunderstorm—one of the abrupt, swiftly descending electrical
storms that have terrified her since she was a child. If a storm comes, she wants to be at home in
(20) her own place.

       She walks back to the center of the room, aware now that the idea of sharing the apartment
has actually begun to repel her. Still, she knows she will have to become accustomed to the notion,
because her savings are nearly gone and the small trust fund left by her father, exhausted. She has
a low-paying job, and, while she has considered seeking another (perhaps something connected
(25) with music—in her childhood she had played the flute and people had said she was gifted), she
has found herself dragged down by a strange inertia.

       Besides, although her job pays poorly, it suits her. She is a typist in a natural history museum,
with an office on the top floor and a window onto the nearby aviary. The man for whom she works,
a curator who is rarely in, allows Sylvia to have the office to herself. The aviary consists of three
(30) enormous, white rooms, each with a high, vaulted ceiling. The birds themselves, so beautifully
mounted they seem alive, are displayed in elaborate dioramas. Behind glass, they perch in trees
with leaves of sculpted metal, appearing to soar through painted forests, above painted rivers and
marshes. Everything is rendered in exquisite detail. Glancing at the birds and up through the skylight at the limitless outdoors keeps her mild claustrophobia at bay.

61. Which of the following best describes Sylvia's mood as depicted in the story passage?
- **a.** anxious
- **b.** angry
- **c.** serene
- **d.** embittered

62. It can be reasonably inferred from the passage that Sylvia's job suits her because:
- **f.** her office is tastefully decorated.
- **g.** she is musical and enjoys the singing of birds.
- **h.** she is able to work alone in a space that feels open.
- **j.** it is challenging, and offers the opportunity to learn new skills.

63. When Sylvia looks out her window, the weather appears:
- **a.** ominous.
- **b.** spring-like.
- **c.** inviting.
- **d.** serene.

64. It can be reasonably inferred from the passage that Sylvia's behavior in relationship to other people would be:
- **f.** distant.
- **g.** overbearing.
- **h.** malicious.
- **j.** patient.

65. What can be reasonably inferred about Sylvia from the description of her workplace?
- **a.** Because her job requires concentration and attention to detail, it shows why she is annoyed by Lola's lateness.
- **b.** The fact that it is light and airy and filled with beautiful dioramas reflects Sylvia's youth and her wish for something better.
- **c.** Some part of the story, perhaps a love affair between Sylvia and her boss, will probably take place there.
- **d.** Everything in it, though beautiful and tasteful, seems frozen or removed from life and reflects some aspect of Sylvia's character.

66. Why was Sylvia unable to avoid the meeting with Lola?
- **f.** She missed her chance to tell her the apartment was rented.
- **g.** She is running out of money.
- **h.** She is too concerned with what others think about her.
- **j.** She could not spot her through the window early enough.

67. The word *exhausted,* as it is used in line 23, most nearly means:

    a. impotent.

    b. stocked.

    c. spent.

    d. tired.

68. According to the passage, Sylvia waited for Lola instead of going out and leaving her a note because:

    f. Sylvia could not afford the rent on her own.

    g. Sylvia thought it would rain.

    h. she knows Lola will not be a suitable roommate.

    j. she thought it would be rude.

69. What can be inferred about Sylvia's dominant emotion in paragraph 3?

    a. timidity

    b. curiosity

    c. irritation

    d. sadness

70. The statement that "the air is oppressively still" in line 17 reflects the viewpoint of:

    f. the author.

    g. Lola.

    h. Sylvia.

    j. the reader.

> **HUMANITIES:** *This passage is taken from the personal memoirs of Ulysses S. Grant, 1885–86.*

(1)   The Cause of the Great War of the Rebellion against the United States will have to be attributed to slavery. For some years before the war began it was a trite saying among some politicians that "A state half slave and half free cannot exist." All must become slave or all free, or the state will go down. I took no part myself in any such view of the case at the time, but since the war is over,

(5)   reviewing the whole question, I have come to the conclusion that the saying is quite true.

Slavery was an institution that required unusual guarantees for its security wherever it existed; and in a country like ours where the larger portion of it was free territory inhabited by an intelligent and well-to-do population, the people would naturally have but little sympathy with demands upon them for its protection. Hence the people of the South were dependent upon keep-

(10)   ing control of the general government to secure the perpetuation of their favorite restitution. They were enabled to maintain this control long after the States where slavery existed had ceased to have the controlling power, through the assistance they received from odd men here and there throughout the Northern States. They saw their power waning, and this led them to encroach upon the

(15) prerogatives and independence of the Northern States by enacting such laws as the Fugitive Slave Law. By this law every Northern man was obliged, when properly summoned, to turn out and help apprehend the runaway slave of a Southern man. Northern marshals became slave-catchers, and Northern courts had to contribute to the support and protection of the institution.

This was a degradation which the North would not permit any longer than until they could get the power to expunge such laws from the statute books. Prior to the time of these encroach-
(20) ments the great majority of the people of the North had no particular quarrel with slavery, so long as they were not forced to have it themselves. But they were not willing to play the role of police for the South in the protection of this particular institution.

In the early days of the country, before we had railroads, telegraphs and steamboats—in a word, rapid transit of any sort—the States were each almost a separate nationality. At that time
(25) the subject of slavery caused but little or no disturbance to the public mind. But the country grew, rapid transit was established, and trade and commerce between the States got to be so much greater than before, that the power of the National government became more felt and recognized and, therefore, had to be enlisted in the cause of this institution.

It is probably well that we had the war when we did. We are better off now than we would
(30) have been without it, and have made more rapid progress than we otherwise should have made. The civilized nations of Europe have been stimulated into unusual activity, so that commerce, trade, travel, and thorough acquaintance among people of different nationalities, has become common; whereas, before, it was but the few who had ever had the privilege of going beyond the limits of their own country or who knew anything about other people. Then, too, our republican
(35) institutions were regarded as experiments up to the breaking out of the rebellion, and monarchical Europe generally believed that our republic was a rope of sand that would part the moment the slightest strain was brought upon it. Now it has shown itself capable of dealing with one of the greatest wars that was ever made, and our people have proven themselves to be the most formidable in war of any nationality.

(40) But this war was a fearful lesson, and should teach us the necessity of avoiding wars in the future. The conduct of some of the European states during our troubles shows the lack of conscience of communities where the responsibility does not come upon a single individual. Seeing a nation that extended from ocean to ocean, embracing the better part of a continent, growing as we were growing in population, wealth and intelligence, the European nations thought it would
(45) be well to give us a check. We might, possibly, after a while, threaten their peace, or, at least, the perpetuity of their institutions. Hence, England was constantly finding fault with the administration at Washington because we were not able to keep up an effective blockade. She also joined, at first, with France and Spain in setting up an Austrian prince upon the throne in Mexico, totally disregarding any rights or claims that Mexico had of being treated as an independent power. It is
(50) true they trumped up grievances as a pretext, but they were only pretexts which can always be found when wanted.

71. According to the passage, which of the following statements is/are true:

    I.   The North was always against slavery.

    II. The North was indifferent toward slavery as long as they were not forced to support it.

    III. The North always supported slavery.

    a. I only

    b. II only

    c. II and III

    d. III only

72. According to the passage, which factors contributed to the North's rejection of slavery?

    I.   the introduction of rapid transit

    II. the legal obligations to support slavery

    III. their moral obligation to defend what is right

    f. I and II

    g. II only

    h. III only

    j. II and III

73. Once of the main points the author makes in the first paragraph is:

    a. slavery must be abolished.

    b. the entire country must either be for or against slavery.

    c. the North and the South can never live in peace.

    d. slavery was an accepted practice.

74. According to the second paragraph, what were the effects of the Fugitive Slave Act?

    f. It freed the slaves.

    g. It angered the South

    h. It forced the North to enforce laws it did not necessarily believe were right.

    j. It forced the North to fight the South.

75. As it is used in line 19, the word *expunge* most closely means:

    a. law.

    b. holding one against his will.

    c. powerlessness.

    d. remove.

76. According to the passage, the South enacted the Fugitive Slave Law because:

    f. they had too many runaway slaves.

    g. slavery was important to the livelihood of the North.

    h. the South was afraid that slavery would be abolished.

    j. they needed help from the North in keeping slavery alive.

77. According to the second to last paragraph, one of things that changed after the war was:

    a. slavery was abolished.

    b. Europeans were exposed to different cultures.

    c. runaway slaves were captured without the help of the North.

    d. the North and the South were united.

78. According to the last paragraph, the author believes that the European countries felt:

    f. threatened by our unified strength.

    g. slavery was wrong.

    h. they owed us money.

    j. betrayed by the United States.

79. The phrase "rope of sand" in line 36, most nearly means:

    a. weakly connected.

    b. shackled.

    c. broken in two.

    d. tightly bound.

80. The author believes that war:

    f. should be avoided at all costs.

    g. is the best way to end disputes.

    h. can have beneficial results but should be avoided.

    j. is morally wrong.

▶ Practice Questions Answers and Explanations

BABBITT

1. Question type: detail

Choice **c** is correct. The best way to handle this question is to go through the possible answers and eliminate the incorrect ones. The first line states that "there is nothing of the giant" in Babbitt, which eliminates choice **d**, because he was not tall. Line 9 says he was not fat, but he was "well fed," which eliminates his being overweight (choice **a**) or skinny (choice **b**).

2. Question type: detail

Choice **h** is correct. The passage rattles off a number of occupations that Babbitt does not perform, but lines 5–6 says what he does do: sell houses.

3. Question type: inference

Choice **a** is correct. The reader knows that on this particular day, Babbitt is having a difficult time getting out of bed. Does this mean he is lazy? It could, but later we learn that the poker game he went to the night before may have something to do with it. We are never given any indication that Babbitt works hard at his job, but lines 5–6 say he was "nimble in the calling of selling houses for more than people could afford to pay." In other words, that he was good at his job, not that he worked hard at it.

4. Question type: inference

Choice **j** is correct. This question asks that you infer something about the relationship that Babbitt has with his wife by paying attention to how they interact. We know that they do not openly dislike each other because Babbitt's wife tries to wake him by cheerfully calling him "Georgie boy." But in the same line Babbitt refers to this cheerfulness as detestable to him, so we know it is not romantic and passionate, but that Babbitt has strong feelings about his wife (thus eliminating choices **f** and **h** as possible answers). Line 43 comes the closest to stating Babbitt's feeling toward his wife (and family), saying that he disliked them and disliked himself for feeling that way.

5. Question type: vocabulary

Choice **d** is correct. The biggest clue that the meaning of *patina* is color is the fact that the word *gold* immediately precedes it.

6. Question type: cause and effect

Choice **g** is correct. There are many things that wake Babbitt from his sleep, but the first one can be found on line 20. We know that the noise of the milk truck wakes him because the next line is "Babbitt moaned; turned over; struggled back toward his dream." All the other options may have woken Babbitt, but choice **g** is the first and therefore correct.

7. Question type: generalization

Choice **a** is correct. It is perfectly clear that Babbitt wishes to return to sleep, but this fact has nothing to do with his blanket. His blanket may indeed offer him warmth and comfort, but the passage does not say as much and we know that Babbitt bought this blanket for a camping trip he never took.

8. Question type: cause and effect

Choice **f** is correct. When the alarm goes off, what keeps Babbitt in bed is stated in lines 42–43, that he "detested the grind of the real-estate business." This makes it clear that Babbitt hates his job. And although the next line refers to his dislike of his family, we cannot assume that he is in a fight with his wife (she seems cheerful enough when she calls him "Georgie boy" to wake him). We also learn in the lines immediately following that he went to a poker game and drank too much beer, so it is safe to assume that he has a hangover.

9. Question type: inference

Choice **b** is correct. Lines 14–19 give the best clues as to the meaning of Babbitt's dream. The fairy sees Babbitt as nobody else: a "gallant youth," or young. He also escapes from his wife and friends who attempt to follow him in this dream (he is free).

10. Question type: generalization

Choice **f** is correct. This question asks you to find a more succinct way of stating lines 32–33, which basically say that as a boy Babbitt was more interested in life. Even if you do not know what the word *credulous* means here, you can still assume that it is something different from the way he is now just from the way the sentence is phrased. We know that now he is not interested in life, or "each new day."

Diabetes

11. Question type: detail

Choice **b** is correct. The answer to this question lies in line 7 of the passage, which states that people with Type II diabetes "may feel tired or ill without knowing why, a circumstance which can be particularly dangerous because untreated diabetes can cause damage to the heart, blood vessels, eyes, kidneys, and nerves." Therefore choice **b** is correct. Choices **a** and **c** are incorrect because they are not examples of the danger of diabetes, but rather facts relating to the disease. Choice **d** is an incorrect statement; the passage states that diabetes does *not* interfere with digestion.

12. Question type: comparison

Choice **f** is correct. The first paragraph of the passage discusses both types of diabetes and the last line states: "both types can cause the same long-term health problems."

13. Question type: detail

Choice **d** is correct. There are a lot of organs doing a lot of different things in this passage, which means that if you do not read carefully you may confuse them. Lines 17–18 state that "glucose that the body does not use right away is stored in the liver, muscle, or fat," and the only one of these that is a possible answer is choice **d**, the liver.

14. Question type: detail

Choice **h** is correct. The last paragraph of the passage discusses the dietary recommendations for people with diabetes. Line 39 specifically says that "50 to 60 percent" of their diet should come from carbohydrates (and 12 to 20 from protein and a maximum of 30 percent from fat), making choice **h** the correct answer. The passage also says that raw foods are better than cooked (choice **j**), but not that the diet should be dominated by them.

15. Question type: detail

Choice **a** is correct. Using the information given in the passage that glucose is sugar, the answer to this question can be found in lines 16–17: "insulin is released into the bloodstream and signals the body tissues to metabolize or burn the glucose for fuel."

16. Question type: main idea

Choice **g** is correct. From statements made in the last paragraph, we know that choices **f** and **j** are factually incorrect. Choice **h** may be a true statement, but it is not the main idea of the passage because a majority of the passage is about Type II diabetes, and not about the consequences of not taking insulin shots.

17. Question type: detail

Choice **d** is correct. The answer to this detail question can be found in line 31: "a defect in the receptors may prevent insulin from binding."

18. Question type: cause and effect

Choice **f** is correct. Cause and effect questions do not necessarily have to use the words *cause* or *effect*, which you can see is true in this question. It is basically asking what the immediate effects of glucose are on the body. The answer can be found in lines 14–15: "the normal digestive system extracts glucose from some foods. The blood carries the glucose or sugar throughout the body, causing blood glucose levels to rise," or simply put, *blood sugar levels rise.*

19. Question type: generalization

Choice **c** is correct. This question is asking you to sort through the information given about Type I diabetes and decide on the most concise way of describing them. We know that choices **a** and **d** are factually incorrect, so they can be eliminated as possible answers. Choice **b** is a true statement, but because it refers to both types of diabetes and is not the most important aspect of the disease, it too can be eliminated. Therefore, the best answer is choice **c**.

20. Question type: vocabulary

Choice **f** is correct. We know from reading the entire paragraph that the point of changing person with diabetes's diet is to "alleviate its symptoms." Therefore, we can figure out that a different diet would counteract "the effects" of diabetes.

HOW THE OTHER HALF LIVES

21. Question type: main idea

Choice **a** is correct. The first part of the paragraph explains how the rich were unaware of the plight of the poor and therefore did not care " 'one half of the world does not know how the other half lives.' That was true then. It did not know because it did not care." But the paragraph goes on to say that it was only when conditions became so bad did it become "no longer an easy thing" for the rich to ignore them. Although choices **b**, **c**, and **d** may be correct statements, they do not sum up the main idea of the whole paragraph.

22. Question type: inference

Choice **j** is correct. The meaning of this phrase can be found throughout the passage, but since the name of the passage is "How the Other Half Lives" and it is about the conditions of the poor, one can reasonably assume it refers to the poor.

23. Question type: cause and effect

Choice **b** is correct. For this question it is important to sift through a lot of details to get to the main point of the statement, which is that a majority of crimes are committed by those "whose homes had ceased to afford what are regarded as ordinary wholesome influences of home and family." In other words, without good housing there can be no good family values, which in turn led to increased crime.

24. Question type: detail

Choice **j** is correct. There are a lot of numbers mentioned in the passage, but the number specifically attributed to the number of people living in tenement housing can be found in line 26, "more than twelve hundred thousand persons call them home," or 1,200,000.

25. Question type: vocabulary

Choice **c** is correct. Because the secretary's statement refers to the living environment of the poor, it can be assumed that the word *domicile* can be defined as "living place."

26. Question type: generalization

Choice **h** is correct. The word *line* refers to the sentence immediately preceding the one in the question: "the boundary line of the Other Half lies through the tenements." It is important to find and understand this reference before you can make sense of the question. Here the line refers to those living in tenements. Therefore, if the "line" no longer divides the population evenly, more than half live in poverty.

27. Question type: inference

Choice **a** is correct. The only reference in the entire passage to a way out of poverty can be found in lines 27–28, "The one way out—rapid transit to the suburbs—has brought no relief." But because it also says it has "brought no relief" and the statement immediately following reads "we know now that there is no way out," you can infer that the author believes there is no way to escape poverty.

28. Question type: detail

Choice **h** is correct. The statement in lines 36–37, "the nurseries of poverty and crime that fill our jails and courts" make statement I true, and immediately prior to that statement it says the tenements "are the hotbeds of the epidemics that carry death to rich and poor alike," making II true. There is no reference to rich living in tenements in the passage, therefore III is incorrect.

29. Question type: inference

Choice **b** is correct. The easiest way to answer this type of question, which really refers to the entire passage, is to eliminate answers you know are wrong. The author makes no statement that crime is over reported, nor does he say how criminals should be punished, or whether they should be punished at all, therefore choices **a**, **c**, and **d** are incorrect. And because throughout the passage, crime is blamed on life in the tenement, it can be reasonably assumed that it is as unavoidable as life in the tenement itself.

30. Question type: point of view

Choice **f** is correct. The first clue that the author is not being objective is that he uses words like "greed and reckless selfishness" (line 10). And because the author says that poverty is inescapable in line 28, "We know now that there is no way out," one can only conclude that his opinion is sympathetic.

ILLUMINATED MANUSCRIPTS

31. Question type: main idea

Choice **a** is correct. Although choices **b** and **c** are correct statements, they are not the main points of the passage, but rather details that explain some of the passage. Choice **d** is incorrect because although many illuminated manuscripts were religious, nowhere is it stated that they should be considered sacred because they are of ancient origin. Choice **a** is the best choice because it summarizes many of the statements made throughout the passage.

32. Question type: generalization

Choice **j** is correct. In general, each paragraph of the passage moves forward in time when describing the evolution of the illuminated manuscript, making the answer choice **j**, *chronological order.*

33. Question type: vocabulary

Choice **d** is correct. We know from reading the second half of the sentence, that illuminated manuscripts originated in Egypt. The word *although* at the start of the sentence clues us in to the fact *apogee* should mean the opposite of *origins.* And because the word *beginning* can mean *origin,* choice **a** is not the right answer. Neither *crises* nor *rarity* can be the opposite of *origins,* but *peak* can, which makes **d** the best choice.

34. Question type: detail

Choice **f** is correct. The answer to this question can be found in lines 47–48 (1450 is during the Renaissance).

35. Question type: detail

Choice **c** is correct. The second paragraph supplies many facts about the Book of the Dead, but nowhere is the significance of the pyramids explained, which makes choice **c** the best answer.

36. Question type: main idea

Choice **g** is correct. If you read too quickly through the paragraph, it would be an easy mistake to think that choice **h** is correct. The last line in the paragraph (choice **h**) refers to manuscripts produced after the twelfth century, not between the tenth and twelfth, as the question asks. Choice **f** refers to illuminated manuscripts throughout much of history, and so does not specifically refer to the tenth and twelfth centuries. And choice **j** is simply an incorrect statement. Lines 26–28 make the point clear that the manuscripts of this time explained the meaning of the text.

37. Question type: generalization

Choice **b** is correct. If you skim through the passage, you can quickly see that almost all the illuminated manuscripts were bibles or religious texts of some sort, making **b** the best choice.

38. Question type: inference

Choice **h** is correct. Because illuminations are a form of art, and are treated as such in the passage (there are many references to perspective and representation), it can be inferred that one would also learn about advancements in art, or choice **h**.

39. Question type: inference

Choice **a** is correct. Because throughout the passage, it is made clear that creating illuminated manuscripts involved a lot of labor, it is fair to assume that a machine would reduce such labor. Without the costs of labor, mass-produced manuscripts were less expensive (choice **a**).

40. Question type: comparison

Choice **f** is correct. This question asks you to compare the quality of illustration in two periods (and two paragraphs). The third paragraph discusses the manuscripts of the seventh century and the fifth paragraph covers the Gothic period. Line 33 states that illustrations of the Gothic period "became more realistic," making choice **f** the best answer.

KNIGHTS OF ART

41. Question type: cause and effect

Choice **d** is correct. Although it is true that Leonardo's father would punish him if he caught him skipping school (choice **a**), this is not what the question asked. You also know from the text that Leonardo continued to skip school (choice **b**), but whether or not his grandmother knew this would happen is irrelevant. The reason that his grandmother did not punish him can be found in line 48, where she says that she loves to see him happy.

42. Question type: inference

Choice **f** is correct. Because the question refers only to the last paragraph, any opinions that Leonardo's teachers may have elsewhere in the text do not apply. It is true that Leonardo did not get along with the other students (choice **j**), but nowhere does it say that his teachers had any opinion on this. This is a basic inference question in that the last paragraph states that Leonardo's teachers dreaded his questions because they were sometimes "more than they could answer." From this statement, you can infer that they were afraid they would not have the knowledge to answer his questions and therefore afraid he might ask questions they could not answer.

43. Question type: detail

Choice **d** is correct. The text mentions many people as having something to do with raising Leonardo, but line 17 states "It was the old grandmother, Mona Lena, who brought Leonardo up."

44. Question type: generalization

Choice **j** is correct. Although you may know already know that Leonardo da Vinci was a talented artist, this is not mentioned in the text, which means that choice **h** is incorrect. Lines 26–27 show that Leonardo spent the time he skipped school studying nature, which is what interested him.

45. Question type: inference

Choice **a** is correct. When Leonardo was punished for skipping school (lines 54–57), his father locked him in the cupboard, and instead of protesting, he soon found himself lost in his own thoughts. This is how the reader knows that he did not mind being alone, therefore statement I is true. Lines 34–36 show that Leonardo was fascinated by birds and the "secret power in their wings," which makes statement II correct. Lines 22–24 describe Leonardo as not enjoying the company of other boys, from which one can reasonable infer he was not popular, which makes statement III incorrect.

46. Question type: detail

Choice **h** is correct. The only date mentioned specifically in the passage is 1492, which was the year of Leonardo's birth. Lines 20–21 state he was 7 years old when he was sent to school, which would make the year 1459.

47. Question type: generalization

Choice **a** is correct. This question asks you to distill a lot of information about Leonardo as a boy and find the one fact that is incorrect. In lines 24–25, it says that Leonardo found Latin grammar "a terrible task," which makes choice **a** correct.

48. Question type: generalization

Choice **f** is correct. The lines referred to in the question describe an aspect of Leonardo's personality, but the question asks you to sum up exactly what that aspect is. The line says he "loved the flowers," but he still pulled off their petals because he wanted to understand "how each was joined." Therefore his desire to learn how things worked was stronger than his affection for nature.

49. Question type: generalization

Choice **b** is correct. Lines 56–59 describe Leonardo's reaction to his punishment. Specifically, it says he did not kick the door (was not angry), and that he only briefly felt it was unfair to be punished. The best way to describe his reaction was that he accepted it and occupied himself with his own thoughts, or "resigned" himself to his punishment.

50. Question type: cause and effect

Choice **h** is correct. We know that many of the answers in this question are in fact true statements, but they do not answer the question. He may have known that his grandmother would not punish him, but nowhere does it say this had anything to do with his motivation to skip school. The answer can be found in lines 24–27, which state that Latin grammar bored him and continues on to say he therefore skipped school.

MIGRATION OF BIRDS

51. Question type: detail

Choice **b** is correct. Lines 6–7 state that every year the Arctic Tern migrates "from the Arctic to the Antarctic with subsequent return."

52. Question type: detail

Choice **g** is correct. Although the body structure of birds is well suited to migration, it is not the reason they migrate. Lines 9–10 state that this makes "it possible for birds to seek out environments most favorable to their needs at different times of the year."

53. Question type: inference

Choice **a** is correct. Lines 18–19 state that when the first migrating birds were spotted, the fur traders and Native Americans "all joined in jubilant welcome to the newcomers." Therefore it can be inferred that their relationship was a friendly one.

54. Question type: detail

Choice **f** is correct. There are many groups mentioned in association with the migrating birds, but line 34 ("bird investigations are made by the U.S. Fish and Wildlife Service") is where you will find the answer to this question.

55. Question type: generalization

Choice **c** is correct. Lines 43–44 explain that the role of the Survey was to collect data on migrating birds before the Fish and Wildlife service was established.

56. Question type: detail

Choice **j** is correct. Lines 22–24 state that birds ate the insects that were troublesome to farmers, therefore were not threats to the birds.

57. Question type: vocabulary

Choice **c** is correct. The preceding lines explain how the arrival of the birds signaled a change in season and the start of celebrations, therefore even if you do not know the meaning of the word, you can assume that the imminence of spring, means that spring was soon to arrive.

58. Question type: detail

Choice **h** is correct. Although the European fur traders appreciated the migrating birds, they did so because they indicated the arrival of spring, and were around before the increasing population of North America referred to in lines 17–19.

59. Question type: cause and effect

Choice **a** is correct. Immediately preceding the following statement: "We soon realized that our migratory bird resource was an international legacy" (lines 25–26) is a list of reasons people appreciated the migrating birds, and it does not include their being a source of food.

60. Question type: detail

Choice **j** is correct. If you only read the beginning of the last paragraph, you might think the answer is choice **g**, but if you continue reading, you learn that many others help the Fish and Wildlife Service.

SYLVIA

61. Question type: generalization

Choice **a** is correct. The first paragraph gives us the best clues as to Sylvia's mood in the entire passage. The fact that she has pulled the curtain and looked through the window is a good example of someone who is anxious.

62. Question type: inference

Choice **h** is correct. With only the last sentence of the last paragraph, "Glancing at the birds and up through the skylight at the limitless outdoors keeps her mild claustrophobia at bay," we know that she enjoys working in a space that feels open, making **h** the best answer.

63. **Question type: detail**

Choice **a** is correct. When Sylvia looks out the window, what she sees makes her think of "conditions that often precede a summer thunderstorm," which she has always been afraid of. Therefore, the best answer is choice **a**, *ominous.*

64. **Question type: inference**

Choice **f** is correct. In lines 21–22 we learn that "that the idea of sharing the apartment has actually begun to repel her" in addition, she is happy that most of the time at work she has the office to herself and that makes her happy. With these two facts in mind, we can assume she does not like to be surrounded by people.

65. **Question type: inference**

Choice **d** is correct. All we really know about the specifics of Sylvia's job is that she is a typist at a natural history museum. We do not know if it requires "concentration and attention to detail," so choice **a** is not a good choice. Her workplace is light and airy, but nothing in the passage suggests that Sylvia wants for something better, in fact she is quite content with her job, making choice **b** a bad choice as well. Sylvia is happy that her boss is not often in the office, so we know that she unlikely to have a love affair with him, and so choice **c** is not a good choice, either. We do know that Sylvia does not like to be around other people, and the stuffed birds do go along with that personality trait, therefore choice **d** is the best answer.

66. **Question type: detail**

Choice **f** is correct. In lines 12–13, we learn that when Lola called, "the moment for saying the apartment was no longer available slipped past," meaning that she wanted to tell her but missed the opportunity, making **f** the best answer.

67. **Question type: vocabulary**

Choice **c** is correct. In many cases, vocabulary questions will require you to give nonstandard definitions, and this is a good example of such a case. You probably know that the standard definition of exhausted is tired, but as it is used in the passage it means something else. Sylvia refers to her trust fund as "exhausted" and since we know that she is taking a roommate because she is running out of money, choice **c** is the best choice.

68. **Question type: detail**

Choice **g** is correct. It is true that Sylvia could not afford the rent, but this does not answer why she did not leave the house, but rather why she wanted a roommate. Choice **h** is in fact the reason why Sylvia wants to leave. Lola was late for the appointment, so Sylvia believed that she could leave without being rude, making choice **j** a bad choice. Lines 19–20 answer the question by stating "if a storm comes, she wants to be at home in her own place."

69. **Question type: inference**

Choice **c** is correct. We know in this paragraph that Lola is late for the appointment she made with Sylvia, and because Sylvia considers leaving instead of waiting patiently, the best answer is that she is irritated.

70. Question type: detail

Choice **h** is correct. This very first line states that Sylvia is looking out the window and relays what she sees, therefore, it is *her* viewpoint.

ULYSSES S. GRANT MEMOIRS

71. Question type: generalization

Choice **b** is correct. We know that statement I is untrue because line 20 states "the people of the North had no particular quarrel with slavery." Immediately following, the same lines also disprove statement III.

72. Question type: cause and effect

Choice **f** is correct. Lines 19–28 establish the argument that rapid transit was a factor, and lines 20–22 show that the North's unwillingness to legally support slavery. Although some Northerners would agree with statement III, nowhere in the passage is this stated.

73. Question type: main point

Choice **b** is correct. The author agrees with the statement in line 3: "A state half slave and half free cannot exist," which essentially means the entire country must be for or against slavery.

74. Question type: cause and effect

Choice **h** is correct. The passage says that because of the Fugitive Slave Law, Northerners were required to chase down runaway slaves. Later in the passage it says that the North was "not willing to play the role of police for the South" (lines 21–22), therefore the best answer is that it forced the North to enforce laws it did not believe were right.

75. Question type: vocabulary

Choice **d** is correct. Because it is clear that the North did not approve of the Fugitive Slave Law, the power they would be seeking would be to "remove" such laws from the books.

76. Question type: detail

Choice **j** is correct. The answer to this question is found in line 13, simply put "they saw their power waning, and this led them to encroach upon the prerogatives and independence of the Northern States by enacting such laws as the Fugitive Slave Law."

77. Question type: generalization

Choice **b** is correct. Lines 31–33 have the answer to this question. Be careful not to use any outside knowledge of the Civil War, in this case, choices **a** and **d** are in fact correct, but they are not discussed in the paragraph mentioned.

78. Question type: generalization

Choice **f** is correct. The author describes the U.S. as expanding in size, wealth and population in lines 43–44, and then line 45 claims Europe may think the United States would threaten their peace. Another way of saying this is that they are threatened by our unified strength.

79. Question type: inference

Choice **a** is correct. Because Grant goes on to say that it "would part the moment the slightest strain was brought upon it," means that the only appropriate answer is weakly connected.

80. **Question type: point of view**

Choice **h** is correct. In lines 40–41, Grant, in effect, says that we should "avoid war," which makes choices **g** and **j** incorrect. In lines 29–30, he says that we are better off after having the war, which makes choice **f** incorrect, and **h** the best choice.

6 ▶ ACT Science Reasoning Test Practice

▶ Overview: About the ACT Science Reasoning Test

The most important thing you should know about this test is that it is not a science test, but instead a *reasoning* test. Unlike tests that you may have taken in high school, the ACT Science Reasoning Test does not assess your knowledge of a particular science topic. Rather, it is designed to test your ability to understand and learn scientific material. During this test, you will be asked this interpret, evaluate, analyze, draw conclusions, and make predictions about the information presented to you. In fact, whether the passage is about biology, chemistry, earth and space science, or physics will not matter. You will be provided with all the information you need, right in the passage.

Some science topics that you might already be familiar with include:

Biology
- the structure of cells
- molecular basis of heredity
- biological evolution
- interdependence of organisms

- matter, energy, and organization in living systems
- the behavior of organisms

Chemistry
- the structure of atoms
- the properties of matter
- chemical reactions

Earth and Space Science
- geology
- astronomy
- meteorology

Physics
- motions and forces
- conservation of energy and matter
- interactions of energy and matter

To learn more about these science topics, refer to the glossary found on page 318.

You will have 40 minutes to complete the 35 questions on the ACT Science Reasoning Test. When you begin the test, you will see instructions similar to the following:

> *The passages in this test are followed by several questions. After reading a passage, choose the best answer to each question and fill in the corresponding oval on the answer sheet. You may refer to the passages as often as necessary. You are not permitted to use a calculator on this section of the test.*

The "passages" mentioned in the directions will be a main component of the ACT Science Reasoning Test, since they are the basis for answering the questions. There are a total of seven passages each followed by up to six questions. Some passages are longer than others, but you should be able to read each one in about two minutes. It's important to know that "passages" does not only mean written information; there may be text, figures, charts, diagrams, tables, or any combination of these.

The seven passages fall into three skill categories: Data Representation, Research Summaries, and Conflicting Viewpoints.

Data Representation simply means graphs, tables, and other graphical forms. The questions that follow data representation passages test your ability to:
- read and understand scatter plots, graphs, tables, diagrams, charts, figures, etc.
- interpret scatter plots, graphs, tables, diagrams, charts, figures, etc.

- The passages before questions may be a *single* graphic or passage, a *series* of graphics or passages, or a *combination* of both graphics and written passages.
- Some passages might be longer than others. Some may take as long as two minutes to go through.
- A question following a graphic passage may also include a separate graphic.
- Answer choices may include graphics.
- Questions may include some math, but do *not* require a calculator since they can't be used on this section of the ACT.
- Like all the other tests on the ACT, there is no penalty for guessing, so you should always try to answer every question on the test.

- compare and interpret information presented in scatter plots, graphs, tables, diagrams, charts, figures, etc.
- draw conclusions about the information provided
- make predictions about the data
- develop hypotheses based on the data

Research Summaries are descriptions or results of one or more related experiments. The questions that follow research summary passages test your ability to:
- understand the design of experiments
- summarize results
- interpret experimental results
- draw conclusions about the information provided
- make predictions about the research results
- develop hypotheses based on the research

Conflicting Viewpoints are two or more related hypotheses or ideas that are inconsistent with one another. The questions that follow conflicting viewpoint passages test your ability to:
- read and understand several related but inconsistent hypotheses or views
- recognize different points of view
- understand, analyze, and compare alternative viewpoints or hypotheses
- draw conclusions about the information provided

Approximately 38% of the questions are Data Representation, approximately 45% are Research Summaries, and about 17% are Conflicting Viewpoints.

▶ Pretest

As you did with the reading, English, and math sections, take the following pretest before you begin the Science Reasoning lessons in this chapter. The questions are the same type you will find on the ACT. When you are finished, check the answer key on page 257 to assess your results. Your pretest score will help you determine in which areas you need the most careful review and practice. For a glossary of science terms, refer to page 318 at the end of this chapter.

Passage I

The following data table represents the population of both wolves and deer during the years 1955–1980 in a given area.

Table 1

	1955	1960	1965	1970	1975	1980
Wolves	52	68	75	60	45	49
Deer	325	270	220	210	120	80

1. Which of the following statements is true about the years 1955–1980?
   a. The population of the wolves increased over time.
   b. The population of the deer decreased at a constant rate over time.
   c. The population of the wolves increased initially, but decreased after 1965.
   d. The population of the deer decreased over time.

2. Between which years is the greatest difference in the population of wolves?
   f. 1955–1960
   g. 1960–1975
   h. 1955–1975
   j. 1975–1980

3. Which of the following statements is true of the wolf population from 1955–1980?
   a. The wolf population increased at a constant rate until 1975.
   b. The wolf population decreased at a constant rate after 1970.
   c. The increase in the wolf population was a result of the decrease in deer population.
   d. The wolf population increased from 1955 to 1965, decreased from 1965 to 1975, and increased again in 1980.

4. What would be an appropriate title for the bar graph below?

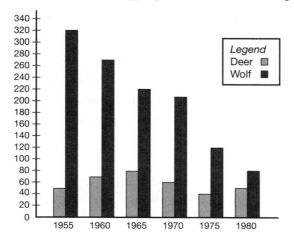

f. The Effects of Hunting on the Deer and Wolf Population, 1955–1980

g. Deer Population over 25 years

h. Deer and Wolf Population, 1955 to 1980

j. Wildlife Population, 1955 to 1980

5. Which of the following would NOT explain the sharp decline in the deer population between 1970 and 1975?

a. The number of registered hunters in the area increased by 60%.

b. The number of wolves also declined.

c. A major forest fire occurred in 1972.

d. Over 150 new homes were built in the deer's habitat.

Passage II

Mark's chemistry project was to study the structure of crystals of the amino acids glycine and L-alanine. First, this involved growing large enough crystals for analysis. Most crystals are grown from supersaturated solutions. Supersaturated solutions have an excess amount of solute dissolved in a solvent at a given temperature. To prepare samples, Mark combined 2 g of water with 40% more amino acid than is normally soluble in that amount of water at room temperature. He then heated the samples until the amino acid completely dissolved and allowed them to slowly cool to room temperature.

With glycine, Mark obtained crystals suitable for analysis in 17 out of 20 samples and he was able to collect the data he needed. With L-alanine, he ran into problems. Namely, none of the L-alanine samples crystallized. He tried to increase the supersaturation by dissolving 50%, 60% and 70% more L-alanine in excess of solubility, to increase the driving force for crystallization in these samples. But that didn't seem to help.

After a few weeks, Mark observed a cotton-like substance in some of his L-alanine samples. He was sure that these weren't L-alanine crystals. After spending some time in the library, he found that the amino acid L-alanine, is prone to bacterial attack. He hypothesized that bacteria were eating his samples and that the cotton-like substance was a bacterial byproduct. He prepared 20 new L-alanine samples. All of the samples were 40% supersaturated in 2 g of water at room temperature. Mark took great care to keep his samples sterile. He used water that had been passed through a 0.22 μm filter and treated by UV rays. Mark was able to obtain crystals from 15 out of 20 solutions.

6. The goal of Mark's research was:
   f. to eliminate bacteria from his samples.
   g. to determine why L-alanine didn't crystallize.
   h. to heat his samples without damaging them.
   j. to grow and analyze the crystals of two amino acids.

7. According to the passage above, what best supports the statement, "40% supersaturation is sufficient for glycine crystal growth at room temperature."
   a. L-alanine is prone to bacterial attack.
   b. When Mark increased the supersaturation to 50%, he obtained crystals.
   c. Crystals formed in 40% supersaturated samples, prepared using filtered and treated water.
   d. Filtering water causes crystallization in all samples.

8. If filtering water through a 0.22 μm filter, without UV treatment, were enough to eliminate the bacterial attack problem, what could be said about the bacteria in Mark's samples?
   f. They are too large to pass through a 0.22 μm filter.
   g. They are too small to pass through a 0.22 μm filter.
   h. After passing through a 0.22 μm filter, the L-alanine stops being a food source for the bacteria.
   j. After passing through a 0.22 μm filter, the bacteria stops being a food source for L-alanine.

9. It can be inferred from the passage that UV treatment is used to:
   a. increase supersaturation in solutions of amino acids.
   b. cause skin cancer in tanning salons.
   c. kill microorganisms.
   d. filter solutions of amino acids.

10. Mark's hypothesis that he wasn't obtaining crystals because bacteria were feeding on his samples:
   f. was probably correct.
   g. was probably incorrect.
   h. was not formed in accordance with the scientific method.
   j. could not be tested.

Passage III

IS PLUTO A PLANET?

Scientist 1

Based on perturbations in Neptune's orbit, the search for a ninth planet was conducted, and Pluto was discovered in 1930. Pluto orbits the Sun just as the other eight planets do, and it has a moon, Charon, and a stable orbit. Based on its distance from the Sun, Pluto should be grouped with the planets known as gas giants. In addition, Pluto, like the planet Mercury, has little or no atmosphere. Pluto is definitely not a comet because it does not have a tail like a comet when it is near the Sun. Pluto is also not an asteroid, although its density is closer to an asteroid than to any of the other planets. Pluto is a planet because it has been classified as one for more than sixty years since its discovery.

Scientist 2

Pluto should no longer be classified as a planet based on new evidence that has come to light in the last few years. When Pluto was first discovered, nothing was known about its orbit or its composition. Pluto has an orbit that is not in the same plane as the other planets (i.e., it is tilted) and its orbit is more eccentric, or elongated than any other planet's orbit. Pluto orbits the Sun in the outer solar system, and so should be similar in size and composition to the gas giants, but it is not. Pluto lacks rings that all other gas giants possess. Also, Pluto's moon is larger than any other moon relative to its parent planet. In recent years, new objects have been found which belong to the Kuiper Belt, a region of small solid icy bodies that orbit the Sun beyond the orbit of Neptune and Pluto. A large object called Quaoar has recently been discovered which has a density nearly identical to Pluto, Charon, and Triton. Based on these facts, I conclude that Pluto is a Kuiper Belt object.

11. Scientist 1 states that "Based on its distance from the Sun, Pluto should be grouped with the planets knows as gas giants." Which of the following statements made by Scientist 2 opposes Scientist 1's belief that Pluto is a gas planet?
   a. Pluto's moon is larger than any other moon relative to its parent planet.
   b. A large object called Quaoar has recently been discovered which has a density nearly identical to Pluto, Charon, and Triton.
   c. Pluto has an orbit that is not in the same plane as the other planets (i.e., it is tilted) and its orbit is more eccentric, or elongated than any other planet's orbit.
   d. Pluto lacks rings that all other gas giants possess.

12. What do both scientists agree upon?

    f. Pluto is like Mercury.

    g. Pluto is a Kuiper Belt Object.

    h. Pluto orbits the sun.

    j. Charon is a planet.

13. Which of the following are reasons why Scientist 2 believes Pluto should NOT be classified as a planet?

    I. Pluto has no atmosphere.

    II. Pluto is similar in composition to Quaoar.

    III. Pluto has the most eccentric orbit of all the planets.

    IV. Pluto's orbit is not in the same plane as the orbits of the other planets.

    a. II and III only

    b. I, III, and IV

    c. III and IV only

    d. II, III, and IV

14. Based on composition and density, Pluto is a:

    f. Kuiper Belt Object.

    g. Earth-like planet.

    h. comet.

    j. gas giant planet.

15. Based on the information presented by Scientist 2, what is a possible origin for Neptune's moon, Triton?

    a. Triton is a natural moon of Neptune.

    b. Triton is a captured Kuiper Belt Object.

    c. Triton is a captured asteroid.

    d. Triton is a captured comet.

► Pretest Answers and Explanations

Passage I

1. d. As seen in Table 1, the deer population decreased over time, but not at a constant rate.

2. g. The greatest difference between the numbers of population among the choices is from 1960–1975 which was 23. All other choices were less than 23.

3. d. If you look at the top row of Table 1, you see that the wolf population increased in the first 10 years from 52 to 75. From 1965 the wolf population decreased from 75 down to 45 in 1975, and finally increased again in 1980.

4. h. The bar graph shows nothing about the effects of hunting (choice **f**) nor does it show any other animals besides deer and wolves (choice **j**). Only choice **h** is an appropriate title for the bar graph.

5. b. A major forest fire, the decrease in habitat, as well increased hunting could all explain the sharp decline in the deer population. Just because the wolf population also decreased is not enough to indicate a cause for the decrease in deer.

Passage II

6. j. The goal of the project is stated in the first sentence of the passage. Eliminating bacteria (choice **f**) and determining why L-alanine didn't crystallize (choice **g**) sidetracked Mark for a while, but his goal remained unchanged. While not overheating the samples is probably a good idea (choice **h**), there was no mention of it in the passage, and it wasn't the ultimate goal of the experiment.

7. c. The statement is best supported by the fact that Mark eventually did get crystals at that supersaturation. Choice **a** is true, but unrelated to the statements under quotation marks. Choices **b** and **d** are not true.

8. f. Filtration separates particles by size. Water molecules are small enough to pass through the filter, but the bacteria are too large.

9. c. UV was used to sterilize the solutions, to rid them of bacteria, also known as *microorganisms.* Choice **a** is incorrect because there was no mention of the UV when Mark tried making the supersaturation higher, and there was no mention of supersaturation when he treated the solutions with the UV. Choice **b** was not mentioned in the text. Choice **d** is not correct because while the UV and filtration were used for the same purpose (getting rid of L-alanine munching bacteria), there was no mention that these two methods were connected.

10. f. Before adopting the technique to eliminate bacteria, the student didn't get any crystals. Once he reduced the possibility of bacterial attack, he obtained crystals in most of the samples.

Passage III

11. d. Only the statement "Pluto lacks rings that all other gas giants possess," opposes the statement made by Scientist 1.

12. h. If you read both passages carefully, only one fact appears in both. Scientist 1 states, "Pluto orbits the Sun just as the other eight planets do," and Scientist 2 states, "Pluto orbits the Sun in the outer solar system."

13. d. According to Scientist 2, the factors that separate Pluto are its different density, composition, and orbital characteristics, which are more like those of the Kuiper Belt Objects than the planets.

14. f. Pluto, Charon, and Neptune's moon Triton all have densities and compositions similar to the newly discovered object Quaoar. This infers that they are all bodies originally from the Kuiper Belt.

15. b. Triton's similar density and composition to Quaoar are evidence that indicate that it is an object that was captured by Neptune's gravity at some point in the early formation of the solar system.

▶ Lessons and Practice Questions

Types of Scientific Reasoning Test Questions

The science component of the ACT is a test in reasoning. You will do well if you hone your skills in:

- recognizing a pattern in scientific data.
- understanding and analyzing scientific material.
- interpreting graphs, charts, tables, and diagrams.
- summarizing observations of an experiment.
- making generalizations.
- making comparisons.
- supporting a generalization or hypothesis.
- predicting behavior given a pattern or trend.
- making inferences based on the information provided.
- drawing conclusions based on the information provided.

The following lessons will help you master these skills, so that even if you have never taken physics, you will be able to answer a physics question correctly, just by carefully reading the passage.

While it's a good idea to get comfortable with a basic science vocabulary, memorizing your science textbook and every equation in it will not necessarily help you. To prepare for this exam, you shouldn't study, you should practice, practice, practice. This means, review as many examples as you come across, and take as many practice tests as you can get your hands on. Make sure that after scoring your practice tests, you go back to the questions you answered incorrectly or to the questions you were unsure about. Read science-related articles in newspapers and technical journals. Think about the charts, graphs, and diagrams you come across, even if they are not science related. This way you will get used to dealing with unfamiliar technical terms and interpreting graphical information. Sound good? Let's begin.

DATA REPRESENTATION

Graphics are a concise and organized way of presenting information. Once you realize that all graphics have some common basic elements, it will not matter whether the information presented in them is in the area of biology, chemistry, earth and space science, physics, or even bubble gum sales.

Consider the following train schedule:

	A.M.	A.M.	A.M.	A.M.	P.M.	P.M.	P.M.	P.M.
Congers Station	12:21	3:20	6:19	9:19	12:19	3:19	6:19	9:19
New City	12:32	3:30	6:30	9:30	12:30	3:30	6:30	9:30
Valley Cottage	12:39	3:37	6:37	9:37	12:37	3:37	6:37	9:37
Nyack	12:48	3:45	6:46	9:46	12:46	3:46	6:46	9:46
West Nyack	12:53	3:53	6:54	9:54	12:54	3:54	6:54	9:54
Bardonia	1:06	4:03	7:05	10:05	1:05	4:05	7:05	10:05

By looking at the table, you can determine:

- the times the trains leave Congers Station (12:21 A.M., 3:20 A.M., 6:19 A.M., 9:19 A.M., 12:19 P.M., 3:19 P.M., 6:19 P.M., and 9:19 P.M.).
- the times they get to West Nyack (12:53 A.M., 3:53 A.M., 6:54 A.M., 9:54 P.M., 12:54 P.M., 3:54 P.M., 6:54 P.M., and 9:54 P.M.).
- how often the trains run (about every 3 hours).
- how long it takes the train to get from New City to Valley Cottage (7 minutes).

Imagine how many lines of text would be required to describe this schedule without using a table, and how much more confusing and complicated it would be for a passenger to get the basic information in the examples above. The point is that tables, graphs, charts, figures, and diagrams are useful and without realizing it, you analyze graphical information on a daily basis.

The only difference between these everyday encounters of graphical information and the ACT is that on this test the information in the graphics will be of a scientific nature and you may run into words or concepts you have never heard of before. But just because you don't know what a diffusion coefficient, a refractive index, or a stem cell is, it doesn't mean that you won't be able to analyze graphical information in which these unfamiliar concepts are mentioned. Did you need to know where Bardonia is to analyze the train schedule above? No. All you did was realize that each row (horizontal) listed the times at which the trains arrive at that station, and that each column (vertical) listed the times at which one train that left Congers Station would arrive at other stations on the way to Bardonia.

You see? You don't need an amazing science vocabulary to do well on the ACT. In fact, using information not presented in the exam question could harm you, since test instructions tell you to only use what you are given. Going back to our train schedule example, if you happen to live on the Bardonia line, you may know that the trains on that line leave every 30 minutes (not every 3 hours) during the day. But if the schedule were on the exam, and you were asked how often the train runs, based on the information provided, your answer would be marked wrong if you answered that it runs every 30 minutes.

In the following sections, you will learn to recognize the common elements and trends in information presented in graphical form. You will also read some suggestions on approaching the types of graphical representation questions that often appear on the ACT.

Table Basics

All tables are composed of rows (horizontal) and columns (vertical). Entries in a single row of a table usually have something in common, and so do entries in a single column. Look at the table below that lists the thermal conductivities (in Watts per meter Kelvin) as a function of temperature (in Kelvin).

ELEMENT	TEMPERATURE [K]					
	100	200	300	400	500	600
Aluminum	300	237	273	240	237	232
Copper	483	413	309	392	388	383
Gold	345	327	315	312	309	304
Iron	132	94	80	69	61	55
Platinum	79	75	73	72	72	72

You only need the table to answer the following questions.

1. Which one of the metals listed has the highest thermal conductivity at 300 K?

2. At what temperature does gold have the lowest thermal conductivity?

3. How does the thermal conductivity for aluminum change in the range of temperatures given?

To answer question number one, you would look at the column that lists the thermal conductivities at 300 K. You would see that the highest number in that column is 398. You would place your finger on that number and use the finger as a guide across the row, all the way to the left to see which metal has a conductivity of 398 watts per meter Kelvin. And you would see that the row you selected lists the thermal conductivities of copper.

Question number two is very similar to question number one, but now you are asked to find the maximum number in a row (gold), and determine to which column it corresponds. In the row listing the thermal conductivities of gold, the highest number is 345. Put your finger on it and use it as a guide, straight to the top of that column to see that the thermal conductivity of gold is at the maximum at 100 K.

In question three, you are asked to describe a trend. This is another common question type. Is there a change? Do the numbers increase? Decrease? Randomly change (no trend)? Looking at the row of data for aluminum, you can conclude that the thermal conductivity for this metal first increases, and then between 300 K and 400 K, it begins to decrease.

Graph Basics

The most common types of graphs are scatter plots, bar graphs, and pie graphs. What follows is an explanation of each, with examples you can use for practice.

SCATTER PLOTS

Whenever a variable depends continuously on another variable, this dependence can be visually represented in a scatter plot. Examples include a change in a property or an event as a function of time (population growth) and change in a property as a function of temperature (density). A scatter plot consists of the horizontal (x) axis, the vertical (y) axis, and collected data points for variable y, measured at variable x. The variable points are often connected with a line or a curve. A graph often contains a legend, especially if there is more then one data set or more than one variable. A legend is a key for interpreting the graph. Much like a legend on a map lists the symbols used to label an interstate highway, a railroad line, or a city, a legend for a graph lists the symbols used to label a particular data set. Look at the sample graph above. The essential elements of the graph—the x- and y-axis—are labeled. The legend to the right of the graph shows that dots are used to represent the variable points in data set 1, while squares are used to represent the variable points in data set 2. If only one data set exists, the use of a legend is not essential.

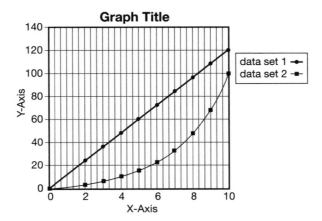

Now let's see how we can answer graphical representation questions effectively by understanding and analyzing the information presented in a graph. Look at the example below.

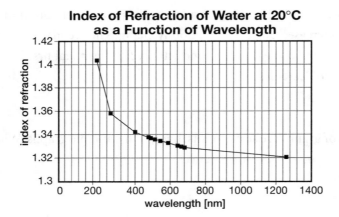

The variable on the *x*-axis is the wavelength. The index of refraction of water is the variable on the *y*-axis. The thick black line connects the data points collected by measuring the index of refraction at different wavelengths.

What can you tell about the index of refraction of water from the graph above? For one, you can get an estimate of the refractive index at a particular wavelength. How would you find the index of refraction at a wavelength of 500 nm? First, find 500 nm on the horizontal *x*-axis. But there is no 500 nm! Sure, 500 nm is not explicitly labeled, but you can expect it to be exactly between 400 nm and 600 nm, which *are* labeled. There are four grid divisions between 400 and 600, so each division corresponds to a 50 nm increment. Once you locate 500 nm, put your finger on it to use as a guide. Move it up along the gridline until it meets the thick black line connecting the data points. Now, determine the index of refraction that corresponds to that wavelength by carefully guiding your finger from the point where the 500 nm gridline crosses the data curve to the vertical y-axis, all the way on the left. The refractive index of water at 500 nm is almost 1.34.

By looking at the graph, you can also say that the index of refraction of water ranges from 1.32 to 1.4. What can you say about the trend? How does the index of refraction vary with increasing wavelength? It first rapidly decreases, and then slowly levels off around 1.32. For practice, try to look for scatter plots with different trends—including:

- increase
- decrease
- rapid increase, followed by leveling off
- slow increase, followed by rapid increase
- rise to a maximum, followed by a decrease
- rapid decrease, followed by leveling off (as in the wavelength example)
- slow decrease, followed by rapid decrease
- decrease to a minimum, followed by a rise
- predictable fluctuation (periodic change, such as a light wave)
- random fluctuation (irregular change)

Do you see how you didn't need to know a thing about refraction to understand the graph?

There are also graphs on which several different variables are plotted against a common variable. See the following chart with levels of three different hormones in the female body (FSH, LH, and progesterone) throughout the menstrual cycle.

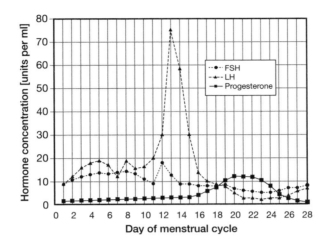

Here, there are three different sets of data, one set for each hormone. Different sets are labeled using different symbols for data points—a circle for FSH, a triangle for LH, and a square for progesterone, as shown in the legend in the top right corner of the graph.

Using this graph you can determine the concentration of a particular hormone on a particular day in the cycle. For example, the concentration of FSH on day 12 of the cycle is about 20 units per ml. To obtain this answer, first find the data line that corresponds to FSH, and then locate the point at which day 12 grid-line intersects the FSH line. Finally, slide your finger from the point of intersection to the *y*-axis, and read the corresponding concentration.

You can also use the graph to make general statements about the change of hormone concentrations throughout the cycle. For example, the concentration of LH is highest around the day 13 of the cycle. Using the graph, you can also compare the concentrations of different hormones on the same day. For example, the concentration of progesterone is higher than the concentration of FSH on day 21 of the menstrual cycle.

BAR GRAPHS

Bar graphs are similar to scatter plots. Both have a variable *y* plotted against a variable *x*. However, in bar graphs, data are represented by bars, rather than by points connected with a line. Bar graphs are often used to indicate an amount or level, as opposed to a continuous change. Consider the bar graph on the next page. It illustrates the prevalence of hypertension among different age groups.

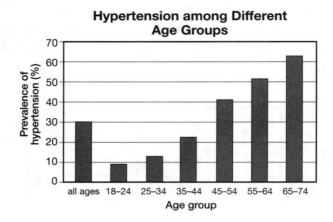

Hypertension among Different Age Groups

You could immediately see that hypertension is more prevalent in older age groups. You could also say that at the prevalence of hypertension in the 45–54 age group (more than 40%) exceeds the average prevalence among all age groups (30%). This graph could have been packed with more information. It could have included the hypertension prevalence among men and women. In that case, there would be three bars for each age group, and each bar would be labeled (for men, women, and both sexes) by using a different shading pattern, for example.

Some bar graphs have horizontal bars, rather than vertical bars. Don't be alarmed if you see them on the ACT. You could analyze them using the same skills you would for analyzing a bar graph with vertical bars.

PIE GRAPHS

Pie graphs are often used to show what percent of a total is taken up by different components of that whole. The pie chart below illustrates the relative productivity (new plant material produced in one year) of different biomes (desert, tundra, etc.).

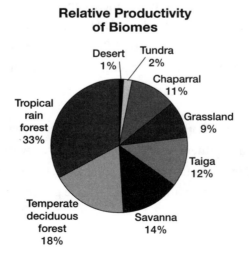

Relative Productivity of Biomes

If this chart appeared on the ACT, you could be asked for the percent of total world productivity of a specific biome. For example, savannas make up 14% of the total productivity. Or you may be asked which biome is the most productive (tropical rain forest) and which one is the least productive (desert). You could also be asked to compare the productivity of two different biomes. For example, you could state that temperate deciduous forest productivity (18%) exceeds the taiga productivity (12%).

A test passage may also present you with two different, but related, pie charts and ask you to compare them. For example, humans can have one of four different blood types (A, B, AB, and O). The percent of people with a particular blood group is different in different geographic (gene pool) areas. You could be asked to compare a pie chart illustrating the blood group distribution in Europe with another pie chart illustrating the blood group distribution in Asia.

Diagrams

Diagrams could be used to show a sequence of events, a process, the setup of a science experiment, a phenomenon, or the relationship between different events or beings. Here are some examples that you might find in your science textbooks:

- diagram of the phases of cell division (Biology)—sequence of events
- diagrams showing the oxygen and nitrogen cycle (Earth and Space Science)—process
- diagram illustrating the titration technique (Chemistry)—setup of an experiment
- diagram showing the focusing of a lens (Physics)—phenomenon
- pedigree diagram for color-blindness (Biology)—relationship between events

When you see a diagram, first ask yourself what the purpose of it is. What is it trying to illustrate? Then look at the different labeled parts of the diagram. What is their function? How are they interrelated? Take a look at the diagram below:

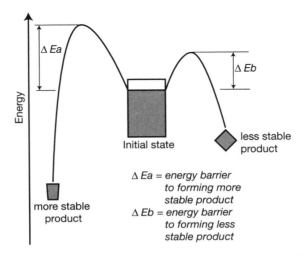

In this diagram, we can see an initial state, connected to two different products. Immediately, we can say that two different products can form from the initial state. And, according to the label, the product represented by the diamond is less stable than the product represented by the cup shaped figure. We also notice that the top portion of the curve connecting the initial states to the products is an energy barrier (explained in the legend in the lower right corner of the diagram). All the way on the left of the diagram, there is an arrow, pointing up and labeled "Energy." Putting all this information together, we should be able to state the following:

- The diagram shows the energy of an initial state and the two products that can result from it.
- The energy of the less stable product is higher than the energy of the more stable product.
- The energy of the initial state is higher than the energy of either product.
- The energy barrier for the formation of the less stable product is lower than the energy barrier for the formation of the more stable product.

The Main Idea

To quickly answer ACT questions on data representation, it's important to get the big picture, or main idea of the graph, table, or diagram before you get bogged down in the details. The best way to do this is to first look at the title of the graphic you are presented with, if there is one. This will give you a summary of what the graphic is showing. The names of some of the graphics used in preceding examples were left out. Can you come up with appropriate titles for those graphics? After looking at the title, look at the axes, if there are any. What are the variables? Then look at legends and labels if they are included. Only when you understand what the graph is portraying and how the information is organize should you look for specific, detailed information. In the long run, this strategy will save you time and provide you with a sense of purpose and direction.

Types of Data Representation Questions

Most data representation questions on the ACT fall into one of these categories:

- Interpretation (reading a table, graph, or diagram)
- Comparison (making a statement about two or more different data points)
- Making predictions (interpolation and extrapolation)
- Drawing conclusions (using data to make a general statement)

We will discuss each question type separately in the paragraphs and examples that follow.

INTERPRETATION

Questions about one specific piece of information presented in a graphic are usually interpretation questions. Questions of this type tend to be easier, and involve only reading the graphic correctly. Examples (using graphics already reviewed in this chapter) include:

1. What time does the train that leaves Congers Station at 12:19 P.M. arrive to Nyack?

2. What is the thermal conductivity of iron at 400 K?

3. What is the index of refraction of water at 400 nm?

4. What is the concentration of LH on the day 15 of the menstrual cycle?

5. In which age groups is the prevalence of hypertension less than 20%?

6. What is the relative productivity of grasslands?

Answer these questions for practice and then look at the answers below to check how you've done.

Answers
1. 12:46 P.M.
2. 69 W/m K
3. about 1.34
4. 30 units/ml
5. 18–24 and 25–34
6. 9%

COMPARISON

Comparison questions involve making a statement about the relative magnitude or relative change in magnitude of two or more data points, or about the trends in different sets of data. The best strategy for answering this type of question is to first find the data you are asked about, and then to compare them. Here are sample questions, based on graphics used as examples in previous sections.

1. Does it take more time to get from Congers Station to New City, or from New City to Valley Cottage?

2. Which metal has the lowest thermal conductivity at 100 K?

3. Is the concentration of progesterone greater in the first or the second half of the menstrual cycle?

4. Which biome has a productivity that is closest to the productivity of taiga?

Answers

1. Congers Station to New City takes more time

2. Platinum

3. It's greater in the second half

4. Chaparral

MAKING PREDICTIONS

ACT questions that require you to make a prediction tend to be the most difficult, since they require true understanding. However, if you learn to interpolate and extrapolate, you will improve your ability to answer even the most difficult questions.

To interpolate means to estimate the value of y for a value of x (or vice versa) between tabulated or graphed points. An example of interpolation would be estimating the thermal conductivity of copper at 250 K. What you would need to do is to is locate the adjacent temperature data points (200 K and 300 K) and read the thermal conductivity at those temperatures. That would give you a range in which the thermal conductivity at 250 has to fall in. If the change of thermal conductivity with temperature were linear (constant slope, i.e. constant change with a fixed increment in temperature), it would be sufficient to get an average of the thermal conductivities at the adjacent temperatures. But if two choices on the ACT were both in the acceptable range of thermal conductivities, you would probably need to make a rough scatter plot of a few data points (with the temperature on the x-axis, and the thermal conductivity on the y-axis). Connect the points with a line or curve, and then determine whether the conductivity at 250 K is closer to the conductivity at 200 K, or to the conductivity at 300 K. That should help you reduce your choices to the correct answer. Here is the quick scatter plot just described.

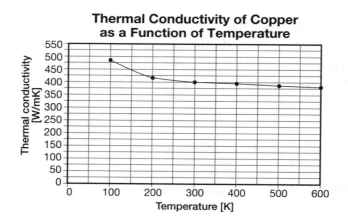

As you can see, the thermal conductivity of copper at 250 K is 400 W/m K, much closer to the thermal conductivity at 300 K, than to the thermal conductivity at 200 K.

To extrapolate means to estimate the value of a variable beyond the range of the data provided. When you extrapolate, you assume that a trend you have observed extends all directions (future, past, increasing temperature, decreasing temperature, etc.). Most commonly (and conveniently) data extrapolation is performed on scatter plots. Here is an example. The scatter plot shows the concentration of a reactant (consumed in a chemical reaction) as a function of time.

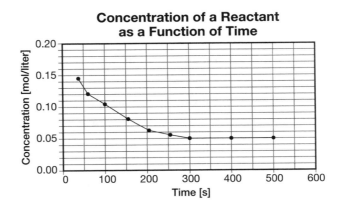

Notice that data were not taken at the beginning of the experiment (zero seconds) and beyond 500 seconds. If you assume that the thick line will maintain its shape in both directions, you can solve this problem. At the beginning of the experiment the concentration of the reactant was at a maximum. Therefore, it had to be higher than 0.15 mol/liter. If you extend the thick data line to the *y*-axis (the gridline corresponding to zero seconds), while maintaining the shape of the curve, you can estimate the initial concentration of the reactant was about 0.18 mol/liter. How about the concentration at 600 seconds? At 300 seconds, the concentration of the reactant seems to have leveled of at 0.05 mol/liter. It stays the same at 400 seconds, at 450 seconds, and 500 seconds. Wouldn't you bet that the concentration will remain 0.05 mol/l at 600 seconds?

DRAWING CONCLUSIONS

To draw a conclusion, we take all available facts into account, and make a decision or statement based on all these facts put together.

> *Question:* Did he do it?
> *Facts:* The accused had a motive, no alibi, and the unfortunate luck of being seen by the nosy neighbor.
> *Conclusion:* The accused is guilty.

In the case of science, in very much the same way, we need to pull all the information available together, sum it up, and make a judgment or prediction.

Example 1

Question: If you were looking for a metal whose heat transfer properties didn't vary much over a wide range of temperature, which metal from the list in the preceding example would you use?

Facts: Thermal conductivity of platinum hardly changes with temperature. The variation of other metals with temperature is greater.

Conclusion: Platinum.

Example 2

Facts: The average woman ovulates on the 14th day of her cycle. Release of the ovum from the ovary is hormonally stimulated.

Question: Which hormone is most responsible for ovulation?

More facts (after looking at the scatter plot): The concentration of LH, rapidly increases from the day 11 to day 13 of the cycle, immediately preceding the ovulation event, and then it rapidly drops.

Conclusion: The concentration of LH increases to stimulate ovulation. Once ovulation occurs, the concentration of LH decreases, since more stimulation is not required. One ovum is enough.

Summary

In this lesson you learned about different types of graphical representation, including tables, scatter plots, bar graphs, pie graphs, and diagrams. You now have an idea of which graphical representation is most useful for a given scenario, that for example, pie graphs are used to show the portion of a whole taken up by a subset of that whole. You know how to locate the essential elements of graphical representation (axes, labels, titles, and legends), and how to find and interpret the information you are asked about. You can look for trends (such as increasing and decreasing), compare different sets of data, interpolate and extrapolate, as well as draw conclusions and make predictions. However, having these skills up your sleeve is only a start, you will need a great deal of practice. (See page 283 for ACT Science Reasoning Test practice questions.)

RESEARCH SUMMARIES

Research Summary passages require you to read one or more related experiments and to analyze them to correctly answer the questions that follow. Each experiment has more or less the same structure. There is a purpose—to prove or disprove some hypothesis, to determine what material is best for an application, what conditions are favorable, or to find what might be causing problems with an experiment.

This lesson will help you develop skills you will need to:

- read and understand descriptions of one or more related experiments.
- draw conclusions and make predictions based on the research results.

Reading with Understanding

As you are reading descriptions of experiments, stay focused on what you are reading by underlining key concepts, making notes on the side of the text, and keeping the following questions in mind:

- How many experiments are discussed in the passage?
- What is the purpose of the experiment(s)?
- What are the variables in the experiment?
- Which variables are controlled by the scientist, and how?
- Which variables are measured or observed, and how?
- Were any calculations performed?
- Is there an experimental control? If so, what is it?
- If more than one experiment is presented, how is each experiment similar/different?

Take a look at the following example:

Example 1

A student working in an optics lab needs a filter that will transmit (pass through) more than 90% of green light, while absorbing (getting rid of) 95% of near-infrared light. She finds six filters in the lab, but they are not labeled, so she is not sure whether any of them will work.

She has a 632 nm green laser, a 1,064 nm near-infrared laser, and a suitable detector. She decides to measure the intensity of each laser with the detector, and then to mount different filters in the path of each of the lasers, recording the transmitted intensity with the detector.

The data she obtains are tabulated below:

Filter	Laser	Initial Intensity [Units of Intensity]	Transmitted Intensity [Units of Intensity]	% Light Transmitted	% Light Absorbed
1	near IR	500	35	7	93
2	near IR	500	200	40	60
3	near IR	500	15	3	97
4	near IR	500	300	60	40
5	near IR	500	100	20	80
6	near IR	500	400	80	20

Filter	Laser	Initial Intensity [Units of Intensity]	Transmitted Intensity [Units of Intensity]	% Light Transmitted	% Light Absorbed
1	green	400	358	92	8
2	green	400	320	80	20
3	green	400	388	97	3
4	green	400	280	70	30
5	green	400	160	40	60
6	green	400	80	20	80

Have you read the passage and looked at the data carefully? Answer the relevant questions listed at the beginning of the lesson.

1. How many experiments are discussed in the passage?
   Just one.

2. What is the purpose of the experiment(s)?
   To find a filter that satisfies specified criteria.

3. What are the variables in the experiment?
   There are six different filters and two different lasers (of different intensity and wavelength—green and near-IR). Amount of different type of laser light transmitted by a particular filter is also a variable.

4. Which variables are controlled by the scientist and how?
   The wavelength is controlled, using two different lasers. Different filters are aligned in the path of the lasers.

5. Which variables are measured or observed and how?
   The initial intensity of each laser is measured using a detector. Intensity of light (for each of the lasers) transmitted through each filter is measured using the detector as well.

6. Are any calculations performed?
   The table lists the percentages of light transmitted and light absorbed. That information was neither measured nor given, so it must have been obtained using a calculation.

As you can see, quickly answering for yourself these few simple questions enables you to determine the functions of different parts of the experiment, and to stay focused on what is important. Here is another example:

Example 2

Meal moths are one of the most common pantry pests. They often nest in flour, cereal, pasta, seeds, and dried fruits they find in kitchen and pantry cabinets. A scientist decided to compare the effectiveness of different methods of ridding the household from this pest. The scientist wanted to know how the total number of adult moths would vary over time when

1. all food is removed.
2. a commercial pesticide is used but ample food is provided.
3. bay leaf, an alleged natural moth repellant is used but ample food is provided.
4. all food is removed and a commercial pesticide is used.
5. all food is removed and bay leaf is used.
6. ample food is provided and no pesticide or repellant is used.

For each of the six experimental settings, the scientist designed a closed container (10 cubic feet) with ample air supply, and conditions such as temperature and light adjusted to resemble an average kitchen. He then placed 10 adult moths (both male and female) in each container, along with the appropriate amount of food and bay leaf. He sprayed pesticide in the containers of Group 2 and 4 once a day. The data he collected over 7 days are tabulated below.

GROUP	CONDITIONS			NUMBER OF ALIVE ADULT MOTHS						
	Food taken away	Bay leaf	Pesticide	Day 1	Day 2	Day 3	Day 4	Day 5	Day 6	Day 7
1	YES	NO	NO	10	8	3	1	3	0	0
2	NO	NO	YES	10	6	5	3	6	8	9
3	NO	YES	NO	10	8	8	7	8	7	6
4	YES	NO	YES	10	6	3	1	1	0	0
5	YES	YES	NO	10	8	3	1	0	0	0
6	NO	NO	NO	10	10	10	10	12	12	12

Now that we have read the passage, underlined or marked key information, made notes in the margins of the text, and analyzed the data in the table, answer the relevant questions from the beginning of the lesson:

1. How many experiments are discussed in the passage?
Only one.

2. What is the purpose of the experiment(s)?
To compare the efficiency of different methods of meal moth extermination.

3. What are the variables in the experiment?
The variables are food, pesticide, bay leaf, time, and the number of moths in a container.

4. Which variables are controlled by the scientist and how?
The scientist controls the contents of each container—food, pesticide, bay leaf, and the initial number of moths.

5. Which variables are measured or observed and how?
The number of moths in each container is observed over the course of seven days.

6. Were any calculations performed?
No calculations were performed.

7. Is there an experimental control? If so, what is it?
The experimental control is the group of moths (6) in the container where ample food is available, and no pesticide or bay leaf is present. It corresponds to the situation where nothing is being done to eliminate the moth population.

You may still not understand all the details of this experiment, but the questions above probably helped you organize the information that was presented to you, and you can now proceed to the more challenging task of interpreting the experiments and the experimental results.

Analysis

When reading Research Summary passages you will have to think about the following questions: What do the results show? What do they mean? How does the measured or observed variable depend on the controlled variable?

Let's look at the data in Example 1. What can we say about the tabulated information? First, there are two different tables. One is for the data taken using the near-IR laser, and the other for data taken using the green laser. The initial intensities of the two lasers are different, the near-IR has an intensity of 500 units, while the green has an intensity of 400 units, but the initial intensity of each laser does not change. The higher the transmitted intensity, the higher the percent transmitted. In fact, the percent transmitted is the ratio of the transmitted intensity to the initial intensity. The higher the transmitted intensity, the lower the absorbed percent. In fact, percent transmitted and the percent absorbed always sum up to 100%, which means that the light is either transmitted by the filter or passed by the filter.

Now let's find the solution to the filter problem. Which filter best satisfies the criteria? Looking back at the criteria, we see that the filter must transmit at least 90% of the green, while transmitting, at most, 5% of the near-IR. Which of the filters satisfy the first requirement? Look at the table that outlines experiments with the green laser. Filters that transmit 90 or more percent of the green are Filter 1 and Filter 3. Do any of these two satisfy the second requirement? Check Filter 1 and Filter 3 transmittance of near-IR light. Filter 1 transmits 7%, which is above the criterion, while Filter 3 transmits 3%, passing the both criteria, and making it the filter to use.

Drawing Conclusions

What conclusions can we draw from the research summary presented in Example 2? When the number of moths in a container is zero, the moths have been exterminated. Three out of the six conditions lead to extermination. Groups 1, 4, and 5, exterminated by the end of the 7-day period, all lacked food. The moth populations exposed to pesticide or bay leaf, but given ample food, did not die off by the end of the experiment. We can conclude that the extermination of this particular moth within seven days requires the removal of the food supply.

What if you were asked how pesticides and bay leaves affect the moth population? To answer this question, we could place marks in the table to indicate whether the population increases, decreases, or stays the same as on the previous day. Look at the example marks in the table below; +, -, and = signs were used to mark an increase, decrease, and no change in population from the previous day, respectively. The data points that represent the extermination of a population have been boxed with a thick line.

GROUP	CONDITIONS			NUMBER OF ALIVE ADULT MOTHS						
	Food taken away	Bay leaf	Pesticide	Day 1	Day 2	Day 3	Day 4	Day 5	Day 6	Day 7
1	YES	NO	NO	10	8 -	3 -	1 -	3 +	0 -	0 =
2	NO	NO	YES	10	6 -	5 -	3 -	6 +	8 +	9 +
3	NO	YES	NO	10	8 -	8 =	7 -	8 +	7 -	6 -
4	YES	NO	YES	10	6 -	3 -	1 -	1 =	0 -	0 =
5	YES	YES	NO	10	8 -	3 -	1 -	0 -	0 =	0 =
6	NO	NO	NO	10	10 =	10 =	10 =	12 +	12 +	12 +

In experimental science, it is always important not to change too many variables at the same time. If too many variables change, it is difficult to attribute the change in the measured or observed variable to any one variable. When analyzing experimental data, it is also important to compare data sets that are closely related. For example, it wouldn't make much sense to compare Group 3, provided with ample food and exposed to bay leaf, with Group 4, exposed to pesticide and not provided with food.

Making Predictions

To truly understand something means to be able to predict it. Here is a prediction question:

1. According to the data collected in Example 2, which of the following strategies would be most effective if the object was to reduce the number of moths as quickly as possible and to completely exterminate them as quickly as possible, without excessive exposure to pesticide?
   a. Remove all accessible food, spray pesticide every day.
   b. Spray pesticide every other day and lay out bay leaf around the kitchen.
   c. Remove all food, lay out bay leaf around the kitchen, and spray pesticide only on the first day.
   d. Remove all food, and lay out bay leaves on the fourth day.

The correct answer is **c**. The data show the effect of each variable independently. You are asked to integrate all the variables to produce the desired change (quick decrease in the number of moths and quick extermination without excessive use of pesticide). Food removal is essential, since as data show, as long as food is present, the moth population can be sustained. Bay leaf helps reduce the moth population slightly and steadily and it has an effect on the new moth generation (after day 5, it keeps reducing the number of moths). So bay leaf should be used. Pesticide, however, most dramatically reduces the population when it is originally applied. Since quick reduction of the moth population is required in addition to the extermination, pesticide should be applied the first day. In order to make a prediction, you will need to consider all the information provided.

Summary

In this lesson you learned to recognize the important elements of an experiment. You also learned to analyze experimental data, draw conclusions, and make predictions based on the experimental information.

Remember, research summary passages are often a combination of data representation passages and reading passages. Use the skills you developed for the Reading Comprehension section, as well as the Data Representation lesson when answering research summary questions, and make sure to get as much practice as you can.

CONFLICTING VIEWPOINTS

This lesson will help you develop skills that you can use to score well on the Conflicting Viewpoints passages on the ACT Science Reasoning Test. These include: understanding the question posed at the beginning of the sample, quickly locating the pertinent detail information in the text, and choosing the best answer. You will also learn to read and understand facts and opinions, as well as recognize, understand, analyze and compare alternative hypotheses or views in order to draw conclusions about the information provided.

Reading with Understanding

Conflicting Viewpoints passages are two or more separate passages from different scientists, on the same or related topic. Each passage includes both opinions and facts. In this section, you will learn to focus on what is important in such passages to increase your overall understanding of the passage. As a start, take a look at the following example.

Is a Vegetarian Diet Healthier?

Article 1: Health Benefits of Vegetarian Diets

A vegetarian diet offers a wide range of health benefits. Research has shown that vegetarians are less likely to suffer from heart disease, hypertension, obesity, diabetes, certain cancers, gall stones, kidney stones, and osteoporosis.

High blood cholesterol is a primary risk factor in cardiovascular disorders, the number one leading cause of death in the United States. Studies found vegetarians to have cholesterol levels 10% lower than health conscious non-vegetarians, which may explain a lower incidence of heart problems among vegetarians.

Cancers, such as colon, breast, and prostate, are often diet related. In a study of over 88,000 women 34 to 59 years old, women eating red meat daily ran twice the risk of developing colon cancer than women eating red meat less than once a month. Reduced incidence of colon cancer in vegetarians may be attributed to dietary differences that include increased fiber intake, increased consumption of fruit and vegetables, and decreased intake of saturated fat.

In addition, 50,000 cases of food poisoning are reported every year and the actual incidence of food poisoning is estimated to be ten times higher. Meat, eggs, and dairy products are the source of 95% of food poisoning.

With the benefit of avoiding the diseases linked to meat diets, vegetarianism is clearly the superior choice.

Article 2: Health Benefits of Vegetarian Diets Are Not Meat Related

There is no evidence that the absence of meat in vegetarian diets is causing the reported reduced health risks in vegetarians. Recent research has demonstrated the importance of antioxidants including beta-carotene and vitamin C and E found in fresh fruit and vegetables. Many researchers now believe that these nutrients, rather than a lack of meat, reduce the risk of heart disease and cancer in vegetarians.

Another concern with meat consumption is that antibiotics and other drugs, including steroids and growth hormones, are added to animal feed or injected directly into the animals. People who eat meat absorb these drugs into their bodies. Reduced effectiveness of antibiotics for human use may be linked to overuse in animals.

Scientists also found that some diseases could be passed from animals to humans through food. Not every piece of meat passes an inspection, and it is possible that meat of a diseased animal ends up in our kitchens. By avoiding meat, vegetarians avoid a potential source of disease.

However, that does not mean that a meatless diet is healthier. Meat offers important nutrients, including, iron, protein, and vitamin B_{12}, which are not easily obtained in vegetarian diets. The benefits of vegetarian diets could be gained just by increasing the fruit, vegetable, and fiber intake, without eliminating meat. The problem with meat isn't that it's inherently unhealthy. The problem is the meat industry, which has sacrificed healthy animal conditions, sustainable environment, and quality control for profits. Vegetarians are avoiding this problem, but they are not fighting it in the most efficient way. A healthy diet should include some healthy meat and we should demand its availability.

Getting Started

When you are reading the Conflicting Viewpoints passage, make sure you carefully consider the introductory question. It will usually give you some idea of where the conflict is. Reading the introductory passage will give you a frame for the texts that follow it. What could you learn from the introductory passage in the example?

- The passage is about vegetarian diets.
- It deals with the impact of a vegetarian diet on health.

As you are reading the different viewpoints, keep track of the arguments used to support each viewpoint. In many cases you will be able to pair an argument in one passage with a counterargument in the other. Sometimes, the passages will be in agreement except in some sticking point. It is also essential that you understand when a viewpoint is being supported by fact and when by an opinion. Arguments supported by facts are generally considered more convincing. For a discussion on the differences between facts and opinions, read the next section.

Facts and Opinions

The science community is trained to examine and present facts—data and information that can be tested, observed, and reproduced. Scientists argue against a conflicting viewpoint by presenting conflicting facts. Alternatively, they expose a fault in the facts obtained by those supporting the other viewpoint—for example, that the facts were obtained under unusual conditions or circumstances. A scientist should be able to repeat the experiment another scientist performed and come up with the same facts. Nonetheless, scientists do have opinions and have a right to express them. It is important to distinguish opinions from facts when reading about different scientific viewpoints.

An **opinion** is a statement not necessarily supported by scientific data. Opinions are often based on personal feelings or beliefs and are usually difficult, if not impossible, to measure and test.

Remember that your agreement with a stated opinion does not turn that opinion into a fact. Here is a list of opinions:

- London weather is beautiful.
- The grass is always greener on the other side of the fence.
- Auckland should be the capital of New Zealand.

Can you come up with a list of opinions from the example passage? After you write your own, look at the list below.

- Vegetarianism is clearly the superior choice.
- The problem is the meat industry, which has sacrificed healthy animal conditions, sustainable environment, and quality control for profits.
- Vegetarians are avoiding this problem, but they are not fighting it in the most efficient way.
- A healthy diet should include healthy meat, and we should demand its availability.

A **fact** is a statement based on scientific data or objective observations. Facts can be measured or observed, tested and reproduced.

Here are some facts:

- It rains often in London.
- Grass in the majority of North American backyards is green.
- Wellington is the capital of New Zealand.

Can you come up with a list of facts from the passage? Here are a few:

- Research has shown that vegetarians are less likely to suffer from heart disease, hypertension, obesity, diabetes, certain cancers, gall stones, kidney stones, and osteoporosis.
- In a study of over 88,000 women 34 to 59 years old, women eating red meat daily ran twice the risk of developing colon cancer than women eating red meat less than once a month.
- Meat, eggs, and dairy products are the source of 95% of food poisoning.
- Recent research has demonstrated the importance of antioxidants including beta-carotene and vitamin C and E found in fresh fruit and vegetables.
- Meat offers important nutrients, including, iron, protein, and vitamin B_{12}.

Let's match up the arguments presented in the two conflicting viewpoints.

1. Article 1 says vegetarian diets are healthier.
   Article 2 says this is due to increased fruit and vegetable intake.
2. Article 1 says that animal products are the source of most food poisonings.
   Article 2 says that this is due to poor quality control, rather than the inherent nature of meat.

Article 2 states that meat contains important nutrients. It also states that these nutrients are difficult to obtain from vegetarian diets, but doesn't back that statement with facts. Here, article 2 changes focus from a discussion of healthy diets to the politics of the meat industry.

Types of Conflicting Viewpoints Questions

The questions on conflicting viewpoints usually fall into a category that you are bound to encounter over, and over. The categories are:

- comparison of different hypotheses or viewpoints
- finding detail in the passage
- making an inference or drawing a conclusion

COMPARISON OF DIFFERENT HYPOTHESES OR VIEWPOINTS

When asked to compare different hypotheses or viewpoints, you will be analyzing how are they similar, and how they differ. Let's take an example.

1. In the passage, what do the two viewpoints have in common?
   Both passages agree that certain health risks are lower in vegetarians. Can you find the statements that support this in both articles? The second article states that the vitamins found in fruits and vegetables are responsible for the health benefits of vegetarianism. Which statement in the first article supports this viewpoint as well? Both passages also seem to agree that there are unresolved quality control issues with meat. Article 1 discusses food poisoning, while Article 2 discusses lack of sufficient inspection and the overuse of antibiotics and other drugs.

2. How do the viewpoints differ?
   Article 1 supports the view that given the benefits of vegetarian diets and the health risks associated with eating meat, vegetarianism is a good choice. Article 2 supports the view that the benefits of vegetarianism can be enjoyed by increasing fruit and vegetable intake, that meat has important nutritional value not easily obtained from a vegetarian diet, and that demanding quality meat is a better solution than becoming vegetarian.

FIND DETAIL IN THE PASSAGE

Finding detail in the passage questions, asks you exactly that—to find or recall some piece of information that was buried in the passage. You have had practice with this already. Here's a practice question from the example.

1. Which argument was NOT used to support the viewpoint that a vegetarian diet is a good choice?
   a. Vegetarians have a lower incidence of many diseases.
   b. Animal products are the major cause of food poisoning.
   c. Beans and nuts contain plenty of protein.
   d. Vegetarians have lower cholesterol levels than health conscious non-vegetarians.

   The correct choice is c. While it is true, it was not mentioned in the passage.

INFERENCE AND CONCLUSION

Deal with inference and conclusion questions in this section using the same skills you used for this type of question in data representation and reading passages. In other words, get the facts straight, put them together, and make a prediction. Specific to the conflicting viewpoint passage, however, is a common question in this category: one that makes a statement and asks you to determine which viewpoint that statement would support. Or, you could be given a set of statements and asked which of the statements listed would best support one of the viewpoints. As an example, consider the passage presented at the beginning of the lesson once more. Here is a question:

1. Which statement best supports the viewpoint presented in the second passage?
   a. The healthiest diet would be one with lots of fruits and vegetables, as well as healthy meat.
   b. Mad cow disease is a prime example that the meat industry is out of control.
   c. Essential antioxidants can be found in citrus fruits and carrots.
   d. Energy drinks often consumed by vegetarians contain too much sugar, which is bad for the health.

The correct choice is **a**. While statements **b**, **c**, and **d** could be true, the main purpose of Article 2 is to show that a diet that includes meat would be healthier than a vegetarian diet if good quality meat were available.

Summary

The skills outlined in this chapter have given you some idea on how to handle conflicting theory passages. You have learned to obtain an overview of the conflict from the introductory paragraph, to recognize and match up conflicting arguments, to distinguish facts from opinions, and to recognize common types of Conflicting Viewpoint questions on the ACT. Make sure you experiment with these strategies and determine which ones work best for you.

▶ Tips and Strategies For Standardized Tests

If you have read the overview of the ACT Success, you already know lots of tips and strategies to help you succeed. These include making sure you:

- learn about the test.
- know what to do before the test.
- take notes on the test.
- never leave an answer blank.
- read each question carefully.
- read all of the answers carefully.
- answer the easiest questions first.

- pace yourself.
- ignore all distractions.
- spot-check your answers.

For Multiple-Choice Questions

When answering multiple-choice questions, don't forget to:

- circle or underline key words in the passages.
- cross out clearly incorrect choices.
- beware of distracter techniques.
- make sure you know what is being asked.
- watch out for absolute statements.
- answer the easiest questions first.

For Science Reasoning Questions

Here are the best tips from the Science Reasoning lessons.

- Skim the questions before you read the passage or analyze the data, to get a sense of what information to look out for.
- As you are reading the passage or looking at data, don't be intimidated by technical words that are unfamiliar to you.
- Underline unfamiliar concepts and make notes in the margins of the passage to help you locate essential information if you need to return to the text after reading the questions.
- Ask yourself questions to help you focus on the important elements of the description of an experiment, data set, or theory.
- When looking at data representation passages, determine what is changing and how.
- When looking at data representation try to observe a trend.
- If asked to make a prediction, assume that whatever trend you have observed will continue.
- Look at graph, chart and diagram titles, labels, axis names, and legends to get a quick overview of important facts.
- When several experiments or theories are described, think about how they are different and how they are similar.
- Think of a quick summary for a passage or for data.
- Practice, and practice, and practice some more.

► Practice Questions

Directions

Each passage on this practice section is followed by several questions. After reading a passage, choose the best answer from the choices given. When you are taking the official ACT Science Reasoning Test, it's a good idea to first mark all of your answer choices on your test booklet, and then transfer them to your bubble answer sheet. This will keep you focused on the test questions (and not on filling in bubbles), and will also reduce your chances of misnumbering your answers.

Passage I

A mixture that is made by dissolving one compound (solute) in another (solvent) is called a solution. The amount of solute that can be dissolved in a solvent at a given temperature is called solubility. For most substances, solubility increases with temperature. When the amount of solute dissolved in a solvent exceeds the solubility, the solution is called supersaturated. Rock candy can be made by dissolving as much sugar in water, as solubility would allow at a high temperature, and then slowly cooling the solution to room temperature. If a thin string is dipped into it and left in the solution, the sugar in excess of the solubility at room temperature will form sugar crystals around the string, making the sweet rock candy. The solubility (in grams of sugar per 100 grams of water) as a function of temperature (in degrees Celsius) is plotted in the graph below.

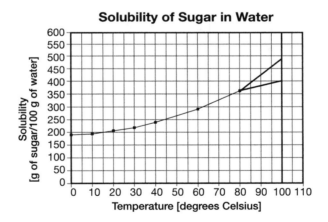

Solubility of Sugar in Water

1. A solution of sugar in water is NOT supersaturated when 300 g of sugar and 100 g of water are mixed at a temperature of:
   a. 20 degrees Celsius.
   b. 40 degrees Celsius.
   c. 50 degrees Celsius.
   d. 70 degrees Celsius.

2. In order for 250 g of sugar to completely dissolve in 100 g of water, the temperature of the solution would have to be at a minimum of:

    f. 15 degrees Celsius.

    g. 25 degrees Celsius.

    h. 45 degrees Celsius.

    j. 65 degrees Celsius.

3. At 100 degrees Celsius the solubility of sugar in water would most likely be:

    a. less than 250 g of sugar in 100 g of water.

    b. between 250 g of sugar and 350 g of sugar in 100 g of water.

    c. between 350 grams of sugar and 400 g of sugar in 100 g of water.

    d. more than 400 grams of sugar in 100 g of water.

4. In order to produce rock candy at 20 degrees Celsius from a solution of 300 g of sugar not completely dissolved in 100 g of water, the solution must be:

    f. first heated above 60 degrees Celsius, then slowly cooled to 20 degrees Celsius.

    g. slowly stirred at 20 degrees Celsius.

    h. slowly cooled to 0 degrees Celsius.

    j. slowly cooled below 0 degrees Celsius, then heated to 20 degrees Celsius and stirred.

5. How much sugar must be added to a solution of 50 g of sugar in 100 g of water at 45 degrees Celsius in order for the solution to be supersaturated?

    a. more than 10 grams

    b. more than 20 grams

    c. more than 100 grams

    d. more than 200 grams

6. Solubility is defined as:

    f. a supersaturated mixture.

    g. a mixture that is made by dissolving a solute in a solution.

    h. the amount of solute that can be dissolved in a solvent at a given temperature.

    j. the temperature that causes supersaturation.

7. What is the *approximate* difference in temperature for the solubility of 200 grams of sugar/100 grams of water and 250 grams of sugar/100 grams of water?

    a. 10 degrees Celsius

    b. 20 degrees Celsius

    c. 30 degrees Celsius

    d. 40 degrees Celsius

8. In a solution of sugar and water, which is the solvent and which is the solute?

    f. solvent: sugar; solute: water

    g. solvent: rock candy; solute: water

    h. solvent: water; solute: sugar

    j. solvent: water; solute: rock candy

Passage II

You set up an experiment to investigate the different rates at which soil and water heat and cool. You use the following equipment:

    Thermometers (measuring in °C)

    Container of soil

    Container of water

    Radiation Lamp

    Timer

You obtain the temperature of the soil and water over a period of time and collect the following data:

DATA TABLE I: During Heating-up Period

TIME (MIN)	SOIL TEMPERATURE (°C)	WATER TEMPERATURE (°C)
0	20.0	20.0
1	21.0	20.5
2	22.0	21.0
3	23.0	21.5
4	24.0	22.0
5	26.0	22.0
6	27.0	22.5
7	28.5	22.5
8	30.0	23.0
9	31.0	23.0
10	32.0	23.0

DATA TABLE II: During Cooling-off Period

TIME (MIN)	SOIL TEMPERATURE (°C)	WATER TEMPERATURE (°C)
11	32.0	22.5
12	31.0	22.5
13	30.5	22.0
14	29.5	22.0
15	28.0	22.0
16	27.0	21.5
17	26.0	21.5
18	25.0	21.0
19	23.5	21.0
20	22.0	20.5

The following graph was then made using the data.

Temperature of Soil and Water versus Time

9. Based on the results of the experiment, what is true about the heating and cooling rates of soil and water?

   a. Water heats faster, but cools slower.

   b. Water heats and cools faster.

   c. Soil heats faster, but cools slower.

   d. Soil heats and cools faster.

10. During the heating-up period, which surface was raised to a higher temperature?

    f. soil

    g. water

    h. They were raised in temperature by equal amounts.

    j. You cannot tell based on the data given.

11. If you repeated this experiment but you let the water and the soil heat for 20 minutes and then cool for 20 minutes instead of the 10 minutes used in this experiment how would you expect the graph of temperature versus time to change?

    a. Only the soil temperature curve would change. The water temperature curve would remain the same.

    b. Both the soil and the water temperature curves would change so that they would have the same basic shape but higher maximum temperature values.

    c. Both the soil and water temperature curves would change shape but maintain the same maximum temperature values.

    d. Only time for the experiment would change. The soil temperature and water temperature curves would remain the same.

12. Based on this experiment, compare the heating and cooling of air masses above the ocean and the land.

    f. The air above the ocean and land heats and cools at the same rate.

    g. The air above land heats and cools faster.

    h. The air above the ocean heats and cools faster.

    j. The air above the land heats faster but the air above the ocean cools faster.

13. Predict the relative air temperature over ocean and land during the day and night.

    a. During the day: air above the land is warmer, above the ocean is cooler. At night: air above the land is cooler, above the ocean is warmer.

    b. During the day: air above the land is cooler, above the ocean is warmer. At night: air above the land is warmer, above the ocean is cooler.

    c. During the day: air above the land is cooler, above the ocean is warmer. At night: air above the land is cooler, above the ocean is warmer.

    d. During the day: air above the land is warmer, above the ocean is cooler. At night: air above the land is warmer, above the ocean is cooler.

14. A sea breeze is a breeze blowing from the ocean onto the land. Air moves from cooler regions to warmer regions. When would a sea breeze occur?

    f. Sea breezes occur during the night.

    g. Sea breezes occur during the day.

    h. Sea breezes occur during the night and the day.

    j. Sea breezes never occur.

15. You complete this experiment a second time, and find that the water reached a higher temperature than the soil. Which of the following could be used to explain why your results are different?

    a. The water was unfiltered.

    b. The soil came from your garden.

    c. The heating lamp was faulty.

    d. You used different sized containers in the second experiment.

16. What is the difference in temperature between soil and water during the 13th minute?

    f. 7 degrees Celsius

    g. 7.5 degrees Celsius

    h. 8 degrees Celsius

    j. 8.5 degrees Celsius

Passage III

The heart is an organ that pumps blood throughout the circulatory system in the body. Red blood cells are a tissue in the body that carry nutrients to the body's cells and waste away from the body's cells. The heart rate increases or decreases depending on the body's needs to transport nutrients and waste.

In an experiment, a female had her heart monitored. For one minute, she sat in a chair quietly. At the end of the first minute to the end of the third minute she did jumping jacks. Finally, she sat again in the chair and waited until her heart rate went back to her resting heart rate as measured in the first minute. After performing this experiment, the following graph was created.

Graph 1

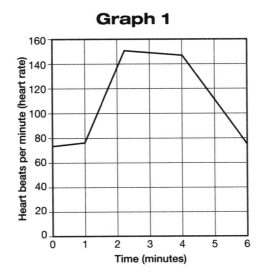

17. How long did it take for the resting heart rate to return after the exercising stopped?
   a. 1 minute 15 seconds
   b. 1 minute 30 seconds
   c. 1 minute 45 seconds
   d. 2 minutes

18. How long did it take for the heart rate to respond to the initial exercise?
   f. 1 minute
   g. 45 seconds
   h. 30 seconds
   j. 15 seconds

19. Which of the following is an accurate pattern found in Graph 1?
   a. The recovery time is shorter than the time it took for the heart rate to peak, due to the increase in exercise.
   b. The recovery time is longer than the time it took for the heart rate to peak, due to the increase in exercise.
   c. The recovery time is equal to the time it took for the heart rate to peak, due to the increase in exercise.
   d. The recovery time was equal to the resting heart rate time.

20. Which of the following statements is true?

I. During exercise the blood needs to carry less nutrients throughout the body.

II. The body does not need any nutrients when at rest.

III. Waste is carried away from cells only during exercise.

IV. During exercise the blood needs to carry more nutrients and wastes throughout the body.

  f. I and III

  g. III only

  h. II and III

  j. IV only

21. Using the data in Graph 1, what will the heart rate be in the 8th minute if the person continued to rest?

  a. The heart rate will be above the initial resting heart rate.

  b. The heart rate will be at about the same as the initial resting heart rate.

  c. The heart rate will be below the initial resting heart rate.

  d. The heart rate will be falling at a faster rate than during the resting period after exercise.

22. Which of the following tables accurately displays the information found in Graph 1?

f.

Minutes	0	1	2	3	4	5	6	
Heart rate	76	78	138	148	146	106	77	

g.

Minutes	1	2	3	4	5	6	
Heart rate	78	138	148	146	106	77	

h.

Minutes	1	2	3	4	5	6	7	8
Heart rate	78	138	148	146	106	77	77	76

j.

Minutes	0	1	2	3	4	5	6	7	8
Heart rate	76	78	138	148	146	106	77	77	77

23. If this experiment were to be recreated using a male participant, what would you expect the graph to look like?

  a. Exactly the same, everyone has the same resting heart rate and peak heart rate.

  b. The resting heart rate will be higher and the peak heart rate will be lower.

  c. The graph would show a similar pattern, but would reflect the amounts recorded for that participant.

  d. Both the resting heart rate and peak heart rate will be higher because males need more nutrients pumped through their bodies.

24. What would be an appropriate title for Graph 1?
- **f.** Female Heart Rates
- **g.** Heartbeats per Minute during Rest and Exercise
- **h.** Female Exercise Patterns
- **j.** Rest and Exercise

Passage IV

Lorna noticed that the amount of time needed to boil water was related to the shape of container she was using. She decided to measure the time necessary to bring 500 ml of water at room temperature to a boil on preheated hotplates. She used five cylindrical 500 milliliter Pyrex glass containers, each having the same wall thickness but a different base radius and height. In other words some containers were narrow and long, others were wide and shallow. This is the table she prepared to record her data.

Container	Radius [cm]	Height [cm]	Volume [ml]	Time to Boil [min]
1	2.0	75.0	300	
2	3.4	26.0	300	
3	4.0	18.8	300	
4	5.0	12.0	300	
5	1.0	3.0	300	

She placed each container containing the same amount of water on a hotplate, and placed a thermometer in each one to monitor the temperature. She noticed that the temperature was increasing faster in the containers with a larger radius. After some time, she observed boiling in the 10 cm radius container. She was about to record the time in the table she had set up, but noticed that there seemed to be less water in that container than she originally put in. She transferred the water into a graduated cylinder, and indeed found that the volume was below 300 ml. She proceeded with her experiment. The boiling in container 5 was followed by boiling in containers 4, 3, 2, and 1, in that order. Lorna checked the volume of the water in each container and found that it was lower than 300 ml. She also found that the decrease in volume was highest in the container with the largest radius. In container 1, volume decrease was barely detectable. While the decrease in volumes prevented her from getting meaningful data on boiling, they gave her an idea of how container shapes affect boiling times. In addition, she got an idea for her next project—evaporation from containers of different shapes.

25. The experiment suggests that:

    a. as the container radius is increased, the time required to boil the water in the container is increased.

    b. as the container radius is increased, the time required to boil the water in the container is decreased.

    c. there is no correlation between the container radius and the boiling time for water.

    d. there may be a correlation between the container radius and the boiling time, but due to the volume decrease, it is not possible to state what the correlation is.

26. The decrease in water volume is most likely the result of:

    f. malfunction in the hotplate.

    g. evaporation.

    h. a careless spill.

    j. microorganisms.

27. What is a fair objection to Lorna's experimental setup?

    a. The water she used was not distilled.

    b. She didn't stir the water.

    c. She used different hotplates for different containers.

    d. She set up a data table before she performed the experiment.

28. Preliminary results suggest that:

    f. the rate of evaporation of water is higher from containers with a larger radius.

    g. the rate of evaporation of water is lower from containers with a larger radius.

    h. the rate of evaporation of water is the same from containers with a different radius, as long as the volume of water in the containers is the same.

    j. the rate of evaporation can't be measured with the equipment Lorna used.

29. From the passage it can be inferred that a graduated cylinder is used:

    a. by students only.

    b. to measure how cylindrical a container is.

    c. to measure the rate of evaporation of water.

    d. to measure volumes.

30. 300 mL of water, placed in a 7.0 cm radius container, and heated as the rest of the water in the experiment described in the text would most likely boil after:

    f. the water in container 2.

    g. the water in container 3.

    h. the water in container 4.

    j. the water in container 5.

Passage V

Why does an arrow shot from a bow eventually hit the ground?

Impetus Theory

The ancient theory of impetus was used to explain why objects continue to move even when they were no longer acted on, for example, an arrow shot by a bow. The theory of impetus says that the bow imparts a certain amount of the property of motion to the arrow. This property of motion is called *impetus*. Impetus is then a property of the bow that is imparted to the arrow. This is what causes the arrow to fly through the air. According to the theory of impetus, only a limited amount of motion is imparted to the arrow by the bow. Once this runs out, the arrow will fall abruptly to the ground. You can think of this theory as being similar to a gas tank. The action of the bow fills the tank of the arrow with a certain amount of "motion" or impetus; once the tank is empty the arrow doesn't move anymore. Furthermore this theory predicts that the impetus is used up at a steady rate. So when it runs out, it runs out abruptly. This yields the prediction that when the arrow uses up the impetus imparted to it by the bow it will stop in mid air and then fall straight down to earth. For an object to continue moving forever in a straight line the impetus theory predicts that it would have to be given an infinite amount of impetus.

Inertia Theory

Inertia is the property of an object to remain at rest or in motion with constant velocity unless acted on by a net force. According to the theory of inertia, an arrow will continue to move in its state of motion with constant velocity unless acted on by a force. The force in this case is the gravity of the Earth acting on the arrow. The force of gravity gradually causes the arrow to fall toward the earth as it travels horizontally, which means the arrow follows a parabolic path. Finally, according to the theory of inertia, if an object is not acted on by a net force, it would continue moving forever in a straight line at constant velocity.

31. In which theory is the reason the arrow continues to move a property of the arrow itself and not something given to it by the bow?
    a. the impetus theory
    b. the inertia theory
    c. both the impetus and the inertia theories
    d. neither the impetus nor the inertia theories

32. Which theory would correctly predict the path of a projectile such as an arrow?

   f. The impetus theory says the impetus runs out gradually at a decreasing rate. This would explain why the projectile follows a parabolic path.

   g. The inertia theory says the inertia runs out gradually at a decreasing rate. This would explain why the projectile follows a parabolic path.

   h. The impetus theory says the force of gravity is acting on the projectile causing its motion to change and creating the parabolic path.

   j. The inertia theory says the force of gravity is acting on the projectile causing its motion to change and creating the parabolic path.

33. Which of the following statements are true?

   I. In the inertia theory, the net force acting on the arrow to cause it to slow down and fall to the earth is the force of the bow on the arrow.

   II. In the impetus theory, the arrow gains an infinite amount of impetus and will never slow down and fall to the ground.

   III. In the inertia theory, the net force acting on the arrow to cause it to slow down and fall to the earth is the force of gravity on the arrow.

   IV. In the impetus theory, the impetus imparted to the arrow by the bow is used up and that is why the arrow falls to the ground.

   a. I and II

   b. II and III

   c. III and IV

   d. III only

34. According to the impetus theory, for an object to continue moving in a straight line at constant velocity what conditions must be true?

   f. According to the impetus theory, the object must be given infinite impetus.

   g. According to the impetus theory, the object must have no net force on it.

   h. According to the impetus theory, the object must be given infinite impetus.

   j. According to the impetus theory, the object must have gravity providing the impetus.

35. According to the inertia theory, for an object to continue moving in a straight line at constant velocity, what conditions must be true?

   a. According to the inertia theory, the object must be given infinite inertia.

   b. According to the inertia theory, the object must have an infinite net force on it.

   c. According to the inertia theory, the object must have gravity as the net force acting on it.

   d. According to the inertia theory, the object must have no net force acting on it.

36. Which of the following statements is correct?

f. Impetus is a property of the object in motion.

g. Impetus is a property of motion that is transferred to the object in motion by the object that acts on it.

h. Impetus is used up gradually.

j. Impetus is the tendency of an object at rest to remain at rest unless acted on by a net force.

37. Gravity is a type of:

a. net force.

b. impetus.

c. inertia.

d. parabolic path.

38. According to the impetus theory, if you throw a rock:

f. it will immediately hit the ground.

g. gravity will act on the rock.

h. it will continue to fly forever.

j. your arm gives the rock the property of motion.

Passage VI

Background Information

If a characteristic is expressed in an organism, that is the organism's *phenotype*. The genes that determine that phenotype are called the organism's *genotype*. A characteristic is determined by the organism's genes that were passed down by the parents. If a gene is dominant, that gene will be expressed in the phenotype. If a gene is recessive, it will only be expressed in the phenotype when two recessives are present in the genetic makeup of that organism.

Description

A cat breeder is losing money because customers are buying cats that do not have white paws, and the cat breeder has mostly white-pawed cats. She decides to experiment with breeding with the six remaining cats that do not have white paws to see if she can produce litters of kittens without white paws. A cat without white paws can be either pure for the non-white pawed cats (homozygote) or a carrier for white paws (heterozygote). The trait for having white paws is recessive.

A homozygote for the non-white = WW (non-white cat paws)

A heterozygote for white = Ww (non-white cat paws)

A homozygote for the white = ww (white cat paws)

You can create Punnett Squares to show the phenotypes that would result from two parent cats breeding.

WW x WW cross yields all non-white pawed kittens.

	W	W
W	WW	WW
W	WW	WW

WW x Ww cross yields all non-white pawed kittens in the first generation; however, $\frac{1}{2}$ will be carriers for white paws.

	W	w
W	WW	Ww
W	WW	Ww

Ww x Ww cross yields a ratio of 1 homozygote non-white paws to 2 heterozygote to 1 homozygote white paws for the first generation.

	W	w
W	WW	Ww
W	Ww	ww

Experiment

Group 1

The cat breeder breeds two cats that do not have white paws. She finds that the first generation of kittens in this group does not have any white paws. When the first generation of cats was bred, she finds that the second generation of these kittens is $\frac{1}{8}$ white-pawed and $\frac{7}{8}$ not white-pawed.

Group 2

The cat breeder breeds two different cats that do not have white paws. She finds that the first, second, and third generations of kittens in this group did not have any white paws.

Group 3

The cat breeder breeds two different cats that do not have white paws. She finds that the first generation of kittens in this group has $\frac{1}{4}$ with white paws and $\frac{3}{4}$ without white paws. She does not breed for a second generation in this group.

39. Which group contains parent cats that may be pure for not having white paws?
   a. Group 1
   b. Group 2
   c. Group 3
   d. None of the groups

40. Describe the most likely genetic makeup of the parents in Group 1.
   f. The cats were both pure for not having white paws.
   g. One cat was pure, while the other cat was a carrier for the white paw trait.
   h. Both cats were carriers for the white paw trait.
   j. It cannot be determined.

41. If the cats from Group 1 were to continue breeding:
   a. the number of white-pawed cats would eventually outnumber the cats without white paws.
   b. the number of white-pawed cats would decline until no more white-pawed cats existed.
   c. the number of cats without white paws would decline until no more cats without white paws existed.
   d. the number of white-pawed cats would decline over time, but white-pawed cats would still be found in newer generations.

42. If a gene is recessive:
   f. it will only be expressed in the phenotype when two recessives are present in the genetic makeup of that organism.
   g. it will never be expressed in the phenotype.
   h. it will only be expressed in the phenotype when a dominant and a recessive gene is present in the genetic makeup of that organism.
   j. it will always be expressed in the phenotype.

43. How many of the six cats are pure for not having white paws?
   a. 2
   b. 3
   c. 4
   d. 5

44. Based on this data, which of the following is a valid conclusion?

    f. Cats from groups 2 and 3 should be switched between the groups to produce kittens with no white paws.

    g. Cats from groups 1 and 3 when switched would produce all white-pawed cats for all generations.

    h. Cats from groups 1 and 2 should be switched to produce a greater number of white-pawed cats than the original setup.

    j. The cat breeder should not make any changes because a greater number of cats without white paws cannot exist.

45. If this experiment were recreated, inaccurate results could be caused by:

    a. the fact that some people like white-pawed cats.

    b. not all of the cats being fed the same brand of cat food.

    c. a cat from Group 3 breeding with a cat from Group 2 during the experiment.

    d. the parents in Group 1 breeding 1 month later than the cats in Groups 2 and 3.

46. What would the Punnett Square look like for 2 homozygote white-pawed cats?

f.

	w	w
W	Ww	Ww
W	ww	ww

g.

	w	w
W	Ww	Ww
W	Ww	Ww

h.

	w	w
W	Ww	ww
W	ww	ww

j.

	w	w
w	ww	ww
w	ww	ww

47. An organism's genes that determine the phenotype are called:

    a. heterozygote.

    b. characteristics.

    c. genotype.

    d. homozygote.

Passage VII

Graphs I-IV and Data Table I represent the motion of objects in one dimension as detected by a motion detector. Motion in the positive direction represents motion away from the motion detector and motion in the negative direction represents motion toward the motion detector.

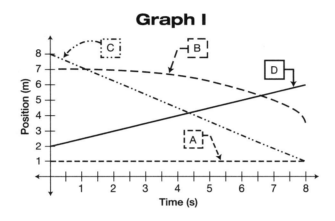

Graph I

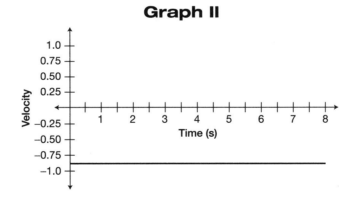

Graph II

Graph III

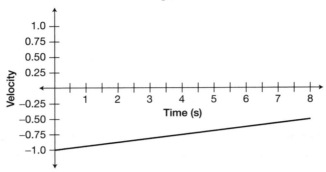

Graph IV

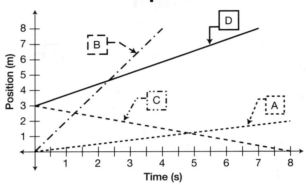

DATA TABLE 1

TIME (S)	VELOCITY (M/S)
0.00	−1.00
1.00	−0.94
2.00	−0.88
3.00	−0.81
4.00	−0.75
5.00	−0.69
6.00	−0.63
7.00	−0.56
8.00	−0.50

48. Which of the objects represented on Graph I is moving at a constant velocity in the positive direction?

    f. A

    g. B

    h. C

    j. D

49. Which of the objects represented on Graph I could also be represented by Graph II?

    a. A

    b. B

    c. C

    d. D

50. Which of the following accurately describes the motion of the object in Graph III?

    f. The object is moving in the positive direction, slowing down.

    g. The object is moving in the negative direction, speeding up.

    h. The object is moving in the positive direction, speeding up.

    j. The object is moving in the negative direction, slowing down.

51. The data listed in Data Table I could be used to construct which graph?

    a. Graph I

    b. Graph II

    c. Graph III

    d. Graph IV

52. If objects A, B, C and D represented in Graph IV were in a foot race, which would win?

    f. A

    g. B

    h. C

    j. D

53. If objects A, B, C, and D represented in Graph IV were in a race, which would come in 3rd place?

    a. A

    b. B

    c. C

    d. D

54. Before conducting this experiment, what would be the most important thing to check to ensure accurate results?

f. the diameter of the objects used

g. the table where you will record the data

h. the weight of the objects used

j. the motion detector

55. According to Data Table I, what was the difference in velocity between minutes 3 and 4?

a. -0.03 m/s

b. -0.06 m/s

c. 0.06 m/s

d. -0.07 m/s

Passage IIX

One phenomenon studied by ecologists is the growth and regulation of populations. Population growth can be restricted when resources are limited. Competition for resources can also have an effect on population growth. Three experiments were conducted on various insects to test the validity of these statements. The table that follows is a summary of all three experiments.

Experiment 1

Two beetle species and caterpillars were studied: Six of each insect were grown in separate vials that contained adequate food supply. Beetle A and Beetle B feed on whole-wheat flour, while the caterpillars feed on fresh leaves. Twenty identical vials were set up for each insect. After ten weeks, both species of beetles grew to an average population of 500 in each vial. There was an average of 20 caterpillars in the vials that contained caterpillars.

Experiment 2

Six beetles from species A and six caterpillars were grown in the same vial containing whole-wheat flour and fresh leaves. Twenty identical vials were set up. After ten weeks, the average population of Beetle A was 500 while there were an average of 20 caterpillars in each vial.

Experiment 3

Six beetles from each beetle species were placed in the same vial containing whole-wheat flour. Twenty identical vials were set up. After ten weeks, the average population of Beetle A was three hundred while the average population of Beetle B was one hundred.

	Experiment 1	Experiment 2	Experiment 3
Beetle A	500	500	300
Beetle B	500	—	100
Caterpillar	20	20	—

The table shows the average population of each insect that is involved in the experiments outlined.

56. Which of the following statements is true of Experiment 1?

    f. Beetle A reproduces quicker than Beetle B.

    g. Caterpillars have a greater number of offspring than beetles.

    h. Beetle B consumed a greater amount of resources than Beetle A.

    j. After ten weeks, there was no difference in population size between the two species of Beetle.

57. Which of the following statements best describes why Experiment 1 is important?

    a. Experiment 1 demonstrates that insects can thrive under the given conditions.

    b. Experiment 1 establishes that both Beetle A and Beetle B eat whole-wheat flour.

    c. Experiment 1 establishes the non-competitive total population of each insect.

    d. Experiment 1 demonstrates that the caterpillar has a much slower growth rate than the beetles.

58. If Beetle A in Experiment 1 was left to grow indefinitely, one would initially observe an increase, followed by a brief plateau, and then a rapid decline in the population size. What would be the most likely cause of the final decline?

    f. other species of insects

    g. limited supply of food

    h. limited supply of minerals

    j. long-term effects of confinement

59. What would happen if, in Experiment 2, Beetle B and caterpillars were put in the same vial?

    a. The caterpillars would die by Week 10 because of overpopulation by Beetle B.

    b. The average population of Beetle B would reach 100 and the average population for caterpillars would reach five because of competition for food.

    c. The average population of caterpillars would reach 50, while Beetle B would die because caterpillars are stronger competitors for food.

    d. The average population of Beetle B would reach 500 while the average population of caterpillars would reach 20, as in Experiment 2.

60. Which of the following statements is true of Experiment 3?

    f. Beetle B is the more dominant of the two beetle species.

    g. Beetle A and Beetle B compete for space, food, or both.

    h. The population size of Beetle B is smaller than Beetle A due to migration.

    j. The population size of Beetle B is smaller than Beetle A due to the absence of the caterpillars.

61. Suppose that, instead of starting with six of each species in Experiment 3, only three of each species were placed in the vial. After ten weeks, what percentage of the total population would the Beetle B species constitute?

   a. 15%

   b. 25%

   c. 75%

   d. 85%

62. Suppose another species of beetle, Beetle C, replaces Beetle A in Experiment 3. After ten weeks, only the Beetle C species can be found in the vial. Which of the following hypotheses does NOT explain the result in terms of competition?

   f. The adult and larval Beetle C species ate the eggs and pupae of the Beetle B species.

   g. The Beetle C species hoarded the food supply and defended it from the Beetle B species.

   h. The Beetle B species was unable to reproduce due to a genetic mutation.

   j. The Beetle C species secretes an enzyme on the food supply that can only be broken down by its own digestion system.

Passage IX

Sedimentary rocks (which form from sediment) are thought to be deposited in cycles that occur in discrete packages called sequences. Each sequence constitutes a complete cycle. The cause for the cyclicity has been linked to sea level change, uplift of continents, climate change, and changes in earth's orbit. These packages are thought to have a duration ranging from 50,000 to 200 million years.

One theory states that the sequences that occur on a scale of every 200,000 to 10 million years are usually caused by changes in the global ice volume. As temperatures increase and glaciers melt, sea level rises and new marine sediment—which is typically coarser-grained than underlying sediments—is deposited along shorelines. As global temperatures decrease and glaciers build up, sea level falls and shoreline environments are eroded.

In order to test this theory, two studies were undertaken which enable us better to understand the relations between glaciations (periods of maximum cooling and glacier build-up) and marine sedimentary sequences.

Study 1

A 400m long core of sedimentary rock from an ancient shoreline in the United States was analyzed. The core represents marine sediments deposited over the last 20 million years. The researchers observed patterns of erosion and change in sediment size and determined that unique sequences occurred every 50,000, 100,000, 5 million, and 12 million years.

Study 2

At several sites beneath the Atlantic Ocean, a 50m core was removed from 500,000-year-old ocean-floor marine sediments. These sediments contained abundant microfossils that can be used in determining the nature of past climates. The researchers studied the abundance and taxonomy of these microfossils and deduced patterns of warming and cooling global temperatures. They found that periods of maximum cooling (peak glaciation) occurred 75,000, 175,000, 375,000, and 475,000 years ago.

63. The characteristics common to the studies is that both:
    a. measured periods of maximum glaciations.
    b. utilized ancient and modern sedimentary rocks.
    c. analyzed data from marine sediments.
    d. measured the depth of the cycles.

64. The two studies support the theory that marine depositional processes are:
    f. controlled by microfossils and local climate changes.
    g. unpredictable in nature.
    h. most likely controlled by the cycling of glacial building and melting.
    j. related to sequences of marine sediments.

65. Which of the following characteristics of a sequence of marine sediments or sedimentary rocks would make it unsuitable for a study such as this?
    I.   an age of only 30,000 to 40,000 years
    II. depth of ocean water
    III. location away from the polar ice caps
    a. I only
    b. II and II only
    c. I, II, and III
    d. I and III only

66. Each of the following is true EXCEPT:
    f. Both studies are compatible with the claim that major climate changes occur at intervals of 50,000 years or more.
    g. Both studies provide support for the claim that cyclic climate changes caused changes in sediment patterns.
    h. Sediment size was a central factor in the results of both studies.
    j. Both studies concerned ancient marine sedimentary rocks.

67. According to the theory discussed in the passage, as glacial melting increases, the sediments along coastlines and microfossils within oceans should respectively show:

a. more deposition and cooler global temperatures.

b. more erosion and cooler global temperatures.

c. more deposition and warmer global temperatures.

d. more erosion and warmer global temperatures.

68. Which of the following hypotheses was investigated in Study 1?

f. Changes in sea level cause sequences of sediments.

g. Cycles occur every 50,000, 100,000, 5 million and 12 million years.

h. The sea level is currently rising.

j. Cyclicity in sediment deposition is the result of changes in global ice volume

Passage X

All proteins consist of a string of amino acids linked together by peptide bonds. Because of its unique sequence of amino acids, every protein is distinct. Each protein folds into a specific conformation when manufactured by cells. All proteins must attain three-dimensional structures to properly function in the cell. While the peptide bonds between the amino acids are relatively rigid, all the other chemical bonds within a protein are flexible and can contort within certain limits. The ability of a protein to fold depends on the flexibility of these chemical bonds. A small protein of about 100 amino acids could undergo an astronomical number of trials and errors before assuming its final structure. This sampling of many conformations before attaining the right one would take far too long and so scientists hypothesize that there must be pathways which guide individual proteins to the right conformations, thereby eliminating total randomness in sampling. Three pathway models of protein folding have been proposed.

Diffusion-collision model

This model suggests that an amino acid within a protein can diffuse within its environment until it collides with its specific partner amino acid, to which it adheres. When all the amino acids, are involved in favorable interactions, the protein ceases to diffuse and the proper conformation is attained.

Nucleation model

This model postulates that the acquisition of the proper fold within several amino acids would trigger the folding process. These amino acids act as nucleation centers and cause a domino effect in promoting protein folding. The protein can be imagined to sequentially acquire its proper conformation beginning from the nucleation centers.

Hydrophobic-collapse model
Out of the 20 different amino acids, some are hydrophobic. A hydrophobic amino acid is one that does not like to be associated with water but does like to be associated with others like itself. In the hydrophobic-collapse model, hydrophobic amino acids in the protein collapse into the center of the protein leaving the hydrophilic (water-loving) amino acids to surround them and interact with water.

69. The final three-dimensional structure of a protein, regardless of the folding pathway models, ultimately depends on:
a. how it is manufactured by the cell.
b. the flexibility of the peptide bonds
c. the number of amino acids.
d. the sequence of the amino acids.

70. A mutation of an important amino acid affects the proper conformation of the protein. Which of the proposed models cannot account for this observation?
f. diffusion-collision model
g. nucleation model
h. hydrophobic-collapse model
j. none of the above

71. A certain mutation of an amino acid, which is thought to play a major role in initiating protein folding, does not affect the general structure of the protein. Which of the proposed models cannot account for this observation?
a. diffusion-collision model
b. nucleation model
c. hydrophobic-collapse model
d. none of the above

72. The nucleation model suggests that some amino acids are more important than others whereas the diffusion-collision model supposes that all amino acids are equally important. Which of the following statements is NOT true?
f. A mutation in an important amino acid in the nucleation model will have no effect according to the diffusion-collision model.
g. A mutation in an amino acid, which is important in the nucleation model, will result in a wrong conformation.
h. A mutation in an amino acid might affect proper protein conformation according to the diffusion-collision model.

j. A mutation in a certain amino acid might have an effect according to both the nucleation model and the diffusion-collision model.

73. Implicit in the nucleation model is the assumption that:
  a. temperature is an important factor for a protein to attain the proper conformation.
  b. the presence of salt promotes a protein in attaining the proper conformation.
  c. the addition of a strong base will destroy the peptide bonds and thus the protein.
  d. the time required to attain the proper conformation is dependent on the length of the protein.

74. A molecular chaperonin is a protein that aids small proteins in establishing their structures. The chaperonin has a barrel-like cavity that provides an unfolded protein an opportunity to fold. If the hydrophobic-collapse model can be used to explain this particular folding process, what can be said about the amino acids of the molecular chaperonin that come in contact with the unfolded protein?
  f. The amino acids in the molecular chaperonins are hydrophobic.
  g. The amino acids in the molecular chaperonins are hydrophilic.
  h. The amino acids in the molecular chaperonins are both hydrophobic and hydrophilic.
  j. The amino acids in the molecular chaperonins are not involved in the folding process.

75. A fourth, all-inclusive view of protein folding is that similar proteins can fold via any of the three models. What cannot be said of proteins that conform to this all-inclusive model?
  a. The structure of a protein can be attained by any model.
  b. The length of the protein does not influence the choice of a model.
  c. The sequence of the protein determines the folding pathway.
  d. A folding pathway that is hindered by a mutation can be compensated by another.

Passage XI

SDS-PAGE is a technique used by scientists to separate proteins according to their size. The compound SDS confers a uniform negative charge to individual proteins, causing these negatively charged proteins to travel toward the anode (positive end) when placed in an electric field. The migrating proteins are further placed in a uniform matrix (PAGE) in order to separate the different sizes. A bigger, heavier protein meets more resistance than a smaller, lighter one while traveling through the matrix, and hence migrates more slowly. The size of a protein is measured in Daltons (Da). The relationship between the logarithm values of the weights of seven proteins and the distances they travel in the matrix in a given period of time is illustrated in the graph. A list of the discrete data point values for each protein, as well as the corresponding weight, is presented under the graph on the next page.

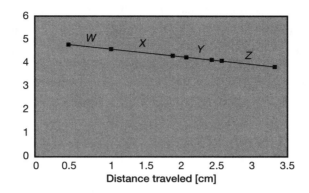

Distance traveled (cm)	Log (Weight)	Weight (Da)
0.5	4.81	65 000
1.0	4.55	35 000
1.8	4.23	17 000
2.1	4.16	14 000
2.5	4.02	11 000
2.7	3.91	8 000
3.3	3.79	6 000

76. Which statement characterizes the migration of SDS-associated proteins?

    f. Diffusion moves the proteins from a region of higher concentration to one of lower concentration.

    g. An electric field causes negatively charged objects to migrate toward the anode (positive end).

    h. The electrical resistance of negatively charged objects determines the speed of migration.

    j. Osmosis of water indirectly causes the migration of the proteins.

77. A protein of weight 45 000 Da would be expected to migrate to the region on the graph marked:

    a. W.

    b. X.

    c. Y.

    d. Z.

78. A protein essential for metabolism has just been discovered. SDS-PAGE reveals that this protein migrates a distance of 1.7 cm. Which statement best characterizes the new protein?

    f. The weight of the protein is somewhere between 6 000 Da and 11 000 Da.

    g. The weight of the protein is somewhere between 11 000 Da and 17 000 Da.

    h. The weight of the protein is somewhere between 14 000 Da and 17 000 Da.

    j. The weight of the protein is somewhere between 17 000 Da and 35 000 Da.

79. Another essential protein in metabolism is made up of two units, each unit traveling a different distance from the other. The combined weight of the two units is approximately 50 000 Da. Referring to the regions W, X, Y and Z on the graph, which combination will NOT give the possible weight of each unit?

 a. X + Z
 b. Y + Z
 c. X + Y
 d. W + Y

80. What would happen if an electric field were to be applied to SDS-PAGE for an indefinite length of time?

 f. Larger proteins will reach the anode before the smaller proteins.
 g. All proteins will eventually reach a limiting resistance in the matrix, at which point they cease to migrate further.
 h. Proteins associated with more SDS will reach the anode while proteins associated with less SDS will stop migrating due to resistance.
 j. All proteins will eventually reach the anode.

▶ Practice Questions Answers and Explanations

Passage I

1. d. One way to solve this problem is to draw a line through the graph along the 300 g of sugar per 100 g of water mark on the graph, as illustrated in the figure below.

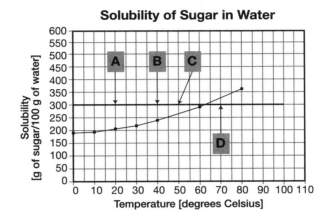

Solubility of Sugar in Water

In the passage, a supersaturated solution was defined as one in which the amount of solute dissolved exceeds solubility at a given temperature. The line going through the 300 mark is above the solubility curve, at all temperatures listed in choices A, B, and C. At temperature D, however, 300 g sugar /100 g of water does not exceed solubility. Therefore, at 70 degrees Celsius, the solution is NOT supersaturated.

2. h. You could use the strategy described in problem 1. If you draw a line through the 250 mark, you will see that it crosses the solubility curve at about 45 degrees Celsius. Below that temperature (choices **f** and **g**), the sugar will not dissolve completely. At 65 degrees (choice **j**) the sugar will dissolve. Choice **j** is incorrect because 65 degrees is above the *minimum* temperature required to dissolve the sugar.

3. d. This question is asking you to extrapolate, make a prediction, based on the given data. The solubility of sugar in water increases, as the temperature increases. You can assume that the trend will continue. So you can rule out choices **a** and **b**. Draw a line through the 100 degree Celsius mark, and extend the solubility curve to that mark, following the trend, as illustrated in the figure below. This should help you rule out choice **c**, since it will require the shape of the curve to change.

Solubility of Sugar in Water

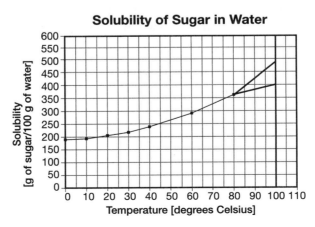

4. f. The question could be answered by going back to the passage. Rock candy is made by first completely dissolving the excess sugar, at a high temperature, then slowly cooling to room temperature. Choices **g**, **h**, and **j** don't describe heating, followed by slow cooling.

5. d. You can solve this problem by drawing a line through the 45 degree Celsius mark. It intersects the solubility curve at about 250 g of solute per 100 g of solvent. In order for a solution to be supersaturated, the amount of sugar has to exceed solubility. Therefore, a total of more than 250 g is necessary. If a solution already contains 50 g of sugar, more than 200 grams are required.

6. h. According to the passage, solubility is defined as the amount of solute that can be dissolved in a solvent at a given temperature.

7. b. The solubility of 200 grams of sugar/100 grams of water is 20 degrees Celsius. The solubility of 250 grams of sugar/100 grams of water is 40 degrees Celsius. Therefore the difference in temperature is 20 degrees Celsius.

8. h. According to the passage, the compound that is dissolved is the solute, while the liquid is the solvent. Therefore in sugar water, sugar is the solute and water is the solvent.

Passage II

9. d. The graphs and the data tables both show that the temperature of the soil increases more quickly during the heating up period and decreases more quickly during the cooling off period. This indicates that the soil heats and cools faster. The correct choice is **d**.

10. f. The graphs and the data table show that the temperature of the soil increases more than the temperature of the water during the heating up period, and the soil reaches a higher maximum temperature.

11. b. Changing the length of time for the heating up period would allow both the soil and the water to reach higher maximum temperature values. The soil will still heat faster than the water so it will still have a higher curve on the temperature versus time graph than the water.

12. g. Since soil heats faster, the air above land should then be heated faster by the heat radiated by the land. This narrows the selection to choices **g** and **j**. Since the soil also cools faster, the air above the land will cool faster as it comes to equilibrium with the cooler ground temperature by losing heat to the ground. This narrows the final choice to **g**.

13. a. Since the air above the land heats and cools faster it will get warmer faster during the day. This means during the day the air over the land will be warmer than the air over the ocean. At night, however, the temperature of the land will cool faster than the temperature of the ocean. This means the air above the ocean will be warmer than the air above the land at night.

14. g. During the day, the air above the land is warmer than over the ocean since the land heats faster than the oceans (as seen by the soil heating faster than the water in this experiment). Since air will move from cooler regions to warmer regions, the cool air over the ocean will move over to the land. This creates the sea breeze during the day.

15. c. It is not likely that unfiltered water or soil from your garden will heat differently than any other water or soil. Also, the size of the containers is not likely to affect the outcome of the experiment. However, if the heating lamp were faulty, it would cause your results to be inaccurate.

16. j. In the 13th minute, the soil is 30.5 degrees Celsius and the water is 22.0. The difference in temperature is 8.5 degrees Celsius.

Passage III

17. c. The exercise stopped at 4 minutes, but the heart rate did not return to its resting rate until about 5 minutes 45 seconds. Remember that between each of the minute lines on the graph, are 60 seconds. So if a point falls halfway between 5 and 6 minutes, that is 5 minutes and 30 seconds.

18. j. The exercise started at the beginning of the 1 minute and by a quarter of a minute later (60 divided by 4 = 15 seconds) the heart rate started its steep incline.

19. b. The total time for the heart rate to reach its peak height was 1 minute 15 seconds, while the total time for the heart rate to go through recovery time was about 1 minute 30 seconds.

20. j. According to the text above Graph 1, the heart rate increases or decreases depending on the body's need to transport waste and nutrients. Therefore during exercise the heart rate increases in order to transport more of these materials.

21. b. As seen in Graph 1, the heart rate decreased until it returned to the initial resting heart rate. Because the participant was continuing to rest, the heart rate would reflect that of a resting period.

22. f. Note that Graph 1 begins at minute 0, and ends at minute 6, therefore the only table that accurately reflects Graph 1 is choice **f**.

23. c. The graph would not look exactly alike because the male participant is likely to have different resting and peak heart rates. There is no evidence to suggest that choices **b** or **d** are correct. Only **c** states what the graph is likely to look like.

24. g. The experiment is attempting to show the heartbeats per minute during rest and exercise, therefore it is reasonable that the title of the graph would be Heartbeats per Minute During Rest and Exercise. There is no mention of the gender of the participant on the graph, so choices **f** and **h** are incorrect, and the title Rest and Exercise is incomplete.

Passage IV

25. b. Water in container 5, which has the largest radius, boils first. Water in other containers confirms this trend. You may have been tempted to choose **d**, because of the statement that Lorna was not able to collect quantitative data. However, there seemed to be a clear trend to support **b** and the statement that she obtained qualitative data means that she was confident that although the exact boiling times could be off, the trend she observed was real.

26. g. There is no mention of problems associated with **f**, **h**, and **j** in the passage. The last sentence in the passage should point you to the correct answer.

27. c. This question required you to remember that it's important to keep the experimental conditions unchanged throughout the experiment. Different hotplates, just like different ovens, may differ in their heating efficiency and could affect the boiling times she was trying to measure. As long as all water used in the experiment came from the same source, it shouldn't matter whether it was distilled or not. Stirring is not necessary since there is nothing to mix. There is nothing wrong with setting up a data sheet before the experiment.

28. f. The statement that the volume change was greatest in the container with the largest radius, and barely detectable in the container with the smallest radius should provide you with the right answer.

29. d. The scientist used the graduate cylinder to check whether and by how much the volume in the container had changed.

30. j. Looking at the unfilled table provided in the text, a container with a 7.0 cm radius has a radius that is smaller than that of container 5, but larger than that of container 4. That tells you that the order in which the water in the 7.0 cm radius container boiled would be between container 5 and container 4. In the text you were told that container 5 boiled first, so the container with a 7.0 cm radius would boil after the water in container 5.

Passage V

31. b. In the impetus theory, impetus is a property of the object imparting the motion. In the theory of inertia, the property of inertia is a property of the moving object itself.

32. j. The theory of inertia correctly predicts the parabolic path of a projectile. This is because the projectile continues to move with constant velocity in the horizontal direction since there is no net force in the horizontal direction. The net force in the vertical direction is the gravitational force of the earth on the object. This causes the object to fall toward the earth as it travels horizontally creating the parabolic path. In the impetus theory, however, the impetus of the projectile would run out abruptly which would then predict that the projectile should keep going in a straight line until it uses up the impetus and then it would be predicted to fall straight down.

33. c. According to the inertia theory, the net force that acts to slow down the arrow is the force of gravity on the arrow. The force of the bow on the arrow is what causes the arrow to begin moving. This means that selection I is false, the force of the bow on the arrow is not the net force acting to slow down the arrow, but selection III is true since the force of gravity is the net force acting to slow down the arrow according to the inertia theory. Selection II indicates that the arrow receives an infinite amount of impetus, but according to the explanation of the motion of the arrow using the impetus theory the arrow only receives a certain amount of impetus from the bow and when it uses up this impetus it will fall to the ground. This means selection II is false, but selection IV which says that the impetus imparted to the arrow by the bow is used up and that is why the arrow falls to the ground is true.

34. f. For an object to continue moving forever in a straight line with constant velocity, the impetus theory requires that the object be given an infinite amount of impetus.

35. d. The inertia theory states that an object will continue moving in a straight line with constant velocity as long as no net force acts on it.

36. g. As defined by the impetus theory, impetus is the property of motion that is imparted to the object by whatever is acting on it. From the example in the reading, the impetus is a property motion of the bow that is transferred to the arrow.

37. a. According to the Inertia Theory passage, gravity is a type of net force. There is no support for the other choices.

38. j. According to the impetus theory, the arm would impart the property of motion to the rock. There is no support for the other choices found in the Impetus Theory passage.

Passage VI

39. b. Since no kittens of three generations had white paws, it is a logical assumption that the parent cats and the kittens, which were bred later to create the newer generations, are all homogeneous for not having white paws.

40. g. The fact that no first generation cats were born with white paws and the second generation of cats had a frequency of 1 out of 8, shows that the original parents had at least one being a carrier. However, if both parents were carriers, then there would have been 1 out of 4 kittens in the first generation with white paws. Thus, it is likely that one of the parent cats is pure and one is a carrier. Furthermore, this indicates that the trait for white paws is recessive because it is not showing up in the parents, but it is showing up in a younger generation of cats.

41. d. Since at least one of the parents is pure for not having white paws and the second parent has both traits in the genotype, the dominant genotypes will statistically be more than the recessive genotypes. However, there will statistically be the chance for the recessive genotype and phenotype to be present if heterozygote cats from the younger generations are allowed to breed.

42. f. According to the Background Information in the passage, if a gene is recessive, it will only be expressed in the phenotype when two recessives are present in the genetic makeup of that organism.

43. b. There is one parent in Group 1, two in Group 2, and none in Group 3 who are pure for not having white paws.

44. j. The cat breeder was very lucky to originally put the two cats together (male and female) who were pure for not having white paws. Any other combination of the six original cats would have produced a lesser number of kittens that are genotypically pure for not having white paws.

45. c. The experiment would not be affected by people's preference in cats, nor would it depend on the food the cats eat. You might think that if the cats from Group 1 bred one month later than the other cats it would affect the outcome, however, the difference in time will not change the genetic makeup of the cats. Therefore, the outcome would be affected by cats from different groups being bred together.

46. h. If you study the Punnett Squares from Passage VI, you would see that the only outcome for a combination of 2 cats with genotype ww, would be to result in cats with the genotype ww.

47. c. According to the Background Information, the genes that determine that phenotype are called the organism's genotype.

Passage VII

48. j. Objects that move with constant velocity have position versus time graphs with constant slope since the object travels equal distances in equal time intervals. The velocity of an object is the slope of the position versus time graph. Of the objects represented on Graph I only objects A, C, and D have straight lines representing constant velocity. Object B has a curved position versus time graph, which indicates it is changing velocity as it travels. This leaves two choices C or D. The graph for object D has a positive slope and the graph for object C has a negative slope. The sign of the slope of the position versus time graph represents the sign or direction of the velocity. This means that object D, which has a positive, constant slope on the position versus time graph represents an object moving in the positive direction with constant velocity.

49. c. The object in Graph II has a constant velocity since the line on its velocity versus time graph is horizontal. It also has a negative velocity since the line is in the negative region of the graph. Since the velocity is negative this means it is moving in the negative direction. So the object should meet the following requirements, it should be moving in the negative direction with constant velocity. The object from Graph I that is moving in the negative direction with constant velocity is object C. As explained above to have a constant velocity on Graph I the object must show a straight line on the position versus time graph. Only objects C and D have straight lines with non-zero constant slopes on the position versus time graphs. Object D has a positive slope on its position versus time graph in Graph I. This means its velocity versus time graph should be in the positive region of the graph. Object C, however, meets both requirements since it has a negative, constant slope on its position versus time graph in Graph I, its velocity versus time graph is a horizontal line in the negative region as represented by Graph II.

50. j. On Graph III, the direction the object is moving in is represented by what region of the graph the line is drawn in. It is important to remember that since Graph III plots the velocity of the object and not its position. Only the sign of the velocity values indicate the direction of motion. The slope of the line on the velocity versus time graph does not indicate the direction the object is moving in. If the object is moving in the positive direction the velocity will be positive, and if it is moving in the negative direction the velocity will be negative. Since the line is in the negative region of the velocity versus time graph the object is moving in the negative direction. This eliminates answer choices **f** and **g**. The slope of a velocity versus time graph represents the acceleration of the object. In this case the slope is positive. This means that while the velocity is in the negative direction the acceleration is in the positive direction. Whenever the acceleration is in the opposite direction than the velocity the magnitude of the velocity will decrease, or the object will slow down. The fact the object is slowing down can also be determined by looking at the velocity values which become closer to zero as time passes indicating the object is slowing down. Object D is moving in the negative direction and slowing down.

51. c. Data table I includes time and velocity information that indicates it would be used to make a velocity versus time graph. This eliminates choices **a** and **d** since Graphs I and IV are both position versus time graphs. Of the two velocity versus time graphs, Graph II shows an object with constant velocity since the line on this graph is horizontal, this indicates that the data table used to make Graph II should have the same value for the velocity for all of the times. This is not the case for Data Table I. This leaves Graph III as the only option. For this velocity versus time graph the velocity decreases in magnitude over time as seen on the Graph III. The values for the velocity in Data Table I reflect this decrease in magnitude.

52. **g.** Looking at the position versus time graph in Graph IV you can determine first the direction each object is moving in. Remember the slope of the position versus time graph is the velocity of the object. Since all of the objects have straight lines for the position versus time graph they are all moving at constant velocity. Objects A, B, and D have positive slopes and are therefore moving in the positive direction. Object C, however has a negative slope and is therefore moving in the negative direction. Object C is going backwards away from the finish line so cannot win the race. The magnitude or steepness of the slope determines how fast the object is moving. Object B has the steepest slope and is therefore moving the fastest. Since it is moving the fastest and they are all moving with constant velocity, object B will win the race.

53. **a.** Object A has the third steepest slope and would therefore come in 3rd in a race with Objects A, B, C, and D.

54. **j.** The weight and diameter of the objects and the table you create will not affect the results, however your motion detector will affect your results.

55. **b.** According to Data Table I, the velocity at minute 3 was -0.81m/s and the velocity at minute 4 was −0.75. If you subtract those numbers, the difference is -0.06m/s.

Passage IIX

56. **j.** After ten weeks, the average population was the same of both species of beetle. All the other statements are not true, or not supported by sufficient evidence.

57. **c.** Experiment 1 is a control experiment that establishes the population size of each insect when provided with an adequate food supply for any size population. This population size is used to compare what happens when there is less food and/or more species eating the same finite supply of food.

58. **g.** The most likely limiting resource that is discussed and applicable to the paragraph is food supply. Over an indefinitely long period of time, the food supply would run out and population size would cease to increase. The population size would eventually start declining due to starvation.

59. **d.** While Experiment 3 suggests that both species of beetles compete for food, Experiment 2 suggests that Beetle A does not compete with caterpillars for food. Therefore, Beetle B should not be expected to compete with the caterpillars for food either.

60. **j.** The decrease in both Beetle A and Beetle B population sizes indicate that there is interspecies competition for resources. All the other statements are not true.

61. **b.** The ratio of Beetle A to Beetle B should remain the same regardless of the initial number of beetles. Hence, Beetle A constitutes 75%, while Beetle B constitutes 25%.

62. **h.** The dearth of the Beetle B species in all the other choices is due to a result of direct influence of the Beetle C species. The failure to reproduce due to a genetic mutation is not a result of competition.

Passage IX

63. **c.** Both studies state that they are analyzing marine sediment. Study 2 makes no mention of sedimentary rocks (ruling out choice **b**). Depth of the cores is irrelevant (ruling out choice **d**) and only study 2 states that it measured peak glaciation (ruling out choice **a**).

64. h. Choices **h** and **j** are tough, but if the student compares the numbers from study 1 and 2, he or she will see that 100,000 years is a common factor to both studies, so choice **h** is the most accurate answer. Choice **j** is too vague, and ignores the results of Study 2. There is no indication that region and micro-fossils control marine depositional processes (ruling out choice **f**). Both studies show that there are patterns in these processes, making choice **g** a poor selection.

65. a. The passage makes no mention of the relevance of ocean depth or proximity to polar ice caps, but it does mention that these sequences have a minimum age of 50,000 years.

66. h. Sediment size was the crucial factor in Study 1, but not Study 2 (where the central factors were the abundance and shape of microfossils).

67. c. As stated in the second paragraph, glacial melting results in deposition and warmer global tempera-tures.

68. j. Study 1's hypothesis was that marine sediments record sequences of sediment that occur in cycles. Choice **g** is the conclusion of study 1, not a hypothesis. Choices **f** and **h** are not discussed in Study 1.

Passage X

69. d. The passage states (in the first sentence) that each protein is characterized by the sequence of amino acids and that this sequence is what makes the protein unique.

70. j. All the models are based on the fact that the amino acid sequence specifies the proper conforma-tion. A loss of a vital amino acid in any of the models would lead to the wrong conformation.

71. b. According to the nucleation model, the mutated amino acid will fail to produce a properly folded protein. However, the protein still acquires the proper fold, suggesting the shortfall of this model.

72. f. Even though the diffusion-collision model does not posit that there are any especially important amino acids, it is still the case, according to that model, that a mutation of any amino acid might affect the folding pathway.

73. d. Since the nucleation method is akin to a domino effect, it follows that the longer a protein, the longer it will take to attain the proper conformation.

74. g. According to the hydrophobic-collapse model, hydrophobic amino acids prefer to interact with themselves. Thus, the interacting molecular chaperonin amino acids must be hydrophilic to promote protein folding.

75. c. Choices **a** and **d** demonstrate that a protein fold can be achieved by any of the three suggested path-ways. While sequence is the only element important in the folding process, hence negating choice **b**, the fact that similar proteins can attain proper conformations via any of the proposed pathways, in this particular case, suggests that sequence does not determine the folding pathway.

Passage XI

76. g. SDS-associated proteins, which are negatively charged, will travel toward the positive end of an electric field. All the other options are true statements, but do not describe the SDS-PAGE context.

77. a. From the table, the weight 45 000 falls between the first two data points. This would correspond to region W on the graph.

78. j. Since a protein weighing 17 000 Da travels 1.8 cm, and since the new protein traveled only 1.7 cm, we can confidently conclude that the new protein is heavier and thus rule out choices **f**, **g**, and **h**. Choice **j** is the only answer allowing for heavier wieghts.

79. b. All the other combinations can be manipulated to give a combined weight of approximately 50 000 Da. The highest weight that Y + Z can attain under 25 000 Da.

80. j. It is consistent with the information provided that, given an indefinitely long period of time, all negatively charged proteins will reach the anode at the rates determined by their sizes. Smaller proteins will arrive at the anode before the larger proteins, ruling out choice **f**.

▶ Glossary of Terms

This glossary is meant as a tool to prepare you for the ACT Science Reasoning Test. You will not be asked any vocabulary questions on the ACT Science Reasoning Test, so there is no need to memorize any of these terms or definitions. However, reading through this list will familiarize you with general science words and concepts, as well as terms you may have encountered in the practice questions. These terms come from all the areas of science found on the ACT (Biology, Chemistry, Earth and Space Science, and Physics), but it is not guaranteed that any of the terms below will be included on an official ACT Science Reasoning Test.

Acceleration—The rate that velocity changes per unit time and the direction it changes in. Computed from the change in velocity divided by the change in time. Common units are meters per second squared (m/s^2).

Acceleration due to gravity—The acceleration of an object that is only acted on by the force of the Earth's gravity. This value is given the symbol g and near the surface of the Earth it has a value of approximately 9.8 m/s^2. The direction of the acceleration due to gravity is vertically downward.

Accuracy—The closeness of an experimental measurement to the accepted or theoretical value.

Acid—A substance that is a proton donor. The pH of an acid is less than 7.

Analysis—A stage in the scientific method where patterns of observations are made.

Aqueous solution—A solution in which the solvent is water.

Arteries—The vascular tissue which carries blood away from the heart.

Astronomy—The study of planets, stars, and space.

Atom—The smallest structure that has the properties of an element. Atoms contain positively charged protons and uncharged neutrons in the nucleus. Negatively charged electrons orbit around the nucleus.

ATP—(Adenosine Triphosphate)—A chemical that is considered to be the "fuel" or energy source for an organism.

Atria—The chambers of the heart that receive blood.

Base—A substance that is a proton acceptor. The pH of a base is greater than 7.

Calibration—The examination of the performance of an instrument in an experiment whose outcomes are known, for the purpose of accounting for the inaccuracies inherent in the instrument in future experiments whose outcomes are not known.

Capillaries—Vascular tissue that receives blood from the arterioles and releases the blood to the venuoles.

Catalyst—An agent that changes the rate of a reaction, without itself being altered by the reaction.

Celestial equator—The extension of the Earth's equator out onto the celestial sphere.

Celestial poles—The extension of the Earth's north and south pole onto the celestial sphere.

Celestial sphere—The imaginary sphere onto which all the stars are viewed as being on for the purposes of locating them.

Cell membrane—An organelle found in all cells that acts as the passageway through which materials can pass in and out. This organelle is highly selectively permeable, only allowing materials to pass through that it "chooses" chemically.

Cell wall—An organelle found primarily in plant cells and fungi cells, and also some bacteria. The cell wall is a strong structure that provides protection, support, and allows materials to pass in and out without being selectively permeable.

Centripetal force—The net force that acts to result in the centripetal acceleration. It is not an individual force, but the sum of the forces in the radial direction. It is directed toward the center of the circular motion.

Chemical change—A process that involves the formation or breaking of chemical bonds.

Chromosome—An organelle that contains the entire DNA of the organism.

Component—The part of a vector that lies in the horizontal or vertical direction.

Compound—A substance composed of more than one element that has a definite composition and distinct physical and chemical properties.

Concentration—A measure of the amount of solute that is present in a solution. A solution that contains very little solute is called dilute. A solution that contains a relatively large amount of solute is said to be concentrated.

Conclusion—The last stage of the scientific method where explanations are made about why the patterns identified in the analysis section occurred.

Constellation—An apparent grouping of stars in the sky that is used for identification purposes. These stars are not necessarily near each other in space since they are not necessarily the same distance from the Earth.

Continental rift—The region on a continent where new crust is being created, and the plates on either side of the rift are moving apart.

Convergent boundary—A boundary between two of the Earth's plates that are moving toward each other.

Cosmology—The study of the formation of the universe.

Crystal—A solid in which atoms or molecules have a regular repeated arrangement.

Current—The flow of charge past a point per unit time; it is measured in Amperes (A).

Cuticle—The top layer on a leaf. It is a non-living layer consisting primarily of wax that is produced by the epithelium, a cell layer directly underneath.

Cytoplasm—A jelly-like substance located in the cell where all of the internal organelles can be found. The cytoplasm consists primarily of water and supports the cell and its organelles.

Cytoskeleton—Organelles that are the internal "bones" of the cell. They exist in thick and thin tubules.

Decibel—A unit of measure for the relative intensity of sounds.

Declination—The celestial coordinate similar to that of latitude on the Earth. Declination measures how many degrees, minutes, and seconds north or south of the celestial equator an object is.

Delta—A fan shaped deposit of material at the mouth of a river.

Density—The mass of a substance for a given unit volume. A common unit of density is grams per milliliter (g/ml).

Displacement—The change in position of an object. Computed from the final position minus the initial position. Common units of measure are meters (m).

Divergent boundary—A boundary between two of the Earth's plates that are moving away from each other.

DNA—Contains all genetic material for an organism. The smallest units of DNA are called *nucleotides.*

Ecliptic—The apparent path of the Sun across the sky over the course of a year.

Electric potential energy—The energy due to an object's position within an electric field.

Electromagnetic wave—A light wave that has an electric field component and a magnetic field component. An electromagnetic wave does not require a medium to travel through.

Electrostatic force—The force that exists between particles due to their charge. Particles of like charge repel, particles of unlike charge attract.

Element—The smallest entity that has distinct chemical properties. It can not be decomposed by ordinary chemical reactions.

Ellipse—A geometric shape that is formed when a plane is intersected with a cone. In this case the plane intersects the cone at an angle so that a shape similar to a circle but stretched in one direction is formed. The orbits of the planets around the Sun represent ellipses.

Endoplasmic reticulum—An organelle that is used to transport proteins throughout the cell.

Energy—The ability to do work or undergo change. Kinetic energy is the energy of motion, while potential energy is stored energy.

Epicycle—Smaller circles on which the planets traveled around the Earth in the geocentric model of the solar system. Epicycles were used to explain the retrograde motion of planets and help make the predicted positions of the planets match the observed positions.

Equilibrium—A state at which the forward and reverse reaction proceed at the same rate.

Focal length—The distance from a focal point to a mirror or lens.

Force—That which acts on an object to change its motion; a push or pull exerted on one object by another. Common units are Newtons (N).

Freefall—An object in one-dimensional motion that is only acted on by the force of the Earth's gravity. In this case its acceleration will be -g or g downward.

Frequency—The number of cycles or repetitions per second. Frequency is also often measured as the number of revolutions per second. The common units of frequency are Hertz (Hz) where one Hertz equals 1/second.

Frictional force—The force that acts parallel to surfaces in contact opposite the direction of motion or tendency of motion.

Functional group—A group of atoms that give a molecule a certain characteristic or property.

Gel electrophoresis—A process used in laboratories to determine the genetic make up of DNA strands. This process involves the movement of chromosomes through a gel from one pole to the other. Magnetism is used to pull the chromosomes through the gel.

Geocentric model—The model of the solar system that places the Earth at the center with the planets and the Sun orbiting around it.

Geology—The study of rocks and minerals.

Glacier—A large mass of snow-covered ice.

Golgi apparatus—An organelle that packages proteins so that they can be sent out of the cell.

Gravitational force—The attractive force that exists between all particles with mass.

Heliocentric model—The model of the solar system that places the Sun at the center with the planets orbiting around it.

Heterogeneous—A mixture that is not uniform in composition.

Homogeneous—A mixture in which the components are uniformly distributed.

Hydrate—A crystal of a molecule that also contains water in the crystal structure. If the water evaporates, the crystal becomes anhydrous.

Hydrology—The study of the Earth's water and water systems.

Hypothesis—A step in the scientific method where a prediction is made about the end result of an experiment. A hypothesis is generally based on research of related data.

Igneous rock—A rock formed through the cooling of magma.

Image distance—The distance from an image to a mirror or lens.

Inertia—The tendency of an object to follow Newton's First Law, the law of inertia. That is the tendency of an object to remain at rest or in motion with constant velocity unless acted on by a force.

Inorganic—A material that is neither plant nor animal in origin.

Intensity—The power per unit area of a wave; measured in Watts/m^2.

Ion—An atom that has either lost electrons to become a positively charged cation, or has gained electrons to become a negatively charged anion.

Isomers—Substances that have the same molecular formula (same number of elements) in different arrangements.

Isotopes—Atoms of the same element, with different numbers of neutrons, and hence a different atomic mass.

Jovian planet—One of the outer planets of the solar system that have characteristics similar to that of Jupiter. They are also called gas planets. They are large, have high mass, have many moons, may have rings, are far from the Sun and each other, have thick atmospheres, are gaseous and have low density, have a composition similar to that of the Sun, have short rotation rates, and have long revolution periods around the Sun. The Jovian planets are Jupiter, Saturn, Uranus, and Neptune.

Kinetic energy—The energy due to an object's motion or velocity.

Land breeze—The breeze that develops on the shoreline due to unequal heating of the air above the land and ocean. Land breeze occurs at night when the air above the land is cooler and the air above the ocean is warmer. The breeze blows from the land to the sea.

Latitude—The coordinate used to measure positions on the Earth north or south of the Earth's equator. Latitude is measured in degrees, minutes, and seconds. Zero-degrees latitude is the Earth's equator.

Longitude—The coordinate used to measure positions on the Earth east or west of the prime meridian, which goes through Greenwich, England. Longitude is measured in degrees, minutes, and seconds.

Longitudinal wave—A wave that has the direction of motion of the particles in the medium parallel to the direction of motion of the wave. Sound is an example of a longitudinal wave.

Mass—The amount of matter in an object; also a measure of the amount of inertia of an object. Common units are Kilograms (kg).

Meander—A broad curve in a river.

Meiosis—A process of cellular reproduction where the daughter cells have half the amount of chromosomes. This is used for purposes of sexual reproduction to produce sex cells that will be able to form an offspring with a complete set of chromosomes with different DNA than the parents.

Meniscus—The curved surface of a liquid in a container, caused by surface tension.

Metamorphic rock—A rock whose crystal structure has been changed through heat and/or pressure.

Meteorology—The study of the Earth's atmosphere and weather.

Mid-oceanic ridge—A region under the ocean where new crust is being created, and the plates on either side of the ridge are moving apart.

Mineral—A naturally occurring element or compound found in the Earth's crust.

Mitochondria—An organelle that produces ATP.

Mitosis—A process in which cells produce genetically identical offspring.

Mixture—A physical combination of different substances.

Mole—The amount of substance that contains as many particles as there are atoms in 12 grams of the carbon 12 isotope (6.022×10^{23} particles).

Molecular mass—The sum of the atomic masses in a molecule.

Molecule—A substance formed by a chemical bond between two or more atoms.

Net force—The vector sum of all the forces acting on an object.

Newton—The metric and System International unit of force. One Newton equals one kg/s^2.

Non-renewable resource—A resource that is not replaced in nature as quickly as it is used. In many cases it is not replaced or re-formed at all.

Normal force—This force acts between any two surfaces in contact. It is the part of the contact force that acts normal or perpendicular to the surfaces in contact.

Nucleolus—An organelle found inside a nucleus that is responsible for the production of ribosomes.

Nucleotide—The smallest unit of DNA. There are five different types of nucleotides: adenine, guanine, thymine, cytosine, and uracil. The arrangement of genes is based directly on the specific arrangement of nucleotides.

Nucleus—An organelle in a cell that contains all of the DNA and controls the functions of the cell.

Object distance—The distance from an object to a mirror or lens.

Oceanography—The study of the Earth's oceans.

Orbit—The path an object takes as it travels around another in space.

Organic—A material that is plant or animal in origin.

Oxbow lake—A crescent shaped lake formed when a meander is cutoff from the river it was part of.

Oxidation—The loss of electrons by a substance in a chemical reaction.

Parallel circuit—A circuit with more than one path for the current to follow.

Period—The time, often measured in seconds, for one complete repetition or rotation.

Phloem—Vascular tissue found in plants that transports mostly sugar and water; can travel either "shoot to root" or "root to shoot."

Photon—A particle of light. A discreet amount of light energy where a single photon of light is the smallest unit of light energy possible.

Photosynthesis—A process by which the sunlight's energy, water, and carbon dioxide are transformed into sugar and oxygen.

Physical property—A property that can be observed without performing a chemical transformation of that substance.

Plate tectonics—The theory in which Earth's crust is made up of many plates that float on the mantle. This theory explains the movement of the continents, the formation of mountains, earthquakes, volcanoes, and the existence of mid-oceanic ridges.

Polymer—A large molecule made up of repeating units of one or more small molecules (monomers).

Position—The location of an object in a coordinate system. Common units of measure are meters (m).

Potential difference—The difference in electric potential energy per unit charge between two points. This is commonly called voltage. The common unit of measure for potential difference is called Volts.

Potential energy—The energy due to an object's position or state.

Precession—The process by which the Earth's axis traces out a circle on the celestial sphere.

Precision—The measurement of the closeness of measurements obtained from two or more experimental runs.

Pressure—Force per unit area. Units used to measure pressure are torr, atmosphere (atm), and Pascal (Pa).

Procedure—A logical list of steps that explain the exact actions taken to perform an experiment.

Projectile—An object in two-dimensional motion that has a vertical acceleration equal to -g (or g downward) and a horizontal acceleration of zero.

Protein synthesis—A process by which DNA will transport its information by way of RNA to the ribosomes where proteins will be assembled.

Qualitative observation—An observation that includes characteristics other than amounts or measurements; may include shapes, colors, actions, and odors.

Quantitative observation—An observation that includes characteristics of measurements or amounts.

Radiation—The emission of energy.

Reactant—A substance that is consumed in a chemical reaction to form products.

Reduction—The gain of electrons by a substance in a chemical reaction.

Renewable resource—A renewable resource is replaced in nature as quickly as it is used.

Resistance—The resistance to the flow of electrons through a circuit. The resistance is dependant on the current flowing through the circuit element and the voltage across the circuit element; resistance in measured in Ohms.

Respiration—A process by which sugar is converted into ATP and carbon dioxide; may include oxygen which is called *aerobic respiration.*

Retrograde motion—The apparent westward motion of objects in the sky from one night to another.

Reversible reaction—A reaction in which products can revert back into reactants.

Ribosome—An organelle where protein synthesis occurs; can be found floating freely in the cytoplasm or attached to the outside of endoplasmic reticulum.

Right ascension—The celestial coordinate similar to that of longitude on the Earth. Right ascension is measured in hours, minutes, and seconds with 24 hours making up 360° around the celestial sphere.

River system—A river and its associated tributaries and drainage basin.

RNA—(Ribonucleic Acid)—Responsible for transmitting genetic information from the DNA to the ribosomes for protein synthesis.

Rock cycle—The rock cycle summarizes how rocks of different types are formed and how they can be transformed from one type into another.

Scalar—A quantity that has a magnitude or amount only.

scientific method—A process by which data is collected to answer an integral question. The major steps are problem, hypothesis, research, procedure, observations and data collection, analysis of data, and conclusion.

Sedimentary rock—A rock made up of sediments that have been deposited, compacted and cemented over time.

Sea breeze—The breeze that develops on the shoreline due to unequal heating of the air above the land and ocean. Sea breeze occurs during the day when the air above the ocean is cooler and the air above the land is warmer. The breeze blows from the sea to the land.

Series circuit—A circuit with only one path for the current to follow. The current in each element in a series circuit is the same.

Solubility—The amount of solute that can be dissolved completely in a solvent at a given temperature.

Solution—A homogeneous mixture of a solute (usually solid, but sometimes liquid or gas) in a solvent (usually a liquid, but sometimes a solid or gas).

Speed—The magnitude of velocity. It measures the rate position changes with time without regard to the direction of motion; common units are meters per second (m/s).

Speed of light—The speed of light in a vacuum is the fastest speed possible. As light travels in other materials it will change speed. The speed of light in any material is still the fastest speed possible in that material; commonly denoted by the symbol c.

Spindle fiber—An organelle used during mitosis and meiosis that separates and "pulls" chromosomes towards the opposite poles of the cell.

Spontaneous reaction—A reaction that does not require an external source of energy to proceed.

Star—A body composed mostly of hydrogen and helium that radiates energy and that has fusion actively occurring in the core.

States of matter—Solid, liquid, and gas. In solids, atoms or molecules are held in place. The shape and volume of a solid usually do not vary much. In liquids atoms or molecules can move, but their motion is constrained by other molecules. Liquids assume the shape of their container. In gasses the motion of atoms or molecules is unrestricted. Gases assume both the volume and the shape of their containers and they are easily compressible.

Temperature—The measure of the average kinetic energy of the molecules of a substance.

Tension—The force that acts and is transferred along ropes, strings, and chains.

Terminal moraine—A ridge of material deposited by a glacier at its farthest point of advance.

Terrestrial planet—One of the inner planets of the solar system that have characteristics similar to that of the Earth. They are small, have low mass, have few or no moons, have no rings, are close to the sun and are close to each other, have thin or no atmosphere, are rocky and have high density, have long rotation rates, and have short revolution periods around the Sun. The terrestrial planets are Mercury, Venus, Earth, and Mars.

Topography—The study of the surface features of the planet primarily through mapping.

Transverse wave—A wave that has the direction of motion of the particles in the medium perpendicular to the direction of motion of the wave.

Uniform circular motion—Motion with constant speed in a circle. Since the direction of the velocity changes in this case, there is acceleration even though the speed is constant.

Valence electrons—Electrons that are in the outer atomic shell and can participate in a chemical reaction.

Vector—A quantity that has both a magnitude (an amount) and a direction. In one-dimensional motion, direction can be represented by a positive or negative sign. In two-dimensional motion, the direction is represented as an angle in the coordinate system.

Veins—In plants, found in the leaves; sometimes called the vascular bundle that contains the xylem and phloem. In animals, tube-like tissue that usually transports blood.

Velocity—The rate that a position changes per unit time and the direction it changes in. Common units are meters per second (m/s).

Ventricles—Chambers found in animal hearts that pump blood away from the heart.

Voltage—Another name for potential difference.

Voltmeter—A device used to measure voltage in a circuit.

Water cycle—The movement of water between the land, oceans, and atmosphere.

Weight—The force of the Earth's gravity on an object. Near the surface of the Earth the weight is equal to the object's mass times the acceleration due to gravity ($W = mg$).

Xylem—Vascular tissue found in plants that transports water in one direction; "root to shoot." This is the water that will be sent to the photosynthetic cells in order to perform photosynthesis.

# Appendix: Additional ACT Resources

This book has given you a good start on studying for the ACT exam. However, as you will find in your future courses, one book is seldom enough. It's best to be equipped with several sources, some general, some more specific.

► English

Azar, Betty. *Basic English Grammar* (Upper Saddle River, NJ: Prentice Hall, 1998).

LearningExpress. *501 Grammar & Writing Questions* (New York: LearningExpress, 2000).

LearningExpress. *501 Word Analogy Questions* (New York: LearningExpress, 2002).

LearningExpress. *501 Synonym & Antonym Questions* (New York: LearningExpress, 2002).

LearningExpress. *1001 Vocabulary & Spelling Questions* (New York: LearningExpress, 2000).

Lewis, Norman. *Thirty Days to Better English* (New York: New American Library, 1991).

Meyers, Judith N. *Vocabulary & Spelling Success: In 20 Minutes a Day, 3rd Edition* (New York: LearningExpress, 2002).

Princeton Review. *Grammar Smart* (New York: Princeton Review, 2001).

Robinson, Adam. *Word Smart: Building an Educated Vocabulary* (New York: Princeton Review, 2001).

Strunk, William and White E.B. *The Elements of Style, 4th Edition* (Boston: Allyn & Bacon, 2000).

The Ultimate Verbal and Vocabulary Builder for the SAT, ACT, GRE, GMAT, and LSAT (Austin: Lighthouse Review, 1998).

▶ Reading

Blachowicz, Camille and Ogle, Donna. *Reading Comprehension* (New York: Guilford Publications, 2001).

Boone, Robert S. *What You Need to Know About Developing Your Test-Taking Skills: Reading Comprehension* (New York: NTC/Contemporary, 1995).

Chesla, Elizabeth. *Read Better, Remember More, 2nd Edition* (New York: LearningExpress, 2000).

Chesla, Elizabeth. *Reading Comprehension in 20 Minutes a Day, 2nd Edition* (New York: LearningExpress, 2001).

Herrell, Adrienne L. and Jordan, Michael. *Fifty Active Learning Strategies for Improving Reading Comprehension* (Upper Saddle River, NJ: Prentice Hall, 2001).

Hoyt, Linda. *Revisit, Reflect, Retell: Strategies for Improving Reading Comprehension* (Portsmouth, NH: Heinemann, 1998).

LearningExpress. *501 Grammar and Writing Questions, 2nd Edition* (New York: LearningExpress, 2002).

LearningExpress. *501 Reading Comprehension Questions, 2nd Edition* (New York: LearningExpress, 2001).

▶ Math

LearningExpress. *501 Algebra Questions* (New York: LearningExpress, 2002).

LearningExpress. *501 Geometry Questions* (New York: LearningExpress, 2002).

Lerner, Marcia. *Math Smart* (New York: Princeton Review, 2001).

Tarbell, Shirley. *1001 Math Problems.* (New York: LearningExpress, 1999).

Weinfeld, Mark. *ACT Assessment Math Flash 2002* (Stamford: Thomson, 2001).

Weinfeld, Mark. *ACT Math Flash: Proven Techniques for Building Math Power for the ACT* (Stamford: Thomson, 2000).

▶ Science

Giere, Ronald N. *Understanding Scientific Reasoning, 2nd Edition* (Austin: Holt, 1998).

▶ Other ACT Study Guides

ACT Assessment Success 2003 (New York: Petersons, 2002).

Bobrow, Jerry et. al. *Cliffs TestPrep ACT Preparation Guide* (Hoboken: Wiley, 2000).

Domzalski, Shawn Michael. *Crash Course for the ACT: The Last-Minute Guide to Scoring High* (New York: Princeton Review, 2000).

Ehrenhaft, George et. al. *How to Prepare for the ACT* (Hauppauge, NY: Barron's, 2001).

Getting into the ACT: Official Guide to the ACT Assessment (New York: HBJ, 1997).

Kaplan ACT 2000 with CD-ROM (New York: Kaplan, 2002).

Magliore, Kim and Silver, Theodore. *Cracking the ACT* (New York: Princeton Review, 2002).

Panic Plan for the ACT (New York: Petersons, 2000).

▶ Study Guides

Fry, Ronald. *Ace Any Test* (Franklin Lake, NJ: Career Press, 1996).

Huntley, Sara Beth and Smethurst, Wood. *Study Power Workbook: Exercises in Study Skills to Improve Your Learning and Your Grades* (Cambridge: Brookline Books, 1999).

Luckie, William R., and Smethurst, Wood. *Study Power: Study Skills to Improve YourLearning and Your Grades* (Cambridge: Brookline Books, 1997).

Meyers, Judith. *The Secrets of Taking Any Test, 2nd Edition* (New York: LearningExpress, 2000).

Wood, Gail. *How to Study, 2nd Edition* (New York: LearningExpress, 2000).

Semones, James. *Effective Study Skills: A Step-by-Step System for Achieving Student Success* (Washington, DC: Thomson, 1991).

▶ Websites

www.act.org— The official ACT site.

www.testprep.compracticehdr.shtml—Provides practice tests for the ACT exam.

www.powerprep.com—Provides strategies, tutoring, software, diagnostic and online practice tests for the ACT exam.

www.review.com—Provides tutoring and test preparation for the ACT exam.

www.kaplan.com—Provides tutoring, test preparation, and general information for the ACT exam.

www.act-sat-prep.com—Provides practice exams and strategies for taking the ACT exam.